OTHER BOOKS BY THIS AUTHOR

The 7 Evangelical Myths: Untwisting the Theology behind the Politics

Rescuing God from Christianity: A Closet Christian, Non-Christian, and Christmas Christian's Guide to Radically Rethinking God-stuff

Spiritual But Not Religious: A Call to Religious Revolution in America

Badass Jesus

The Serious Athlete and a Life of Noble Purpose

by Sven Erlandson

Llumina Press

ISBN: 978-1-60594-307-7 (PB)
978-1-60594-308-4

Printed in the United States of America by Llumina Press

Library of Congress Control Number: 2009904328

- To Mom,

A most patient gardener of
vegetables, fruit, flowers…and people,

who, as a pastor's wife, once said to a 10 year-old boy,
"Sven, don't believe everything you hear in church."

TABLE OF CONTENTS

ACKNOWLEDGMENTS

Thanks to the Llumina staff for your constant professionalism, especially Fina Florez for her terrific support and Joseph Masci for his great cover art.

Thanks to all the coaches, administrators, and athletes I have coached, worked with, worked out with, or had the pleasure to know, over the years, from: the US Air Force Academy, the University of Minnesota, Augsburg College, Gustavus Adolphus College, the University of St. Thomas, the US Women's Olympic Hockey program, USA Powerlifting, the US Bodybuilding Federation, USA Weightlifting, mixed martial arts, as well as college sports, Olympic and pro sports, and countless gyms and high schools.

A special thanks to the ballers and other athletes – as well as the students, faculty and staff – of Augsburg College in Minneapolis for trusting me with not only your workouts but your lives as your coach, friend, counselor, and sometimes-mentor. After years in the business and life of sports and spirituality, this book began to come together in my work with you. It was such a blessing to work with you and learn from you.

Thanks to Jeff Swenson, new Athletic Director at Augsburg and 10-time NCAA National Champion wrestling coach, for your support of passionate old-school coaching that believes in toughness, respect, and a genuine love for the athlete. Thanks to the guys in the football office, especially Chris Bergstrom, Drew Privette and Tony Madline. Thanks, also, to women's soccer coach, Mike Navarre, and women's volleyball coach, Jessica Rinehart, for your friendship.

Special thanks to Mike Matson, All-American football player, who bought into my program without question, who really 'got' the connection of spirituality and intensity, and who became the strongest lifter in the history of Augsburg College, not to mention one of the finest athletes I've had the pleasure to work with; for being a strong enough student of my method that I could entrust the program to you when I left. You were one of the primary inspirations for this book.

Special thanks to Frank Haege, former Arena League Professional Football Head Coach, and present Head Football Coach at Augsburg College, for trusting me with your program, for your friendship, and for supporting my sometimes unorthodox methods.

Thanks to Todd Rens, Dr. James Bland, and my brother, John, for your decades of support for my work and writing.

Thanks to Rev. LeRoy and Charlotte Erlandson, for your ceaseless support as I've fought, over the years, to create relevant spiritual answers for a hungry nation, even though those answers have looked very different from the faith you taught us six kids.

And, to my brother, David, one of the most intensely focused and driven people I've ever known – thank you for being the original badass in my life, and for, long ago, teaching me what it means to take life seriously and work my ass off for what I want and believe in.

As always, thanks to Colbjorn and Svea for loving your Pop. Mostly, thanks for your laughter!

INTRODUCTION

"People Naturally Follow Leaders Stronger Than Themselves"

- Robert Maxwell,
The 21 Irrefutable Laws of Leadership,
Rule #7: The Law of Respect

This book is written mainly for intense male athletes, but also for that rare breed of person who is, by nature, simply ferocious, intense, fierce, inordinately strong, focused, driven, and/or hard-nosed. 'Cuz the truth is, the Christian Church has long sucked at providing us with leaders – men! – we can look up to and truly be inspired, challenged and moved by in our spiritual lives.

Weak, spineless, flat, fat, shifty, soft, and/or uninspiring leaders have been selling only a soft, tender, touchy-feely Jesus. And there's a time and a place for that Jesus. But, the problem is that we've lost the hard-nosed, balls-to-the-wall Jesus – the one you can't help but respect, can't help but be inspired by his hardcore teachings, and can't help but be totally energized by his life and mission.

As a result, men have been running out of churches in droves for a couple of generations.

More significantly, however, we have lost the fiercest of the fierce. We have lost in the church the most intense personalities, the greatest leaders, and those rare types who would foolishly give their lives in radical love and service to others, even though it might profit themselves nothing.

We have long ago lost the badasses. Worse, because people will only follow someone stronger than them, we have lost the capacity to win the badasses back. And I'm not talking about winning them to the church. I'm just talking about winning them back to a life that is bigger, more important, and nobler than a life of consumerism and self-service.

We need the fiercest of the fierce. We need those crazy-ass SOBs who have true fire in their veins. Those are the people who have the innate saltiness and earthy vitamins, as well as the sheer force of character, necessary to carry others. Channel that energy and you can change the world. Get those lead ducks and all the baby ducks who tend to cluster around them will follow.

I'm not just talking about the cliché of the supposedly strong conservative Christian man. In fact, the guys I'm referring to have long since left the building. The badasses I'm referring to probably got sick of religion a long time ago, and have no interest in going back. The dudes I'm referring to can be liberal, conservative, moderate, or nothin'. The guys (and some women) this book is for are in their own league, live their own lives by their own rules, and won't be fenced in by anyone else's rules or ideas of what it means to be alive, be a man, or be a follower of anyone, let alone Jesus.

See, I believe in the power God has given to the fiercest of the fierce. I believe it is not a bad thing or something that needs to be tempered or gotten rid of. I believe it is to be harnessed and channeled. I believe that it is only by the passionate intensity and mad love of the most serious athletes and intense personalities that this world can truly be changed into something new and great. It doesn't have to be the athletes, but it seems like the fiercest and truest leaders tend to gravitate to the extreme challenge of athletics. And it is only with the greatest leaders that great wars are won.

I believe there is a great spiritual hunger in America that is going completely unmet, not just among the great leaders but among all people, just as I wrote in my first book, *Spiritual but not Religious*, ten years ago. And I believe that a radically simple, new understanding of Jesus' core message of love and self-sacrifice is just what is needed to meet this hunger.

<u>One very important note</u>: What your *beliefs* about Christianity, the Bible, Jesus, miracles, and so on are is totally up to you. The truth is, every denomination, every Christian, every non-Christian has very different *beliefs* about Jesus, what he did, and the miracles, creation, the Bible and so on. This book is not about beliefs. You can figure your beliefs out on your own with God. This is for those of any denomination and those outside Christianity. *This book is dedicated to one thing: Bringing you, the seriously intense athlete/leader, into sharp introduction with the core message of Jesus – radical love and a noble life of self-sacrifice for others, so that they might truly live and so that your life might, in the end, mean something.* This book is simply about what he, himself, called his two first and greatest commandments: Love God and love neighbor.

If you like soft, squishy Jesus, this is not the book for you. Put it down now. You'll hate it.

If you want a Jesus you can fall in love with, this is sooooo not the book for you. Please put it down or you'll only end up vomiting on its pages.

If you're a lamb, this book is not for you. If you're a wolf in sheep's clothing, this book is not for you. If you're a wolf in wolf's clothing, read on.

Yes, if you're looking for a true badass that you can totally respect and model your life after, Jesus and his powerful message of radical love are it. And you've found what you're looking for in this book.

But, please understand, this isn't some long Jesusy book. It's not some Christiany book, either. In fact, it's very un-Christian in most ways. In addition to years as a pastor, I'm a former college head strength and conditioning coach, a former D1 athlete, and former military. This is hardcore stuff. This is a book of stories about my athletes, the lessons they learned (or taught me), and how their lives relate to the greatest teachings on love and self-sacrifice. Pretty straightforward.

My hope is that it will inspire you and push you to a life bigger than yourself. My hope is that you will engage your power, your time, your life, your energy, your crazy, your fire, and your everything for a life of noble purpose….just as Jesus did, and just as he would have you do!

Kick some ass!

Sven
Spring, 2009

Chapter 1

MEANT TO BE LIONS

Prior to their lifts that day, in the early weeks of my tenure at the college, I brought parts of the football team back into a corner of the weightroom. It was no more than ten feet by teen feet with a very low ceiling. There, saying nothing, with these inner-city college players packed tightly around me, I pulled a can of cat food out of my pocket, opened it, and let the smell spread. Cat food has a foul smell in any setting, but quickly filling that space it seemed unusually acrid. The young men winced.

I then instructed them to pass it around, with each one to stick it up to his nose and take a big whiff. At first, they balked. But, knowing I do not tolerate insubordination, they did as I said.

Some grimaced and coughed as the can made its way around. While the smell sat in their nostrils and in the enclosed air, I explained to these college-age boys, "Gentlemen, this is who you are. This is who you have been trained to be. This is what you have become. This is life as you know it."

I continued,

> "You have been raised by your mothers, your teachers, and some of you have even had involved fathers. But in this society you have been raised to be kittens. In this society we have turned boys and young men into kittens. Soft, easy to get along with, controllable, cute, cuddly, and warm. You have been told since a very young age that no matter what you think or feel like, you are a kit-

ten. And just as the smell of your food – your kitten food for your kitten spirit – is repulsive to your nose, the idea of you being a kitten is repulsive to your very soul!"

With that said and the kitten food having made its way around the group, I slowly extracted from my bag a very, very large piece of raw steak meat (roughly a foot and a half long) that had been cut and hacked, such that it appeared to have been pulled from the cow by an amateur butcher with a dull knife and then nearly shredded by someone's teeth.

As I raised the slab of meat from some dead animal, I said to the boys,

"But this is what you really are, gentlemen. You have been taught to be kittens, but you are lions, gentlemen. You were not made to eat kitten food, gentlemen; but raw meat. You are lions. Deep in you is an animal – a ferocious, untamed animal waiting to come out. Inside you are rage, crazy, anger, and hatred in some cases, but mostly massive, massive amounts of power.

"The goal of life, my young lions, is not to kill the lion inside and become a kitten, as society wants to do with you. Granted, there are times when you must be a kitten – when playing with your young children one day, when interacting with old people, perhaps when intimate with your wife, or when encountering someone who is hurting or bearing their soul to you. There are kitten times, gentlemen. But the goal of this time of your life is to let the lion out and to learn to harness that lion energy and that lion power inside you. It is to be able to turn it on and turn it off. For, if you don't, gentlemen, if you don't find your lion spirit, you will die from the inside out. Your spirit and soul will become depressed and weak. Or, the rage and fight that are part of being your age and part of being you will spill out in all sorts of wrong ways.

"Yes, the goal of this time of your life, and in fact one of my tasks as your strength coach is to find and release that lion inside of you, and then to teach you how to harness and channel it. I am not here to teach you how to lift weights. Any monkey can do that. I am here to unleash and harness your inner lion. Despite what you've been told, the goal of life is not to become good boys, gentlemen. The goal of life is to take all those things inside you – all those salty, earthy vitamins, like rage and fight – that look bad to most people, and to put them to work for great good!

"This is not about being macho or a tough-guy just for the sake of acting tough. This is sooo much bigger than that. This is about finding yourself and mastering yourself. It is about discovering and focusing all parts of who you truly are, including that fire and mad strength you have inside you.

"The goal is to find the greatness inside you and harness it. There is fight inside you, gentlemen, and I will find it. And I will challenge you, day in and day out, throughout our workouts and time together, to put that fight and that power to great use! You must become the lion that God made you to be! And I'm here to make that happen."

We had a killer workout that day and for the weeks and months following. Slowly – ever so slowly – my boys began to find and unleash their lion spirit. Slowly, my boys were becoming men.

Ride the Wild Horses

One of the greatest books I have ever read, and one of the few I actually keep on my bookshelf, was written over a half-century ago by a preacher from Florida, named J. Wallace Hamilton. The book, *Ride the Wild Horses*, is a collection of sermons he gave on what he considered the godly use of 'our untamed impulses.' In it he radically asserts that our desires – such as the desires for greatness, to be in front of the crowd, take gambles, or constantly want more – are not curses, but are gifts from God to be harnessed and put to use for greater good.

Hamilton asserted that the central figure of the Christian story, Jesus, was no kitten or soft spirit; nor did Jesus attempt to make men into kittens. Instead, Jesus sought to bring out the lion and the wild horses in men, and harness that power – not tame it, but harness it! – to accomplish great good on behalf of those who most need the help of a man of character, passion, and power.

Unfortunately, we live in a culture today where young women are taught to be strong and young men are taught to be weak. Strength in women is a great thing. But we do everything we can to neuter young men. We cut off anything that looks even remotely like pre-feminism patriarchal man.

Worse, the Christian Church has done everything it can, it seems, to turn Jesus into a nice guy rather than a leader. Thus, it has, by extension, turned our leaders, particularly our men, into kittens when the leader spirit cries out to be the lion. We have so neutered Jesus that the leaders who are to bring us to Jesus' teachings have become impotent themselves. Or maybe the neutering of the leader caused the castration of Jesus. Whatever the case, we have lost the fierce spirit that drove Jesus' ministry, drove the titans of the Christian faith, and drove others who sacrificed themselves so that those in need might live. We have lost the lion spirit.

We fail to realize that inside young men is the power to change the world. Inside young men are the rage, crazy, anger, discontent with injustice, and aggressiveness that, if channeled properly, can be used to right the world's wrongs and create valiant warriors for noble causes. More importantly, inside young men is also a powerful sense of honor just waiting to explode out of them and be harnessed, if only they had someone – someone stronger than them, someone they respected – to grab them by the scruff of the neck and lead them, challenge them, teach them, kick 'em in the arse, and transform them.

But, because of the evolution of the sensitive man (an altogether necessary, if overdone, movement), rather than teaching young men the balance of strong and kind, we have near-completely lost males now in older adulthood who can teach young men to tap into their inner lion. We have lost male leaders who can bring out the fight in young men, direct it to solid and noble use, *and* teach them to be gentle and kind when the situation calls for it.

Caveat

I come from a long line of very strong and even powerful women. My maternal grandmother told her country pastor to 'stick it,' and started her own house church, roughly around the time of the Great Depression. My paternal grandmother raised 4 boys and a girl through WWII on a 1500-acre farm that was granted AAA-1 rationing status by the government. And, when her successful and innovative husband gave her pearls, furs, or other such gifts paid for with the profits of this enormous farm and his patented invention, she often demanded that he take the gifts back and re-invest the money in the farm or use it to help the church.

My mother raised 5 boys and 1 girl and later had her own successful career as a religious educator, seminary professor, and wise old woman. Today, my sister is highly integral to running highest-level, day-to-day operations of a mid-size American corporation so successful that it has been featured multiple times on 'Oprah.'

Both of my wives were ferociously strong women. One was a lawyer; the other a professional dancer/actor whose dance career extended ten years beyond the 30 year-old retirement of most dancers.

My point in mentioning all these strong women in my life is that I have tremendous respect for women of fierceness and passionate spirit.

If you are a fierce woman, this book may speak to you. I salute you and give thanks to God that this book could help you.

However, one of the great problems in our society is that we have lost ourselves as a society in no small part because we have lost the conquering male spirit that seeks not only to be strong, but do so in service of something greater than oneself. We have lost the lion male spirit that fiercely seeks to give of himself so that others may live.

In the past, this spirit was used to conquer nations, subject peoples, subdue nature, dominate women, and control children. Today, that same spirit can be harnessed not to dominate others, but to fiercely serve others and change the world for those who are weak and need a fighter to wipe away all that would oppress them. What is needed is men of character, fight, and power who have tapped into their lion spirit, and who want to live the noble path of self-sacrifice and other-service.

So, while I salute the strong in women. This book is written for the lion spirit in young male athletes and that same spirit in other men who have long let it lay dormant. For, it is the belief of this author that when Jesus' core teachings penetrate a man they awaken in the man the fire to become more than himself. Jesus' life and example ignite in a man the passion and fire to go beyond his smallness and live a life of noble purpose.

"Some men die by shrapnel
Some go down in flames
But most men perish, inch by inch,
Who play at little games."
-- author unknown

Badass Jesus!

When most people hear the term 'badass' they think it is some sort of put-down. You have the word 'bad' and the semi-swear word 'ass.' So people think 'badass' must be an insult or a curse. Or it is just a 'bad' word that shouldn't be used in polite company.

But athletes – real athletes – know that 'badass' means something completely different in sports. *Badass,* quite simply, is a compliment. It refers not to someone who is mean or harsh. Though the term does imply some strong measure of toughness, a badass is someone who excels at what he does, who is focused and driven in doing so, and who has some measure of inner ferocity that you can see in his eye. And any toughness the badass has is not a meanness toward others, at all. A badass might be gruff at times. But, more importantly, he has a singular focus and commitment to excellence that require prioritizing one's life and eliminating the trivial. The badass is the one who knows why he's here, knows he has a job to do, and isn't afraid to kick some tail in his work ethic, discipline, and focus to make it happen! To be called a badass is a high, high compliment among serious athletes. It is an honoring of the very essence of the athlete, a term of respect for the caliber of the man's character.

Jesus was the ultimate badass! There has never been anyone more focused, more driven, and more willing to get his own ass kicked and kick some ass to get the job done than that 30 year-old carpenter from Nazareth.

Jesus was not some one-sided pansy, lover boy, and cute Jack Russell Terrier that most churches have made him out to be. He was not and is not a soft and tender lamb that we are supposed to fall in love with and gently stroke, as far too many pastors would have us believe. He had a kind and loving spirit, to be sure. But he was a whole lot more than just that.

Jesus was a mixture that was often unpredictable, violent, and upside-down. He was filled with rage and tenderness, intensity and relaxedness, ferocity and passivity. Whether you believe in all the beliefs and trappings of Christianity or not, it is simply undeniable that all of Jesus – ferocious and gentle – was channeled toward bringing love and justice to a hurting world. His entire life – in all its dichotomies – was intent on using that inner fire to relieve the suffering of others.

His love was not so much that of a lover for a mate, but was the love of a player for a great coach. It was the love of a young man for an old mentor. It was the love of a Secret Service agent for the office of President – the man he is sworn to protect with his life! In truth, it was the passion of a servant for a master he has grown to both love and respect. His fire, his passion, his great love in life was to fight, rage, humble himself, teach, challenge, and lead for the people he served.

Jesus' love and rage flowed together in a passionate desire to serve, and therein found their greatest joy and power.

But we are very, very seldom taught this in our churches. We are told of the lover side of Jesus, but, oh, so rarely the ferocious love side.

We are so quick to ignore the 'other side' of a Jesus who:

- Spewed venom at his own friends, such as when he called Peter, one of his closest disciples, 'Satan' (Matthew 16:23);

- With cool calculation raged white-hot and then flipped-out in the temple when the injustice of the money-changers was being perpetrated (John 2:13-17);
- Drank alcohol and did so to the point where others even called him a drunk (Matthew 11:19; Luke 7:34);
- Advised his disciples to, quite literally, take on the mentality of, “to hell with them” if a particular village or household didn’t want to hear the message the disciples preached (Matthew 10:14-15);
- As his first miracle he turned 175 gallons of water into wine (John 2:1-11);
- Went-off on the religious leaders, calling them the equivalent of rapists, hypocrites, snakes, and fools (Matthew 15:6-9; 23:13-36);
- Hung out with and defended the gangsta rappers, meth users, AIDS patients, Hell’s Angels, and the porn stars of his day – the outcasts whom no one else stuck up for (Matthew 9:11; Luke 15:2);
- Said such things as, “I came to cast fire upon the earth” and “Do you think that I have come to give peace on earth? No, I tell you, I came to bring division…” (Luke 12:49,51);
- Was a carpenter, who worked with his hands, and was earthy and not uncomfortable around the rough and tumble side of life;
- Told people they must become slaves to others if they truly wish to follow God’s will for their lives (Matthew 20:27);
- Selfishly allowed a woman to rub him with expensive oil – oil which could have been sold for a very high price and the money used to feed the poor (Matthew 26:6-13);
- Basically blew off his own mother, telling people that she was not so special just because she had given birth to him! Instead, the people who love and serve God are his brothers and mother (Mark 3:31-35);
- Told people they must hate their own parents and family if they are to truly love God (Luke 14:26).

We are quick to ignore anything uncomfortable about Jesus. In so doing, we are quick to ignore and demonize anything uncomfortable about ourselves and especially our young men. Rather than teaching them to use all of their impulses and instincts for the glory of God, we hold up Jesus as the ultimate pussy that our young men should be like. We teach them to squelch the very parts of them that make them strong and able to endure and fight for that which God calls humanity to defend. We have lost the development of young men of fire, passion, fight, and servant love. Or, we have young men out of balance with hate and anger, unable to channel those passions for a noble purpose or a loving cause, instead choosing mindless violence and rage.

Our spiritual diet cannot be one that is solely niceness and flowers. We are beckoned by the example of Jesus to be lions for the call inside each one of us, fighters for justice and the work of God, and filled with channeled anger against that which defiles the spirit of the lowly, weak and outcast. We are called to use everything in our arsenal – every gift, every talent, every instinct, every desire, every power, every dream – to bring love to those who are most in need, whether physically or spiritually, and to help people grow in their own relationships with God.

We have gotten so hooked up and spun around into this belief that following Jesus is about 'being good' when it most certainly is not! Following the life and teachings of Jesus is about changing the world and being an instrument of love and energy in the lives of others. It is more about 'doing good' *for others* in great amounts than 'being good' little boys and girls.

'Being good' is self-focused. It is placing my own 'holiness,' my own navel, my own 'getting into heaven' as the highest directive in life – placing my own concerns squarely in the center of the universe, when Jesus and the Bible (especially the First Commandment) call us to do precisely the opposite – pull ourselves out of the center of the universe. 'Doing good' for the world (and especially for those in need who can benefit oneself in no possible way) is other-focused.[1]

---

[1] In an article, entitled *Leaving Niebuhr,* that I wrote awhile back for Associatedcontent.com I overturned the long-held belief taught at nearly every seminary (and many colleges) of every Christian denomination that Christians are called to be "in but not of" the world – participants in but still 'above' the slop and decay of society. According to Reinhold Niebuhr, Christians are called to be moral people in an immoral society – in but not of that society. I argue, then and now, two primary points: 1) No matter how much Christianity clicks its red heels together and wishes otherwise, 1950s-vintage

The goal of life is not to become perfect or sinless. The goal is to find your greatness and pursue it. It is to find your awesome potential and tap it, putting it to service for others. It is to become your lion self for those who are most in need, knowing full well you will make mistakes and accidentally do some harm along the way. The goal is not to live a life of perfection, constantly making sure you offend no one. The goal is not to so fear offending others that you refuse to take risks. The goal is to live boldly, knowing you will occasionally step on toes, cause offense, or just plain screw up. But it is to do so in service of some great cause that can at least justify such an offense, even while it strives to reduce the number of such offenses. The goal of the lion servant is to be flawed yet real, fierce yet other-focused and honest, and always pursuing the nobility of the call – the call to bring love to those who are most in need.

One of the goals of life is to find and live the path that breathes passion into your soul. If there is one thing that nearly all of the characters in the Bible have, and all of the great figures in Christian history have, it is that they were intensely passionate, fierce people! Jesus and his followers were not milk toast, wallflowers, or bland in any way. Martin Luther King, Jr., Malcolm X, Dietrich Bonhoeffer, Pope John XXIII, Martin Luther, John Hus, and St. Augustine, to name a few.[2] These people were full of passion, zeal, and fire in the belly!

---

thinking no longer works today. For, crazy as it may sound, the leader or Christian who is not, at least to some degree, "of the world" – i.e. flawed and sinful – and open about it will not be taken seriously by non-Christians, but will be seen as a hypocrite who is simply hiding his/her flaws. Further, non-Christians today actually respect *more* the person or leader who is flawed but real! To un-churched and de-churched Americans, honesty is seen as a categorically higher virtue than moral purity. 2) "In" the world and "of" the world are, ultimately, self-centered prepositions. The new goal of the follower of Jesus must be to be "for" the world. It must be a life of service, a life bigger than oneself. It's not about personal holiness, but radical other-centered love. And that is a very different primary orientation from Christianity of years past.

[2] MLK stood with a straight spine before entrenched hatred. Malcolm X, raised Christian prior to becoming Muslim, stood in the face of great heat from even his own people to have a powerful counter-balance force to the Civil Rights Movement. Dietrich Bonhoeffer, a German Christian pastor, was imprisoned by the Nazis in WWII for inciting opposition against Hitler. Martin Luther, a German priest/professor, who hung out in bars, drinking and singing, is known for changing the face of Western Civilization by standing up to the Catholic Church, telling it and the Pope to basically stick it. And, one of his most well-known theological quotes is "Sin boldly" (for the greater the sin, the greater the mercy of God that is incurred). John Hus, a monk who came before Luther, was burned at the stake for standing up to the Church. St. Augustine, a Catholic bishop

None of these greats equated Jesus with being a softy or a pushover. Instead, Jesus inspired them to fight for what was right. They used all the fire and passion they had been given by God to be great and grand sources of love to others, particularly those in need. These titans of faith embodied servant love – the love of a servant for his stern, strong, yet benevolent and fair master. The love of a fiercely focused athlete for his demanding coach and mentor.

These greats, like Jesus himself, teach us. It is no sin to have strength of character. It is no sin to have passion. It is no sin to be fully loaded with earthy vitamins! It is no sin to have hell in your veins. It is no sin to be fiery, intense and focused. It is no sin to be salty, aggresive, driven, or badass.

The question is, What do you do with it?

We have so easily convoluted being loving with weakness! Love and weakness are not, not, not, not, not the same thing! The greatest lovers of people, the greatest lovers of life, the greatest lovers of doing good for others are always the strongest, most passionate, biggest believers in others. They are bearers of great love in this lifetime, who feel that passion of God flowing into them, and then flowing out of them to others!!! People like that know power and know love. And they know one cannot long exist without the other.

In fact, the very goal of life is to tap into this lion-nature and *use it for the greatest possible good for the most amount of people!!!* It is the very goal of life to become the focused, intense, driven badass for God that you were made to be. It is the very goal of life to listen for the very voice of God in your heart, and then pursue that calling with all your passion, all your mind, all your body, and all your strength and focus. It is the very goal of life to become the salty SOB that lives, fights, and dies for those who need the transformative power and servant love that God has put deep in your viscera.

For, in living this gutsy, other-centered life, you will know a rush, a joy, a radical adventure, an excitement, and a deep sense of fulfillment

---

in the early centuries after Christ, and one of the most venerated of all Christian saints and thinkers, was known for bold action, as well as saying such things as, "Love God and do what you want" and "The Church is a whore…but she's my mother."

like you have never known! Jesus – the ultimate badass – not only promises you this, he lived it and was killed for it!

The day you begin to tap into that badass, lion nature that finds power and passion in servant love is the day you finally come alive. It is the day you waken from your mommy-lulled, fattened slumber. It is the day you finally begin to become you – the you God meant you to be on the day he created you. And it is the day you finally begin to 'get' the real nature of that ultimate badass from long ago.

Are you ready to be a lion, or are you still convinced that following Jesus is a sign of weakness?

Who or what is holding you back, holding you down, or oppressing your inner badass, your inner lion?

In what areas of life are you most a lion?

Have you stepped your life up to the next level of being a badass with a purpose bigger than yourself?

What are you waiting for?

Chapter 2

ACHIEVE TRUE GREATNESS NOW!

Not everyone I have worked with is an intense athlete. Over the years, I have taught classes, groups, and individuals of novice and intermediate fitness ability, as well. I have been employed to devise everything from simple workout programs to total life fitness plans.

Often, when giving speeches to groups of these novice and intermediate athletic folk I talk on many of the fitness possibilities available for moving one's body and mind into a state of greater fitness fulfillment. But one of the topics I regularly highlight is the benefit(s) of resistance training, or weightlifting.

Despite what their feelings might be about actually doing it, most people know lifting is good for them. But, unlike the advanced athlete, they often don't know why resistance training is generally more effective for achieving fitness goals than simple cardio, which is the fitness default for most novices and intermediates. As a teacher and coach I must put it into language and concepts they understand. Otherwise, there is no way to get them excited about lifting and its features and benefits.

So, one of the playful exercises I do with a group, whether adults or teens, is go to the chalkboard and have them shout out to me all the things they have heard about what weight training does for them. They may know a little or a lot. I, then, make a list. What follows are the features and benefits of lifting that generally round out the list, some they know, but many they don't:

1. Increased physical strength
2. Increased heart capacity
3. Depression-fighting ability
4. Adrenaline release
5. Increased flexibility
6. Increased bone density
7. Increased lung capacity
8. Muscle growth and appearance
9. Sense of accomplishment

The problem, however, is that none of these things are big motivators for most people, at least not in that form. Most people really don't care about increased lung capacity, unless they've quit smoking. Most regular folk don't significantly care about increased strength, unless they have a job that requires lifting, such as raising toddlers or working on a loading dock. Most people don't care about bone density or increased flexibility, in and of themselves.

So, the problem I am confronted with as a teacher/coach/trainer, and the problem each one of us is confronted with as we try to stay motivated in our workouts, is translating these benefits into something more compelling. The task is to take each of the 9 benefits listed above and show how they directly impact the real goals for people's lives. In the chalkboard exercise I will go down the list and ask them to shout out guesses for what each one of these things really means, or what it translates into.

For a simple example, increased heart capacity (#2 above), means increased blood flow, which, at the very least, brings more natural color to your skin, making you look livelier, younger, and more vigorous. In that vein, I have known women who, after getting into a regular fitness/lifting habit, either stopped or greatly reduced their use of makeup, largely because they discovered that their own natural colors were coming out more.

Further, by pumping fresh blood more efficiently and strongly, the body actually takes on and exudes greater energy. Ever been around someone who has a weak or 'blah' energy or aura about them? Ever been around someone who has an exuberant or at least lively energy? Or, ever been around a 65 year-old who has more vivacity and zip than many 25 year-olds? A heart that is used to being pushed and taxed by regular workouts naturally increases energy in the bearer, giving that person an aura of energy, excitement, and zest for life.

After we go through a few on the chalkboard list and they get the hang of it, they begin to see a pattern developing. I can list all the medical and physiological reasons in the world for weightlifting. But to the average Joe or Jenny, all of resistance training (or really any type of training) boils down to basically two things – looking great and feeling great. Unless there are serious medical issues in the equation, most people just want two things: to look better and feel better (which includes increasing the quality and perhaps length of life in older people who may workout). It's that simple: look great and feel great! And unless I translate it into these words and ideas that are important *to them* as a felt need, they will never be motivated to work out when I am not around.

To illustrate this, here is the translation of the benefits listed above:

1. **Increased Strength = Feel Great**: Increased strength means you can carry your own groceries and heavier laundry baskets. You can wrestle around with your kids. You can do your own lifting in the garage when working on your car. You can carry your baby in your arms longer as it gets older. You can hold your own on camping trips with your buddies. Being able to do more of these things means you feel much better about yourself.

2. **Increased Heart Capacity = Feel Great and Look Great**: In addition to the benefits listed above, increased heart capacity also means increased blood flow to your extremities, so you stay warmer in winter. Further, you can go for vigorous walks or engage in waterskiing or other activities that your friends might be doing, or play harder and longer with your own children. It also contributes to long term wellness, so you will look better longer and feel better into older age.

3. **Fight Depression = Feel Great**: Many studies confirm that by challenging your mind to go beyond what it thinks the body is capable of strength-training increases a sense of accomplishment with each workout. For the fitness beginner, resistance training has the effect of decreasing depression-related feelings so often caused by inaction.

4. **Adrenaline Release = Feel Great**: Closely related to #3, working out with weights increases the release of adrenaline/endorphins in the brain, causing an increase in 'good feelings' and happiness. This is a great benefit to people who are not depressed, too. Everybody likes to start the day feeling great, and a workout can accomplish this, making you ready to attack with gusto whatever is ahead. Or, at the end of a hard day of work this can be great for pushing out the stress and anxiety, causing each day to end on positive and peaceful feelings.

    - Interestingly, feeling great after a workout happens in varying degrees to different people. One of my best friends, as well as a great many other people I have worked with, absolutely thrive on the high they get from working out, and the 'feel good' feeling it gives them for hours afterward. Yet, in contrast, I seldom feel great after a workout. Generally, I feel beat and totally spent. So, the 'feel great' of adrenaline release has never been a big motivator for me to lift. I do it for other reasons, such as the ability to eat more of what I really like, and the ability to look the way I want to look. But that's the point, everyone works out for different reasons. *My job as a coach is to find out what excites each different person and translate it into language and goals that particular person understands and is motivated by.*

5. **Increased Flexibility = Look Great and Feel Great**: Increased flexibility lends to better posture and quicker movement and walking. Multi-joint exercises contribute to increased overall body functioning. Studies show that we actually judge people by how freely they move, how loose or tight they are, and how relaxed or strained are their movements – leading us to see them as either 'old' or 'young.' As we age we tend to walk slower, slump a bit when we stand, and be more mechanical and tighter in our movements. Therefore, we not only are chronologically old, but if we don't have flexibility *we actually look old.* And not all older people let themselves look old. Flexibility has the ability to create a physiological look of youthfulness. And looking younger generally contributes to feeling great, as well.

6. **Increased Bone Density = Look Great and Feel Great**: While not as big an issue for men at younger ages, bone density is a huge issue for women as they get into their 40s and beyond. Osteoporosis is a major disease that also contributes to the signs of aging

listed in #5, as well as the body simply becoming more brittle and prone to problems. But high bone density – which can be directly created from resistance training (and running) – causes a person to be less prone to injury, and contributes to an overall feeling of fitness. And in aging people this is one of the single greatest contributors to quality of life. A new knee can be pushed off for years, or avoided altogether, by increasing bone density. Falling no longer automatically translates into a new hip. And, most importantly, increased bone strength (and overall body strength) can reduce the *fear* of falling, which is huge for many people as they age. Thus, they actually feel better psychologically.

7. **Increased Lung Capacity = Feel Great**: Increased lung capacity means more oxygen is getting to the body quicker and more effectively. This contributes to heightened capacity and greater endurance during sex or when playing with your kids, the ability to go up a flight of steps without getting winded, and also greater calmness. Why calmness? The same reason an athlete takes deep breaths before attempting something big: increased oxygen relaxes the body. It's not merely psychological. It's physiological. Increased oxygen flow relaxes muscles and decreases tension. So, by having greater capacity in the lungs there is, daily, the capacity for a greater flow of oxygen and, hence, peacefulness. Increased lung capacity also greatly contributes to recovery from strenuous exercise or movement. That means a second flight of stairs is possible, as well as a fourth or fifth dance at the wedding reception, another romantic go-round with your wife, a good cigar without it clouding your breathing entirely, or the ability to go out and do yard work after a strenuous morning bike ride.

8. **Muscle Growth = Look Great and Feel Great**: Muscle growth increases calorie-burning, even when at rest (an amazing and little-known fact to be looked at later in the book). Thus, your body is essentially working out even when you're not working out. It, therefore, increases your ability to eat more of the foods you like! Still, the most obvious benefit of muscle growth, no matter how far you take it, is that you simply begin to look great!!

9. **Sense of Accomplishment = Feel Great**: For the advanced athlete, significantly increased muscle development demands

mental focus and yields huge changes in one's physical state and state of mind, often taxing a person in ways that mere cardio does not. Beyond just fighting depression, radically increased capacity to focus and increased physical abilities create a sense of having achieved something well beyond the bounds of normal daily living. It is this sense of major accomplishment that lifts the spirit, boosts confidence in other areas of life, and creates a sense of feeling great about life.

The primary point in all of this is not to pitch the benefits of weight-lifting to you, the reader. Instead, it is a roundabout way to show you how it has been necessary for me as a coach, teacher, and trainer to translate any program or plan into concepts my athletes or trainees understand, naturally buy into, and will get really excited about!

The best coaches and teachers understand the mind and the lives of their athletes and students. The best coaches have the ability to translate, say, the medical features and benefits of 1-9 above or the benefits of their sport, into concepts and language that mean something to the hearer, such as in the chalkboard exercise. Unless this is done, the person will never own it for him- or herself after the coach or trainer is gone.

The greatest coaches and leaders are able to translate sport into life, athletics into everyday, and severe physical activity into wisdom. That's the bottom line. They show how the concepts of sport are pointedly relevant in all areas of life. They motivate the beginner or the most advanced by:

1) stepping into that person's world,
2) finding out what things motivate and drive him or her, and then
3) putting the ideas into language the athlete can understand and be motivated by!

Jesus Understood the Athlete Mentality!

Jesus was brilliant at this. He was the ultimate translator, the ultimate relevant coach. In fact, Jesus' message is perfectly suited for the high-level, intense athlete, because he is already speaking the athlete's language.

Interestingly, Jesus made direct or indirect reference countless times to the one thing that motivates all high-caliber athletes – the desire for greatness! It is the desire and drive for greatness, in some form or another, that is intrinsic to the lion nature.

Jesus *knew* what is in the hearts of men, and what drives athletes of both genders. Each one of us desires, to a very large degree, to do great things and be considered great. That's what championships and competition are all about. It is the mad quest for greatness. This is why we immortalize Michael Jordan, Bret Favre, Michael Phelps, Johan Santana, Wayne Gretzky, Jesse Owens, Tom Brady, Martina Navratilova, Nadia Comaneci, Greg Louganis, and Tiger Woods. They are the greatest of the great in the sports world. And each one of us strives for a measure of what they have, or more. We, too, want greatness.

Jesus knew this. This is why he said such things as:

> "Truly, truly, I say to you, you will do **greater works than I have done**!" (John 14:12).

He knew how powerful the desire to do great things is in the hearts of men. But what's interesting is that he didn't try to purge men of this desire or tell them it was a bad thing. Jesus never said that the desire for greatness is a bad thing!

Too often the Christian Church has confused the desire for greatness with arrogance and pride. Too often the Christian Church has sought to strip men of the thing that drives them to accomplish great things and live lives of noble purpose.

Do you think Tiger knows he's the greatest golfer in the world, utterly dominating his opponents? Do you think Kevin Garnett, Kobe Bryant, and LeBron James know they're the greatest basketball players in the world? Further, do you think it would do any of them any good to think they're not the best? No. They may not need to spout it off all the time, but they know inside that they are the best.

Now, do you think Tiger Woods or Tom Brady knew they were the best when they were in college or only amateurs? Well, they didn't have 'proof' yet, but somewhere in them they had to believe in it. Even before they achieved their greatest accomplishments, they had to believe in their own innate greatness. THAT was what drew them forward and drove them to work ever harder – that belief in themselves; that belief in their greatness!

Now, being a jackass and knowing you kick ass are two different things, and most athletes know the difference. But feigning inability or pretending to have only moderate ability does no athlete any good. Modesty is a gift and an honorable trait. In contrast, while mildly entertaining, at times, arrogance is generally unbecoming and ignoble. But outright denying one's own ability and denying one's greatness is a mistake. The greatest athletes, no matter how humble they are, have the swagger of confidence and that inner knowing of what they are truly capable of.

Jesus did talk about lots of things men should *not* be: Self-centered, hypocritical, adulterers, negligent toward the poor and hungry, and untrusting of God, to name a few. But isn't it interesting that he *never* said men should not seek greatness?

In fact, startlingly, Jesus did just the opposite. When dealing with his disciples he used that deep desire for greatness as the primary motivation for life, for faith, for trusting in God, and for *action,* not because it would get 'em into heaven or something, but because Jesus' very definition of greatness was other-centeredness. Truly, it could be well-argued that Jesus' entire ministry and message were about helping people find the immortality of true and lasting greatness. Again, I don't mean just the idea of going to heaven somewhere when you die. Jesus was talking in very real, very right-here-right-now terms.

See, Jesus taught a radical new reality: that the highest echelons of respect and greatness are reserved for those men and women who have given themselves for others. In John 15:13, Jesus states the truth that we all know, the truth that resounded in our hearts as we learned of the bravery of regular Americans in New York, D.C., and Pennsylvania on 9/11:

"Greater love has no man
than to lay down his life for his friends."

This is why even the greatest of sports stars is humbled to be in the company of firefighters, police officers, and military men. These great defenders of the public put their lives on the line every day for meatheads like us athletes. This is why Pat Tillman, a professional football player, was so immortalized in the sports world when he walked away from the money and fame of the pro game to go fight the wars in the Mideast; and even moreso when he later died in one of those wars.

People who 'live to serve' move us and stir us. This is why great leaders of nations were humbled in the presence of the true greatness of Mother Teresa, Gandhi, Nelson Mandela, Lech Walesa, and Martin Luther King, Jr. – people who lived lives sacrificing themselves for the benefit of something greater than themselves. We venerate most the people who sacrifice the most for others.

Even on a team level we know that those who work the hardest always gain the most respect. The ones who sacrifice the most of themselves in the off-season (when they could be lazy or partying instead) just naturally earn the respect and honor of others. The more they sacrifice for the team or for the goal, the more respect they gain.

Jesus knew that people honor the greatness of self-sacrifice and giving oneself for others. He spent his entire life preaching to men and women on how to achieve that greatness. Of course, his teachings on how to do it were completely upside-down, counterintuitive, and all spun-around from what people were used to. But he was right. He knew it. And deep in us, we know it. That is why so many people only go halfway toward buying into Jesus' message of other-centered love and self-sacrifice. They know the truth of Jesus' message, but they also know the cost. For many people the price is just too high.

But for the intense athlete and the fiery personality that is precisely the appeal! Intense athletes think in precisely the terms Jesus was using. Intense athletes do not fear great sacrifice. They love it! They may, indeed, fear it....but they feed on it, nonetheless! They need something they fear. They need sacrifice. They live for it. They live to go to the edge of life. They crave it!

And in going through such trials and suffering these fierce athletes bring out the best in those who have lesser physical ability or lesser courage. They inspire us to greatness in our own realms of influence.

Intense athletes know that everything has a price; and the higher the price, the higher the payoff. That's why so many intense athletes really are attracted to this odd understanding of Jesus' ministry. He is speaking their language. He is singing to the very hearts of the passionate, fire-in-the-belly athletes. And the reason you are reading this book is because he is speaking your language!

"Whoever desires **greatness** among you must be your servant, and whoever wishes to be first among you must be slave of all" (Mark 10:44).

"...Let the **greatest** among you become the youngest, and the leader as one who serves. For which is greater, the one who sits at the table, or one who serves? Is it not the one who sits at the table? But I am among you as one who serves" (Luke 22:26-27).

"...He who is least among you all is the one who is **great**" (Luke 9:48).

"He who finds his life will lose it, and he who loses his life for my teachings will find it" (Matthew 10:39).

"He who is **greatest** among you shall be your servant; whoever applauds himself will be humbled, and whoever humbles himself will be applauded" (Matthew 23:11).

"If any man would come after me, let him deny himself and take up his cross and follow me. For whoever would save his life will lose it; and whoever loses his life for my sake and the sake of my teachings will save it" (Mark 8:34-36).

Don't we all tire of athletes, politicians, and movie stars who think they are 'all that' and more? Don't we tire of people who continually hold themselves up as the greatest? Don't we all admire those people, whether well-known or completely anonymous, who sacrifice themselves for others, especially when it benefits them in no possible way…and who keep their mouths shut?

We expect players like Cal Ripken, Jr., to go into the Baseball Hall of Fame on a near-unanimous vote, because of his incredible history of selfless commitment – his dogged self-sacrifice day-in and day-out for decades, never missing a game, and always being such a team player, on top of the fact that he not only showed up but excelled.

We respect athletes like Mia Hamm, Brandi Chastain, and Michelle Akers of the 1999 World Champion US Women's Soccer team who constantly deflected their much-earned praise to their teammates.

We marvel that Wayne Gretzky can be the greatest hockey player of all time, the all-time leading scorer, *and* be the all-time leader in assists – setting his teammates up for success more than twice as many times as he scored.

We stand in awe of players like Jerry Rice – unequivocally the all-time greatest receiver in the history of football – who walks through life with such humility and integrity. We stand in awe of quarterbacks like Favre, Montana, Bradshaw, and Brady who constantly give/gave praise to their coaches, their offensive lines, and all of their teammates – everyone except themselves, and were often greatly self-deprecating, as well!

There is something innate in us – innate in human nature – that honors great achievement, but even more greatly respects great achievement mixed with humility, other-respect, other-service, and self-sacrifice.

See, Jesus translated the entire message of all of Scripture into a very simple truth, one we all know (even people who aren't real religious): ***True greatness only comes by sacrificing yourself for others!*** And it doesn't just mean dying for others. For it also has the very powerful meaning of *living for others,* and not just you and yours, not just those in your immediate circle, not just your family and friends, but those who can benefit you in no possible way.

This is why Jesus said that his “First and Greatest Commandment” is to love God; and his second one is to love your neighbor as much as you love yourself. True greatness means putting in the center of your life those who are most in need. Jesus goes on to say these words,

“Truly, I say to you, as you do it to one of the least of your neighbors, you do it to God”
(Matthew 25:40).

To show love and respect to your neighbor and to all of humanity is to show love to God. It is to see and honor the Divine in all people.

Every athlete I have ever known has desired in his or her heart to do something great with his or her life. Sure the desire for athletic prowess tops the list, for awhile. But ultimately there is a desire to do something great with the rest of one’s life, something that will last, something that will be beneficial to more than just the athlete, himself, or to his family. At the core, we all desire to create or be a part of something greater than ourselves.

That is where the seriousness and the intensity come from. These things find their origin in orientation to other things outside one’s own personal gain.

The Center of the Universe

It is interesting to note, in this regard, that the first of the Ten Commandments is, “I am the Lord, your God. You shall have no other gods before me.” This is the first commandment because God knows darn well that all other commandments, rules, teachings, and laws basically flow out of this one. Yet, none are so difficult as this one.

All human screw-ups, failings and folly – all ‘sin,’ for those who prefer that religious term – flow out of the fact that we are constantly putting ourselves and our own best interests at the center of the universe. The single most difficult thing to do in life is to take ourselves out of the center of the universe and put others and God there. We so want to put ourselves there. We have such a propensity for making our own selves, our own lives, and our own heaven the most important things in life. Our natural state is one of 'me, me, me.' We so badly want to be the center of life. Our own egos. Our own pride. Our own interests. Our own everything. Heck, marriages fail because we can't even take ourselves out of the center of the universe for the person we say we love the most. It is just so easy, so intoxicating, so addicting to make all of life revolve around me. This is the desire for greatness gone bad.

The push to satisfy one's own needs is important, to be sure. But the very highest levels of fulfillment in life are achieved when one's own joy is finally only accomplished by the service of others.

The center of the universe is a magical, exhilarating, special place to be. And we all want to be there. But, it is ultimately unfulfilling, because experience teaches that we are never satisfied. Those who have lived long and well in the center of their universe – whether they were captains of industry or giants of sport – have often learned and taught essentially the same message Jesus taught. When you're at the center of the universe there is never enough to fill you up inside. The more I make my own happiness the most important thing in my life, the more I realize that I am never happy. I am a bottomless pit of unfulfilled desire. It is ultimately an unfulfilling and non-satisfying place to be.

But there is an experience in life that is very much like that center-of-the-universe experience, but ultimately more fulfilling and ultimately the only way to true peace, power, greatness, joy and sense of purpose. It is Jesus' path.

You can have the greatness you seek, Jesus says. Jesus knows that we desire greatness in our lives. And he doesn't try to tell us that is bad or that we can't have it. He doesn't tell us to get rid of this desire. He just says that those who want *true* or highest levels of greatness, and those who want to do things even greater than he did, must be able to put God and others in the center of the universe.

Jesus says that if you genuinely desire greatness, if you genuinely desire to accomplish something great and lasting – something greater than yourself – you must have the ability to do one thing: You must constantly – daily! – be pulling yourself out of the center of the universe and putting God and those in need – or God in the form of those in need – there in the center. And, even though it is no longer about you, as it was when you were at the center of the universe, it will bring greater joy and fulfillment than the center of the universe ever could.

The Difficulty of the Path

But Jesus knew how hard this can be. Jesus knew our inclination to constantly indulge ourselves, our egos, and our own desire to get fat on life. This is why focus is so important to being a follower of Jesus' most radical teachings; and therefore why athletes make such powerful livers of Jesus' message. It takes constant attention and focus to pull yourself from your self-interest and daily re-orient yourself to the needs, hurts, and longings of those who are most in need. It takes an athlete's level of focus to constantly pull yourself from the center of the universe.

As will be dealt with in Chapter 13, mental focus is not only the key to success in sports and in life; it is the key to greatness in all of life. Jesus said that the only real and highest fulfillment in life comes from following God's calling in your life to serve others. But as long as you allow yourself to be distracted by ongoing self-interest and self-serving pursuits you will never find your true potential or your true fulfillment, peace, and deep joy.

This is not to say that life is to be only drudgery. Certainly not. Surely we, too, may delight in the goodness of life. In fact, we will never last in life if we are not also filling our own tanks, so to speak. But the real challenge and greatest joy in life come from constantly pulling ourselves out of the center of the universe and giving our lives in humble service of those who most need the love, strength, fight, and generosity we can bring to their cause.

To bring love to those in need is another way of showing love to God. And it is self-sacrificial love that is the key to finding the greatness you so desperately seek.

Not only that, Jesus said time and again that it is this same self-sacrificial love of God and love of neighbor that are the keys to abundant life. This message is echoed all throughout Scripture.

This is the message of Jesus' death, as well. At the very least (or most, depending on your perspective), he gave himself up to death so that his spirit would live on in you, just as some like to say that quarterback Tom Brady has Joe Montana's spirit and nature, or how analysts might say Kevin Garnett has a bit of Wilt Chamberlain or Magic Johnson in him. Those who give of themselves live on in the lives of those who are inspired by them and those whom they touched. Their greatness becomes immortal in those who carry on their dreams, goals, and way of living in passionate service.

Even if you don't buy into Jesus' whole "Savior of the World" thing, that's okay. But it is indisputable that Jesus died so that you would be inspired to live for the true greatness that only comes by giving your life in service of others. And each one of us lives and dies so that our spirit of great purpose might live on in others and inspire them to more noble aspirations and greater heights for the benefit of humanity. That is greatness!

In what ways do you put yourself in the center of the universe?

What people do you feel called to put in the center of your universe and give your life in service of? Perhaps, who is it that can benefit you in no possible way that needs your greatness?

What are you great at already?

Are you ready to begin your pursuit of real greatness? Do you have the guts?

Chapter 3

I'M STILL WAITING FOR MY BURNING BUSH

One of the responsibilities I am regularly asked to take on when working at the collegiate level is to speak to groups of high school recruits who are visiting campus for different sports. These young kids are the keys to any college's future athletic success, as well as the future financial viability of the college. And I often find myself in the position of pitchman for the college and the sports programs. Generally, these groups are somewhat large and, more often than not, the recruits are joined by their parents.

Often, I use this opportunity to debunk one of the greatest fallacies ever perpetuated in sports. Every athlete has heard it, at one time or another in his or her sports career, beaten into his head by a ball-busting coach. It goes, "Winners never quit, and quitters never win." And it is this notion, I tell the recruits and parents, that they now must throw out the window, especially at this time in their lives when they are entering college.

I tell them that their single greatest task, now in their late-teens and early- to mid-twenties, is to, in fact, *quit as many things as possible*.

Yeah, you heard me right. Quit!

The goal of this period of their lives (and really it never stops throughout life) is to burn through as many life-options as they can, until they find that one thing, or those two or three things, that I could pay them money to quit and they still wouldn't quit.

Our job as a college is to essentially lay before each student a vast buffet of options – from Chemistry to International Business, from Physician's Assistant careers to Psychology, from sports to feeding the homeless, from chapel to dating, and from studying overseas to learning Arabic – so that each student can go up and down that buffet tasting all the options, until she finds the one or two things that she wants to make a meal/life out of. Unless the student has the courage to quit those things that don't work, she will likely never find the one or two things that really do work, and make her heart sing.

In the past, such a mentality was unthinkable. Quitting, whether it be a job or an area of study or sport, was all but unheard of and unallowable. Quitting has always gotten a bad rap and been looked down upon. Residue from this mentality is still seen in parents who expect their kids to declare and keep a major, unwaveringly. Changes in direction are seen as embarrassments for parents locked in old-school mentalities of one-life = one-career.

But finding one's life calling generally demands weeding out those things that are not one's calling. Sometimes in life we only discover who we are by discerning who we are not. And that means sifting through it all to find the ringer.

There is an old Hasidic Jewish proverb:

***"Each man must carefully observe which way his heart calls him,
And then pursue that path with all his strength."***

And you can never know which way your heart calls, unless you are willing and able to let go of all those directions that your heart is not calling you to, even if you previously thought it was calling you in those directions.

Tenacity, endurance, and determination are admirable and necessary virtues, especially for athletes. I do not tell these young athletes that they are to abandon these qualities. I tell them, instead, that we will help develop them. But the point of tenacity and endurance is not to employ them toward something that holds no meaning for him or her, but to use them in the pursuit of one's own dream, particularly in the down times or hard times. It is to use them to accomplish that which fires your soul! That is the key.

But to apply tenacity and endurance to life paths that are ultimately forced rather than inspired, or externally imposed rather than self-chosen, is to spend one's energy coercing oneself through life rather than using all that energy in a direction one is really and truly excited about going.

Then, speaking more to the parents than the kids, I explain that often the reason people have a mid-life crisis is because they wake up one day to discover they have been living someone else's life or someone else's dream for their life. They have not been living out the calling of their own heart, but have been refusing to quit at their life, even though the life they are living was never really their own choice or what they *really* wanted. A mid-life crisis springs from a heart that does not know itself – a heart that is living what someone, somewhere said it should live, rather than what it, by itself, naturally yearned to do.

The goal for parents when their kids are college age is to give the young adults permission and space to quit that which does not feed their soul. So often kids do what they think they are supposed to do, what their parents encourage them to do, or what other important adults impress upon them. This is especially true for kids who are people-pleasers – kids who so desperately want to be loved that they will do anything with their lives, even if it's not what they want (a far too common occurrence among kids). Though, kids like this have been doing what other people wanted for so long that they often cannot even hear their own voice inside, which is why it's our job as college leaders to help them find that which feels just right to them, regardless of what their parents might think.

Thus, if the parent does not realize the purpose of this time in life as a time of exploration and grant the kid space, the parent will grow exasperated that the young adult has not decided what he is going to do with his life, as if there is some God-ordained mandatory timeline for life's decisions. Then the student will grow even more frustrated that he just can't seem to figure out what he is going to do with his life.

I explain to my recruits and their parents that when a key is struck on a piano that key lifts a hammer which then strikes a string. Deep inside that piano the string resonates with the sound it has been tuned to make with that particular key. Their lives are no different. They must explore life – at this time in life when they have the time and more financial liberty than they might have later – to discover those things that play them like a piano. They must discover those things that resonate deep inside them with the music of who they are.

"To love someone is to learn the song that is in their heart, And sing it to them when they have forgotten."
-- Thomas Chandler

It is like those times in life when someone speaks a truth that just seems to seize us deep inside. We know it is true the second the person speaks it. It's like we've always known it, but never fully heard it crystallized in words. That is what it is like to find one's true calling, or even to find one's true love.

I tell them that is the goal of being this age, even if it means quitting sports. Some of the coaches occasionally ride me about this, but they know it is true. Further, they know that in the long run I am doing them a favor, because one semi-committed athlete quitting generally makes room for another athlete who wants it and who is willing to work hard and with more passion, because football or soccer or baseball is something that resonates deep inside him or her.

I tell them of a very large young man – an ox of a guy – I met while living in Los Angeles. My wife was a principal performer with the Los Angeles Opera at the time, and this young man was a young vocal virtuoso, hand-picked by Placido Domingo, one of the great tenors. This young guy and I were chatting at an after-show party, one evening. There he shared with me that he had actually been on full scholarship as an offensive lineman at a large and extremely successful Division 1 Florida university. Then, in his sophomore year, not prompted by injury or poor grades, he quit. He quit D1 Florida football!!

When I asked why on earth he did this, he responded that he simply wanted to sing. He had realized after lessons from a vocal coach that he had talent – real talent – for singing. On top of that, he really, really loved singing, even more than football.

So here he was, but a few years later, as the principal tenor in the Los Angeles Opera's latest major production. He had followed his heart away from something really good to find something even better, something that brought him to life and enabled him to find his true greatness.

The courage to quit!

Each one of us must have the courage to walk away from that which does not feed our soul, in order to find that which does. For, once that vocation or calling is found, endurance and tenacity come naturally and are not forced. Once we find that which inspires us, all desire to quit fades away. Quitting becomes almost a non-issue. Endurance and tenacity are embraced as tools for achieving one's life dream, not simply that which forces to fruition a path that is not loved from the beginning. They are seen as best friends that can help a person become who he or she was most fully made to be. The work becomes almost effortless; it flows. It's the difference between walking upstream against a strong river current, and the feeling of going with the current, which is pulling you in the direction of your dreams.

Once we find our true passion, quitting ceases to be an option….at least until the next calling comes along, perhaps years or decades down the road, at which time the first calling must be quit just as surely as if it were bleeding one's soul, which it likely is if a new call is felt.

As a culture, we have been so locked into that 1950s-ish mentality that you have one job, one dream, one life direction, and you have it forever. Or, if not that, you at least don't jump from here to there very often. Stability and lack of movement in careers and in life were prized in this old-school mentality. Changing your path was seen as a mark of indecisiveness and childishness.

Fortunately, this notion has been changing for the past few decades as we've grown to realize that life brings freedom and the possibility for great joy on bold new paths in life. Research now indicates that people will change *careers* – not just jobs, but careers! – multiple times in their life.

There is no joy, no greatness, no badass life, until you quit living what is not you, and start living out who God made you to most fully be.

But HOW?

Step One: The Most Important Thing Jesus EVER Said

In Matthew 22: 37-40, Jesus states clearly a saying he goes on to say numerous other times, words that are found countless other times in the Bible, stated by prophets, apostles, and other writers,

"'You shall love the Lord your God with all your heart, and with all your soul, and with all your mind.' This is the Great and First Commandment. And a second like it 'You shall love your neighbor as yourself.' On these two commandments depend all the [Bible]."

Here Jesus lays out his two simple, yet greatest commands for life! These two commands are the very backbone of the Bible, Jesus' entire ministry, and this entire book you have in your hands! He says everything depends on these two core principles.

Well, the second of the two Great Commandments is pretty straightforward. Jesus explains that it means to love those around us who are in need, not just our family or those who can benefit us, but those who need help most. This second commandment will be dealt with more fully in later chapters.

But it's that other commandment – what Jesus calls '**The First and Greatest Commandment'** – that is a bit confusing. For what does it mean to 'love God?' Does it mean to say nice things to the ceiling of your bedroom before going to bed? Does it mean pointing to the sky after scoring a touchdown? 'Love God' sounds simple, but how do you do it?

Step Two: I Got Stiffed on the Whole Burning Bush Thing

The first trick to understanding Jesus' greatest commandment – *Love God* – is to admit to yourself a very real, rock-solid truth.

This may seem a bit strange, but you must, first and foremost, concede that, more than likely, God has not spoken to you in any grand vision in the sky, as he did with many characters in the Bible. The heavens have not parted for you. A dove has not descended from the ethers to speak God's message to you. You have not had a burning bush obstruct your path and then tell you what to do with your life. You have not been struck off your donkey by a light and voice from the sky.

You may have gotten little times when you felt God was there or was helping you or nudging you, or you may have had occasions where coincidence or synchronicity was too uncanny to be anything but God. But you have not had a dream in which God spoke some master plan to you. No angels have appeared in your life bearing good tidings of great joy. God has not spoken to you in the wind, in the clouds, in the dirt, in the waters, in a storm, or in a tongue of fire. You have not been called by a thundering, heaven-sent voice to build an ark, lead people out of slavery, confront a corrupt king, eat locusts and honey, travel to strange lands to make them believers, or do anything else like the people in the Bible.

The thing you must admit is that God has never spoken to you in some grand vision, unexplainable act, or nature-defying miracle or voice. You've never had God come to you and speak some crystallized message of exactly what is expected of you in your specific life.

Odds are, that is probably not a difficult admission for you to make. For, quite simply, it likely has never happened to you. If it had happened, if God had spoken to you some great message from the sky or through an angel, you likely wouldn't be reading this book. You would not be wrestling with an empty soul or some need for greater fulfillment. You would know your course with rock-solid, God-sent assurance.

No, the problem for people like you and me is that God has never spoken some earth-shaking, sky-opening, dove-delivered, donkey-scaring message.

The second thing you must admit is that despite your best efforts you have never found your name, your full name, written anywhere in the Bible or in any other sacred book. You must admit that despite preachers' attempts to make religion relevant to you, you have never read a divine message in a book that was directly worded to you and your exact situation in life at the time.

The suffering and the struggling in your life are the result of this lone fact. You don't know your God-given purpose. You don't know exactly what God wants from you at exactly this time. It's not in a book and it hasn't fallen out of the sky. For if that had happened, and if you did know your true God-given calling, your spirit would find fulfillment carrying it out.

Now, perhaps you knew it at one time, but no longer. And so you hunt and peck, foraging for answers.

God may, indeed, speak through the Bible. God (whatever God is) may even speak through Creation, through other people, and through certain life events. But the point here is that if God does speak through Creation, sacred texts, or some other life experience, it is only in general principles, and you are still left trying to interpret it on your own to *make it specific to your personal experience*. God may have spoken to other people in some grand vision. But the point is that, more than likely, *God has never spoken to you in any specific and clear way.*

Folks like you and me are left fumbling through life trying to make sense of all the conflicting messages and truths that bombard us from a multitude of sources. Rather than getting a divine revelation, burning bush, or divine writing of our exact individual purpose in life, we get a basket of general messages from many sources, and we're left trying to sort it all out.

So, you are stuck! You can do your best to try to make sense of Bible stuff and Jesus stuff, not to mention the well-meaning input from friends and loved ones, but it always seems to fall a little bit short…or a lotta bit short.

So, like the elite through the ages, you maybe have nearly every material thing you want in life, but you do your best to distract and numb yourself from the ache of not knowing what on earth to do with your life. Your life has no deeper meaning. You drink, play, smoke, shoot, work, run, exercise, travel, shop, and everything else you can to make it go away, but it never does.

But, once you admit (or have permission to admit) that you've never had a grand vision from God and that your exact personal message from God is not written anywhere, then you are on your way to finally 'getting' or understanding the great command of Jesus; finally on your way to finding the answer to the plague of emptiness; and finally on your way to the greatness and abundant inner fulfillment you seek.

Step Three: Don't Believe

By acknowledging that when we talk about God and Jesus we don't have to talk about grand visions and perfectly personalized Bible revelations, we open up the possibility…no, we open up the hardcore fact that Jesus spoke in very real, very ordinary, very accessible language to very ordinary and real people, like you and me.

You don't have to believe in voices from heaven. You don't have to believe in miracles. You don't have to believe a guy was dead for three days and came back to life. You don't have to believe in magical, mystical stuff. You can believe in these things if you like, but filling the emptiness of your soul and achieving the greatness you were put on this earth to become does not require belief in anything.

That is another thing that has been lost by religion over the years. Jesus' teachings can radically change your life today, and you don't have to believe a doggone thing.

All you have to do is try his core commandments out and see if they work. Experience them. Take 'em out for a spin, a test drive. If your joy and sense of purpose and fulfillment increase, go with 'em. If you don't like 'em, don't buy 'em. Let your decision be based not on what you're, quote-unquote, supposed to do. Let your decision be based simply upon whether or not the teachings *work!*

What you'll find is that they'll blow you away!

It is about experience. Either the teachings work, or they don't. Either following the teachings transforms your life experience *today* — radically — or it doesn't. You don't have to believe anything – like resurrection or salvation or whatever – just see if the teachings work in making your life, right here and right now, significantly better.

Not having to believe anything starts with not having to believe even in God. You do not have to believe there is a person floating around in space who is really powerful. You do not have to believe that God is any 'thing' at all. You don't have to believe that God is some magical power.

Certainly, you can believe that God is a person in space, if you like. You can believe that God is a spirit or force. Or you can believe that God is simply life itself, if you prefer. Whatever suits you. I use God language in this book because it is a language I am comfortable with and believe in in a way that suits me. But you don't have to buy into someone else's ideas of what God is. Just go with your own understanding of what God is. Go with your own belief. The point isn't the beliefs, but the experience.

Ultimately, the only belief this book is based on is 'whatever God is (whatever the Spirit of the universe is), within God and you is the possibility of a categorically better life for you.' The only thing you must believe in reading this book is that somewhere in the human experience of life there is an answer for what will fill your soul and make your life one of deep, powerful, and lasting greatness and love.

Step Four: Test-driving Jesus

See, what Jesus was trying to get across in his teaching is that the spiritual life is not about believing the right things, saying the right things, or doing the right things. The spiritual life is about growing closer to God by trusting in God's power. The whole Bible ultimately boils down to one story, one theme, one point – God is powerful and can change your life if you but trust and engage. The spiritual life is about tapping into the Divine, the unexplained, and the unknown, and its capacity to change your life. The great joy and peace of life, Jesus taught, come from seeing God's power transform your life as you trust that power more and more.

Jesus simply taught that if you deliberately try to move closer to God you **will** experience greater peace, purpose, joy, hope, love, power, and fulfillment. These are the fruits of relationship with God. And the further and further you move into a state of God-centeredness, away from self-centeredness, the more your joy and ultimate satisfaction with life increase. Counterintuitively, God-centeredness brings an odd fulfillment to self that self-centeredness cannot.

I know this sounds very fuzzy and squishy, right now, and doesn't yet sound different from anything you might hear in a church on any given Sunday. But hang in there. It will become very concrete.

Spiritual masters were called so in the past not because they taught how to make more money, raise a better family, run a better business, or do anything dealing with the tangibles of life. They were called spiritual masters because they taught people about spiritual stuff, non-tangible stuff inside people that could genuinely help them live more fulfilled lives. ***And their teachings worked***. Jesus was a master because he helped people get closer to God and closer to the power that God offers. Jesus has been called a spiritual master, even by non-Christians, because his teachings work in changing people's lives *today*. No one has proof whether his after-death teachings are real, but the ability of his teachings to change lives today is well documented by Christians and non-Christians alike.

Peace, power, purpose, joy, hope, love, and fulfillment are all non-tangible things. You cannot buy them in a store. They are feelings, senses, instincts, and mindsets. They are assets — non-tangible things — that most everyone desires. And the spiritual masters taught ways to tap into them so they will flow into your life.

You're not much different from the people of Jesus' day. Wealthier, yes, but just as hungry for fulfillment. They were seeking, just as you are. You're told that this new car, that new dress, this next vacation hot spot, or that new beer or soft drink will make you feel that power, peace, joy, or hope you crave. But the point of this book is that, like the people of Jesus' day, you are being fed a pack of lies and half-truths. Yes, these things make you feel good for awhile, but the emptiness doesn't go away. And that is why people turned to spiritual masters like Jesus.

Jesus spoke to this exact problem of life's hunger for something more fulfilling when he promised to give the 'living water' after which you will never thirst again (John 7:38) . He said his teachings were the 'bread of life' (John 6:35). He wasn't talking about literal water and bread. He believed his teachings were so powerful, so helpful, and so life-transforming that you would not be *spiritually hungry or thirsty* again, no matter what life threw at you. Jesus was providing a way to fill the void inside. That is what his whole ministry was about – offering deep fulfillment that fills that gaping hole of unfulfillment inside, such that you never have the spiritual hunger/thirst of an unsatisfied soul.

And his antidote, his elixir for filling that giant hole that no car, no drug, and no new vacation or experience can satiate is to fill up by drawing out the greatness that is within each one of us! His answer was not to put something into you, but to draw something out of you, something God placed in you on the day you were created.

As you take Jesus' teachings for a spin you will realize, slowly but surely, that the man was right!

Jesus knew that the single greatest problem in life for so many of us is not lack of food, water or shelter. The greatest problem is lack of spiritual fulfillment. For history has shown (and continues to show every day) that people can endure complete lack. People can go a spell without food, water, shelter, and everything else, if they have something that fills their soul.

"He who has a why can endure any how."
-- Friedrich Nietzsche

People can live in war-ravaged regions. People can lose all the accessories of human importance. People can suffer all sorts of agony and suffering, if they have something inside that fills them.

That 'something' is what Jesus spoke about. Jesus taught about a spiritual food that will fill your emptiness. With that in you, you can withstand any storm, any loss, any heartache, any aloneness, any anything. If you use Jesus' formula, you will find precisely what it is that will fill *you* up, and give you new life.

It is interesting to note in this regard that in most of the religions of the world one of the things that set the gods apart from the mortals was their ability to literally breathe life into nothing and make a living being. Gods can do it; humans can't. In Genesis, for example, God breathed into the nostrils of the clay figure he crafted, and it came alive. Adam was born.

Whether you believe these things literally happened between the gods and humans isn't the point. The point is that it is a powerful metaphor. We consider god-like or god-sent anything that has the power to 'breathe life into us' or give us new passion, new spirit, and new dreams and vigor for life.

Jesus' teachings have that power, spiritually speaking. They have the power to breathe life into you by filling the emptiness that nags at your soul. By exploring what Jesus meant by *Love God and Love Neighbor* we discover a way out of our self-centered lives, and what it is that is calling to us from within, waiting to be expressed. We discover a way to a fulfilled soul.

Step Five: Reading the God-chip

But still, what does it mean to 'love God?'

At the colleges and churches I've spoken at I try to help athletes and others understand that to *Love God* means, more than anything, to love and most fully be the person God created you to be. In the past, the nearest concept to this was called 'being obedient to God.'

But 'being who God created you to be' means something very different from what we've been told or sold in churches over the years. We've been told it means following what the Bible and what the pastor or priest says. Now, while following the Bible can be a very powerful driver in people's lives, the notion of 'being who God created you to be' is so much more than following general principles for living or general morality principles. The true spiritual life is not about 'being good.' It's about being precisely the individual that God created you to be. And that is something altogether different from merely 'being good.'

It's like God planted a computer chip inside of you at your birth. On this 'chip' was written exactly what this individual was to be that God just made: What your dreams are, what your gifts and talents are, what you would be interested in, the foods you would like, what your general body shape would be, the things and activities that would bring you the most joy, and so forth. But, because we're just babies for a good twenty years after we come out of the womb, most of us are not good at figuring out who we really are and what we really feel called to do with this life.

So, we all basically find out by trial and error. Unfortunately, some of us find out by having other people force us down a path that is the exact opposite of what we really want. (A brilliant, though painful, way to figure out what you don't want for life and what you're not called to is to have someone force on you their version for your life.) Some people find out by having a perceptive parent who, when the child is young, picks up on little clues to what is written on the child's chip, and encourages and makes a path for the child to pursue his/her calling (think Tiger Woods or Serena and Venus Williams, and what their parents saw and nurtured at young ages).

To love God is to love and fully live out the creation God made you to be. It is to commit to a life of reading your chip and courageously living it. It is to quit that which is not on the chip, that which doesn't feel right with who you are. It is to follow the calling of your heart, the calling of who God created you to be. You most fully honor God by doing what God 'commanded' you to do the day He made you. To love God is to 'obey' the imprinting of your soul that has been there from the day of your creation.

"...Do the will of God **from the heart**" (Ephesians 6:6).

"I will put my commands within them, and I will write it upon their hearts; and I will be their God, and they will be my people" (Jeremiah 31:33).

"My son, do not forget my teaching, but **let your heart keep my commandments**; for length of days and years of life and abundant life they will give you" (Proverbs 3:1).

"I do not cease to give thanks for you, remembering you in my prayers, that …God may give you a spirit of wisdom and of revelation in the knowledge of him, **having the eyes of your heart enlightened,** that you may know the hope to which he has called you..." (Ephesians 1:15-18).

"…May Christ dwell **in your hearts**" (Ephesians 3:17).

If God is truly in us, then it is impossible for anyone to presume to know what God is speaking to another individual. *Only you* can know what is in you. *Only you* can know the call of God inside you, written on your heart.

Your job in life is simply to read the chip and have the courage to do what it says. And the truth is, you cannot follow the calling of your soul, you cannot live out the life and dreams that are on that chip in your heart, *unless you have the courage to abandon all the things that are* ***not*** *on the chip.*

You cannot know what is on the chip until you clear away everything outside you that does not feel right deep inside you, everything that is not written on your heart. That is what is meant by stepping up to the buffet of life, and tasting and sampling all that life offers, until you find those handful of things that really energize you. That is what it means to quit when you know it is time to quit.

Interestingly, sociologists are saying that a new life stage is developing in America. More and more, people in their twenties are pushing off marriage and child birth in favor of 'finding themselves.' Essentially, the twenties are being used to taste and sample everything at the buffet, quitting that which doesn't feel right, and finally embracing that which does. What they may not have been allowed to do in high school or college they are now making time to do in their twenties.

Yet, despite all the time we Americans spend 'finding ourselves,' whether in our twenties or in mid-life, it is almost more about 'allowing ourselves' to just be on the outside who we are deep on the inside.

See, so many of us are taught (or have it pounded into us at young ages) that each of us has no idea what feels good and feels right for me.

We are taught that we cannot trust our own senses and our own experiences. We are not given 'permission' to feel what feels good to us. 'Permission' is taken away.

Instead, many of us were told as children, teens, or even as adults that this over here is what's supposed to be right for you, feel good for you and be what you are interested in.....even though that over there is what really feels good and feels right for you. We are basically taught that what feels right for me isn't. Instead, I should like what I am told to like.

And some people who really want to be liked or loved will carry on this ruse of trying to like things they don't for years. Some go through their entire lives living this way. They have packed away deep inside them what really feels good to them. And instead, they have chosen that which they are told they're supposed to like.

But, for most people, it is this disconnection from one's own self and what feels good and feels right for me that causes the dissonance. It is this that creates the feeling of un-fulfillment and dissatisfaction in life. It is this that creates the feeling of a hole inside oneself or creates a pervading sense of loneliness.

And the only way out of this despair and discontent with life is not by 'finding oneself.' We are so used to listening to everyone's answers *outside* ourselves. We are so used to thinking the answers for our joy and our peace and sense of fulfillment, not to mention connection with God and humanity, are outside of us – in a book, in a spiritual leader, or in something other than ourselves – that we fruitlessly search for ourselves. But all the while who we are is *inside* us, waiting to come out, waiting to be given permission to be valid, waiting to be given permission to be felt and experienced.

Thus, the key to 'reading the chip' is not about finding yourself. It is about allowing yourself. It is about giving yourself permission to be who you really are, feel what really feels good and feels right for you, and do what really brings joy to you, despite what all others may say.

Joseph Campbell, the great 20th Century writer on myth systems, talked about the Hindi word *neti*. It means 'not this.' Sometimes in life, Campbell explained, we don't know what the right path is for our lives. Instead, all we can say is *neti, neti, neti* – "not this, not this, not this."

Sometimes, the only thing we can know in our lives is what is not right – what doesn't feel right – even as we continue to discern what *is* our right path. Reading the chip is not always about knowing what the path is, but often first what it isn't.

A friend of mine told me of a particular prayer he likes to use when he feels stuck in life or like something isn't quite right. He calls it a 'clearing prayer,' and it simply goes like this, "God, what do you want me to move out of my life? What is bleeding my energy rather than breathing life into me. Please show me, God. What is standing in the way of me being who you created me to be? And give me the courage to let go of or remove that which must go."

Tough stuff. But powerful stuff. For it is only when you clear out the stuff in life that is not-you that you can find the things and ways in life that are you – the things, people, and paths that feel right.

Once a person discovers those one or three things that feel like a piano string resonating deep inside, and once a person commences doing them, he or she discovers something even bigger – that the greatest joy comes not just from doing those things. The greatest joy in life comes from doing that which is imprinted on your chip *and* doing so in service of others, particularly those who are most in need. The greatest joy of life, and the best opportunity to find your own greatness, comes not from using your life's passion to simply amass a fortune for yourself or obtain some sense of financial security as well as toys and the occasional vacation or lake cabin. These things can be well and good, but there is a higher level. Generally, an excess of these things indicates a person living not his own calling, but instead living the desire to prove his value to others, likely an aging or long-dead parent-figure. And, for the rare few who have discovered the higher path of using self in service of others, there is an even greater joy that only comes from 'giving back.'

Stephen Covey, author of the international bestselling business book *The 7 Habits of Highly Successful People*, wrote 10 years later in his follow-up book for successful business people, *The 8th Habit*, that ultimately the amassing of toys, fortunes, and experiences won't fill that void inside. True fulfillment, Covey states, is ultimately only found by giving oneself back to society in the form of those who are most in need and those who can most benefit from all you bring to life.

The greatest sense of fulfillment in life (which is something far greater and far deeper than mere 'happiness') comes from Jesus' second commandment, 'Love your neighbor as yourself.'

To love God is to fully live out and 'obey' the calling God has placed in your heart for who you are to be – i.e. what your traits, loves, abilities, interests, talents, and dreams are. To love neighbor is to use that calling in service of humanity. For that is a path, once started, that you will never desire to quit. To do what you love to do and then do it in service of others will bring joy like you have never known. It will feed your soul. And it will just feeeeel right deep, deep inside you. You will know it as the very truth of your existence. It will feel like your very reason for being alive.

That is the balance and the greatest, greatest joy of life – living in the grand state of doing what you love to do and doing so in service of those who need what you bring to life. That is what it means to *Love God and Love Neighbor.*

That is also the greatest nobility of life – doing that which you love to do, *not so that you might profit, live large, or always be secure,* but so that others might find the joy, hope and peace of a fulfilled life!

But, it cannot happen unless you have the courage to quit those things that are not your calling. It cannot happen unless you hear the voice of God calling to you from deep within, and unless you have the courage to heed that calling, no matter where it leads and no matter who says you're a fool. And that is when tenacity, endurance, and determination – fueled by your own desire and love for your path – will sustain you and move you forward. It is only when following the calling of the God-chip inside that you will create great life accomplishments and have an enduring sense of a noble life well-lived.

What do you feel called to quit? Do you have the courage to do so?

What string is resonating deep within in you? What call do you hear?

What is it that you just cannot quit, no matter how hard you have tried to walk away? What is it that feels right?

Are you allowing yourself to become who you really are and what you really want for life?

What, to you, is the definition of a noble life? What would a noble life look like if you were to live it?

Is your life in alignment with the ‘chip’ inside you?

Chapter 4

You Ain't Really Lifting Unless You Lose a Limb

I had a kid, Tommy, who was a natural bench presser: An enormous barrel chest and short arms. By his senior year he was the bench king of our Division III college. And he was a nice kid. No attitude.

When he first came into my program he had a bench max above anything I personally had ever maxed – mid-400s. I was plenty big at the time, but I wasn't near his numbers on bench. Though I was a former powerlifter, my personal strength had been in squat and dead lift. Thus, I knew it would be an insult for me to presume to tell him anything even remotely related to chest workouts. This kid clearly knew his stuff.

So, I did something I rarely do. I told him that I expected him to stay on his own chest workouts and not use the team program I had created. I told him that he obviously knew chest far better than anyone else, and I wasn't going to disrupt his flow. However, I also told him that I fully expected him to buy into the remainder of my program, including leg, conditioning, and core programs, because he did not know more than me in those areas, as evidenced by his only mediocre performance in squat and powercleans.

Generally, I always want a team working together as a team, everyone on the same page doing generally the same workouts with some variation by position. However, not only did I want to respect Tommy's knowledge and ability, I knew that giving that one lifting leader a bit of freedom to be different from the team would, from day one, win loyalty from him. By somewhat pushing him away, or giving him the freedom to step away on his bench workouts, I was in fact drawing him close in his commitment to my program and the team.

Now Tommy should have been a natural squatter. He looked like a fire hydrant. Short, powerful legs. He was just made to be a lifter. Problem was, he had fallen into the trap that so many young guys do: Bench, bench, bench, bench, bench, bench, and more bench. He should've been squatting 700 pounds, but what he had in natural physical ability he lacked in passion for leg workouts (in no small part because leg workouts demand more mental energy and focus. And despite enormous physical strength, Tommy was still in the developmental stage of acquiring the mental focus necessary to lift beyond himself and lift beyond his ability. Interestingly, Tommy's lifting partner, Mark, who is discussed in Chapter 16, was precisely the opposite: average natural strength that had been turned into huge lifting numbers and size by monster mental focus.).

This quickly changed. In a matter of a month or two, Tommy had fully bought into the leg program *and the bench program* I had for the team! Mondays – squat day – became Tommy's favorite day (as it did for most of the team. The camaraderie, the anticipation, and the electricity of Mondays were intoxicating to the entire team.). A year later, Tommy told me that the reason he had bought into my leg/core program *and the chest program* was because I had treated his program and work with respect. And he both appreciated and respected that!

But the purpose of my mentioning Tommy here is because just as Tommy was growing mentally stronger in our weightroom and being changed by my program, so also did Tommy change us. Totally opposite the cliché idea people have of heavy lifters, Tommy was such a nice kid – big, but nice! In short order, Tommy, a very quiet and reserved offensive lineman, became the new inspiration for all of us. But it wasn't his personality that changed us. Instead, it was one normal Monday squat-day that went seriously awry, and Tommy was in the middle of it.

Prior to Tommy's life-changing day in the squat rack, the weightroom motto of the football team had been, "You ain't really lifting unless you're bleeding," courtesy of Tommy's lifting partner, Mark, who had a knack for losing blood and popping blood vessels when lifting. Tommy changed all that, upping the ante!

While Tommy could just crush the weight on the bench, he was, as mentioned, still learning the extreme mental focus necessary for squatting when I had him in an intense squat workout that day. His body was plenty strong, but it was also beyond his ability at the time to generate enough mental energy when it came to legs.

See, squatting heavy weight (akin to dead lifting, snatch, and so forth) is not so much a physical exercise as a mental one. It demands the capacity to conjure a massive amount of mental focus which manifests itself physically in a 2-second explosion of energy release. To the casual observer it appears that a person is exerting physical energy to lift heavy weight. However, the instant physical explosion starts in the brain. This is not New Age philosophy, or some such thing. This is hard core athletic truth: the body is only capable of doing what the mind has set forth to do. And, to do such large things in a tiny amount of time is impossible without a mind that has been trained and trained and trained to focus and pull from the depths of the person the instant energy of massive physical exertion. Lifting is truly a mental sport, especially as one gets into the higher weights.

Tommy, prior to my work with him, was a brute force lifter. His lifting came from his body, not his mind. And because squatting requires so much more mental focus than benching, it was like starting with a newbie. In my beginning months with Tommy I had to gently move him along 'til his mental strength and focus began to slowly increase, so that he could conjure more and more energy.

Therefore, I was generally careful to keep my mouth shut when he was squatting. Because he was still learning extreme mental focus (as were most of the guys on that team), I knew just about anything could and would distract him, thus dropping the numbers from what his mind and body were truly capable of. But this day I didn't keep my mouth shut.

Tommy had the added mental pressure of being the strongest bench-presser on campus, and therefore always being in the spotlight in the weightroom, no matter what he was lifting. This was part of why I had him off the main platforms that day, and had him squatting in one of our older racks off to the side. I wanted a quiet, solid workout without the hype. All focus, no distractions. And, while all of the safety mechanisms were solidly in place and not about to go anywhere, the rack itself was a bit smaller and allowed less room for maneuvering, especially for the lifter used to the larger, newer racks.

Tommy was working in the upper 400s for multiple reps that day. He was on about 495, and was catching his wind before going down for his fourth rep when I made a comment. As I regularly do with most lifters, even in mid-lift, I reminded him that he needed to focus on his eye placement because that would help carry him through the sticking point on the hard reps. Many lifters tend to drop their eyes and look down when the weight gets heavy. And, without exception, when the eyes come down, the body leans forward and the weight with it. The lifter then 'takes a dive,' falling forward with the weight and landing it on the safety rods designed specifically to catch the weight when the lifter hits the point of failure. So, it is my job to constantly remind lifters to focus part of their mental energy on keeping their eyes up, as well as a few other squatting fundamentals. Further, by occasionally speaking to them in mid-lift I help them acclimate to dealing with distractions and multiple sources of stimuli without losing focus on the task at hand.

Unfortunately, as mentioned, some lifters, such as Tommy in his early months, don't have the focus to handle multiple sources of input. Couple that with a lot of weight on the bar, and, well, bad things can happen....

As I had instructed him, Tommy adjusted his eyes in between reps. But the second he did it, I knew I had thrown off his rhythm and concentration. With blown concentration I knew he wouldn't get this fourth rep. I could see it in advance. I could smell it on him. Something had shifted in his energy. But I wasn't prepared for what was to come next.

Tommy was a wide-gripper on his squat bar. And, moving into the older and somewhat smaller rack meant that prior to his lift a grip adjustment was necessary – moving his hands in toward his body to avoid pinching them when re-racking the weight.

Unfortunately, that never happened. And so, what did happen after that blown rep was precisely what would have been prevented by a grip adjustment: A nasty accident.

Tommy sunk his rep deep, as always, going sub-parallel. As he started coming up he lost his strength and simply set the bar back onto the low iron safety bars. But rather than taking a dive forward, he laid it backward. Whether forward or backward, setting the weight down was standard procedure and fully covered by the simple safety rods of the squat rack. Unfortunately, what wasn't standard procedure was Tommy setting that 495-lb bar on his pinky as it went onto the safety bar!!!!

Lopped that pinky almost clean off! There was just a small strand of skin holding the pinky on. None of us noticed it until Tommy stood up and said, "Let's go boys!" Instantly, his lifting partner, Mark, and I freaked out and charged into action. He ran Tommy to the training room as I ran to call an ambulance. Instant frenzy in the weightroom and athletic area. It was nuts!

Yet, despite the gruesomeness, Tommy was unfazed by the whole thing as he made his way onto the training table. He was the most level-headed one among us. No lie.

The head athletic trainer put the pinky back in place as if it was still attached, then packed and wrapped the whole hand in ice. The paramedics came, took a look at it, and shipped him to the hospital. The next day he went through a many-hour surgery to attach the little bugger. To this day he has near-full movement and almost completely operative nerves and muscles in the digit.

Furthermore, ever since that surgery, Tommy, who was sort of a mad, intense lifter, wore that slightly crooked finger like a badge of honor; or at least the rest of us always looked at it as a badge of honor. It was cool and impressive by any lifter's standards! With that incident Tommy went down in school lore as a true badass.

The new mantra of the gym? "You ain't really lifting unless you lose a limb!"

Blown Anus, Popped Eyeball, and Flying Barbells

After 20+ years in the weightroom as a serious lifter, athlete, and coach I had seen some interesting things, but never anything quite like

Tommy's. In fact, I always tell athletes and coaches of other sports that, actually, injuries rarely happen in the weightroom. Far, far more injuries happen on the field, the court, the rink, or the track than ever happen in the weightroom, because the weightrom is a controlled setting with limited range of movement and no person-to-person contact. Accidents and injuries are very rare.

But, I have plenty of coach friends who after many years have seen wilder things. One dead-lifter while lifting extreme weight blew out his anus and rectum in a bloody mess all over the lifting platform; requiring serious surgery. A bencher in one of my gyms tore a pectoral clean off the bone; a gruesome black and blue sight. One squatter popped his eyeball out from the enormous strain on his body of lifting a massive amount of weight. Every lifting coach has seen at least one hernia in his or her days. I've seen barbells flip and spin because a lifter lost his focus and forgot to put on a clamp or two to secure the weight (and incurred my wrath for his temporary stupidity and the potential danger that stupidity created for everyone in the weightroom). One coach had a lifter's improperly loaded and un-clamped bar literally go flying twenty feet across the weightroom and break a floor-to-ceiling mirror. But again, considering the decades of accumulated stories from multiple coaches, the occurrence of such things is rare in the weightroom.

But crazy stuff is not just limited to lifting and lifters. Every coach in every sport sees a whole lot of crazy stuff on fields, on rinks, on courts, in pools, in arenas, on the track, and so forth. It's just part of sport. Athletes get hurt. Athletes do stupid stuff. Athletes break bones. Athletes get into body-compromising situations. The nature of athletics is such that injury and strange experiences are inevitable. Athletes flip, fall, and fly. Anuses pop, bones break, and blood pours. It's part of the game.

The Rollercoaster Known as the Faith Journey

Faith is very much like athletics, in that regard. Faith, or relationship with God, is an odd thing. Unpredictable. Strange things happen. People sometimes get hurt. But, it is simply a life of challenges, setbacks, overcoming obstacles, triumphs, and a pervading sense of joy, peace, and accomplishment that goes through it all.

Faith ain't what we've been told by many preachers and Sunday School teachers, over the years. It ain't a pretty path. It ain't a sure bet. It ain't secure. It ain't predictable. And it sure ain't nice.

Relationship with the Divine is anything but that. In fact, it can be stated with absolute certainty that unless it is scary, unless it is on odd path, unless it does push you, unless it does feel like a rollercoaster at times, and unless it rivets you and challenges you deep inside, it ain't faith! It may be cute and nice religion, but it sure ain't relationship with or experience of God. That's for sure.

Why? Following that voice of God inside you is unpredictable, risky, scary, mad, life-altering business. It takes us to places we can never predict and may never want to visit again. It takes us through hardships and into situations that we never could have imagined faith would be about.

That is what God does. That is where the voice of God in our lives leads us – "to ventures of which we cannot see the ending, by paths as yet untrodden, through perils unknown…not knowing where we go, but only that God's hand is leading us and God's love supporting us."[3] It doesn't make sense to us.

But any person who has lived a serious and passionate life of faith knows that following the call of God in your life is an anus-blowing, finger-lopping, barbell-flying, eye-popping, upside-down, counter-intuitive, utterly unpredictable way to live..

> "…You may have to suffer various trials so that the genuineness of your faith, more precious than gold which though perishable is tested by fire, may [find its full glory]" (1 Peter 1:6-7).
>
> Paul encouraged the people, "…Strengthening the souls of the disciples, exhorting them to continue in the faith, and saying that

[3] *Lutheran Book of Worship.* Augsburg Publishing House (4th Printing, 1979), Minneapolis, MN. p137.

through many tribulations we must enter the kingdom of God"[4] (Acts 14:22).

The path of faith is not all blood and guts. That is not the point. The point is the inevitable unpredictability and rollercoaster-like nature of it. The path of faith is most certainly one of steep paths, hard decisions, and deep valleys, just as surely as it is one of high summits and grand glorious vistas.

The Apostle Paul survived shipwrecks, trials, imprisonment, beatings, and all other manner of experience. He also lived a chameleon's life – feeling called to become all things to all people so that he might tell as many as possible of the teachings of Jesus. He spoke as a Jew to Jews. He was a weak man when speaking with the weak. He was strong when working with the strong. He was a glutton among gluttons and a drunk among drunks. He felt called by the voice of God in his life to do whatever was necessary to bring people into relationship with God. And sometimes that meant enduring great hardship.

One of the great traditions of the Roman Catholic Church is the reverence for martyrs of ages past (and sometimes present) who endured all manner of hardship in their commitment to their faith.

Centuries ago, Jesuit Catholic monks that first attempted to bring Christianity to Japan met many hardships, as well. They were often captured and imprisoned. Most notably, if they did not renounce their faith, they would be put to death in the slowest, most torturous way possible. They were taken to the beach of the ocean where large posts 18"-24" in diameter and 15' tall had been driven into the ground at low tide.

The monks who had refused to deny their faith were then lashed to the top of the post by their extended arms as their bodies hung down. Then, the tide slowly returned. Wave after punishing wave, they were

[4] It is important to recognize that the phrase "kingdom of God" does not necessarily refer to the standard idea of 'heaven after death.' Many scholars consider it a simple euphemism for the ever-expanding community of love Jesus was trying to create on this earth.

beaten to death by the sheer force of the ocean's rising tide pounding against their fatigued and eventually broken-boned bodies.

Centuries later, in a different part of the world, Dietrich Bonhoeffer was a Lutheran pastor in WWII Germany. One of the few German Protestant clergy to openly stand against the Nazi movement, he wrote and preached of resistance. Insane and necessary as it was, he was also part of a group plotting an assassination of Hitler. Before he could effectively carry out his mission, he was imprisoned. Days before his prison camp was liberated, Dietrich Bonhoeffer was executed by the Nazi guards.

These are all tragic and inspiring stories. But dying for faith is not something that most of us are called to. Instead, we are called to do things that are sometimes more grueling spiritually, mentally, emotionally, or circumstantially, if not bodily. We are called to do things and live lives that yank us out of our comfort zone, out of our sense of security, and away from our clinging to lesser lives of emptiness and lack of fulfillment.

Some Interesting People and Their Interesting Paths

While living in Los Angeles, I was working with a woman who was the Executive Vice President of a marketing firm with offices near the top of L.A.'s tallest building. It was just after 9/11 and the realization of life's frailty caused her to revisit an idea she had had years ago. Since adopting a little girl from China and seeing the deplorable conditions of orphans in China, she had dreamed of opening an orphanage in China. Craziest thing, she would say, because she knew almost nothing about China and precious little about anything outside of the business world. But the call nagged and nagged her.

Eventually, she relented. One of the last sessions we had together was in the fall. She had decided to quit her job and begin the journey of following that bizarre yet true call she had inside. I have not heard from her since I moved from California. But the last news I received was that this woman who was by all accounts not religious in the least had begun the process of following that calling inside and making that orphanage a reality.

Another acquaintance from a church at which I was the youth pastor had been a corporate lawyer for 25+ years, achieving the level of General Counsel to a mid-level U.S. corporation. He enjoyed his work. It had afforded him an excellent lifestyle and the ability to put 3 kids through private college. But in his mid-50s he got an itch that just wouldn't go away.

Two years of enduring the incessant nagging of the call inside led him to finally quit his corporate job, after he had reached the top. Within months he was back in college getting his certification as a teacher. By the start of the next school year he was teaching 3rd grade in a public school in our suburb. 3rd grade! A 52 year-old male! It was an insane decision for an ultra-successful lawyer, one that was questioned by many of his friends and colleagues (and no doubt envied by a few, as well). Yet, he loved it, and felt more alive than he had in years!

A very dear friend of mine, whom I actually went to seminary with for a few years, had an unusual path, as well. He and I dropped out of seminary at about the same time. After doing some writing, I later went back. He didn't.

Derek would follow a very different call from within. Upon leaving seminary, he went on to start his own courier company while getting back into acting. After growing his business and acting for a handful of years, he eventually sold the business, moved to NYC, and landed a starring role in an off-Broadway play.

With the voice still churning inside, he years later moved back to a west coast metropolis, got into a serious relationship, and began building his new-found dream with his mate. He had a calling to start a wellness center which incorporated the fusion of mind, spirit, and body; and then expanding that to several locations.

Their dream began to unfold, bit by bit, over the next few years. He ended up going back for more spiritual leadership training in a completely different religious denomination as he continued to expand himself spiritually. In expanding his potential physically, he was recently named one of the Top 10 personal trainers in his urban area, which has millions of inhabitants. His phone now rings off the hook, and there is a waiting list to get into his program, which has a reputation for total body wellness. Today, Derek's dream of creating a total mind/body/spirit wellness center continues to grow in leaps and bounds.

Craving Security, but Choosing the Adventure

On the journey of faith we are each asked to do all manner of oddities that we could have never predicted in advance. You will be asked by God in your heart to do, endure, and become far more than you can now imagine. You will feel the need to take crazy left and right turns and off-road paths that seem to make no sense *at the time*. But, with time, it all sews itself together in what could only be considered, in hindsight, as a perfectly orchestrated life. And if you knew in advance what you must go through, you might never endeavor the journey. If you knew what God wants you to become and what turns you will be asked to take, you might be reluctant.

The problem is that a part of us so clings to security. We want nice paths. We want decisions that our friends and family don't question us on. We want easy endeavors. We want to know what is ahead. We want choices that have no social consequence or price.

We so crave comfort and security that we often trade peace for it. Comfort and peace are two very different things. The former is outside you; the latter inside. And, to a very large degree, they are inversely proportional. More comfort often means less peace. More peace often means less comfort. I couldn't even count the number of troubled couples I have counseled who, by all outward appearances, 'have it all,' but whose 'all' includes a pervading sense of un-fulfillment and unhappiness in their lives and marriage. Their physical and financial comfort has come at the expense of inner peace.

We spend so much time in life pursuing external comforts and security, thinking these things will quell the inner unrest that is the crown jewel of human experience. But, more often than not, the price of peace is comfort. The price of deep inner fulfillment and spiritual abundance in life is the even greater sacrifice of self, self-interest, and self-security, not in some self-as-martyr way, but more in a self-as-joyful-servant-of-humanity way.

Further, that increased discomfort often comes in the form of looking like a fool to others for carrying out the things God calls us to do. And few things are more reprehensible in America than doing that which looks foolish to others. Few things mean more to people than how they appear to others and what others will think and say. This, for example, is a huge reason why many people prefer to neither be nor be with Christians. The social consequence is perceived as being too high, because the Christian Church has done such a profoundly effective job of offending nearly everyone in American society and much of the world; and, as a result, Christians are often greatly disliked.

But we are never promised smooth sailing on the spiritual path, whether Christian or otherwise. God never promises that we will understand. We are never promised that others will understand and encourage the odd things we might be called to do with our lives.

God never promises anything, except that you will know abundance if you follow the path of loving the voice of God inside and following it with all your strength; and using your gifts and calling to serve others. The abundance is the filling of that ginormous void inside that no amount of stuff, toys, money, or experiences seems to fill.

God promises that the more you endeavor to use your gifts for the betterment of humanity you will know greatness; but a greatness far different from the trivialities of how TV and culture define greatness. With time, you will win the respect of God-folk and non-God-people, alike. Others will see in you the passion and power of someone committed to the in-dwelling of God and the path that inner voices calls to. That will be your greatness.

God promises the greatest adventure you could ever possibly know, if you will only have the courage to trust and follow his voice speaking to you quietly from within! The adventure is in being asked to do things that seem absurd to others, but all promise to fill your soul and give life and breath to others. Therein is your greatness. Therein is your eye-popping adventure. Therein is your deepest fulfillment in life.

If it doesn't make you laugh from the sheer absurdity of it all, it's probably not God's call. If it doesn't scare you with its raw power and scary beauty, it's probably not God's call. If it doesn't make you lose sleep or nag you over years, it's probably not God's call. If it doesn't make you feel like you are jumping off a cliff with no idea what is ahead (except fast-rising ground), it's probably not God's call.

God calls us to all sorts of things, from getting divorces to starting orphanages, from ending a business to having a child, from recording a CD to traveling to a remote village in Honduras. And there is no way to hear and heed God's call, unless we are tuned into the voice of God inside us. And the reason that call comes at such a price is because no one else can hear God's call to you. So everyone else – especially those who love you most – thinks you should do X, Y, or Z. But inside you hear God calling you to do Q or F. And following Q or F or any other odd thing you might hear God calling you to means having the courage to stand counter to those who love you and go where others would say you ought not go.

Life with God to God is not smooth sailing. It is a rollercoaster. The only thing predictable about life with God is that it will be both terrifying and exhilarating. The downs of life, like the downs of a rollercoaster, can be even more exhilarating than the times going up or even being on top. People don't pay to ride rollercoasters for the ride up. People buy tickets to rollercoasters for the fall, for the trip down! So also in life, it is the downs that sharpen our wits and challenge our ability to trust, just as surely as the ups and the climbs are exciting and slow-going.

If it doesn't rivet you and challenge you in ways you could never imagine, it's probably not God's call. If it doesn't require you to leave behind some measure of who you were, it's probably not God's call. If it doesn't cause family to say, "Are you crazy?" it's probably not God's call. If you don't lose a few friends over it, it's probably not God's call to you at this point of your life. If it doesn't scare the bejesus out of you, it's probably not God's call. If it doesn't bring you peace and fulfillment like nothing you've ever known, it's probably not God's call. Lastly, if it doesn't cause you to eventually or at some point say, "This is what I was put on this earth to do!" it's probably not God's call.

***"Everybody has talent.
Rare is the person who has the courage
to go to the dark places where that talent leads."***
-- unknown

Can you hear the voice inside?

To what is God calling you?

Does it terrify you and make you laugh at its absurdity at the same time?

Are you ready to jump, anyway?

Are you ready to sacrifice comfort and security?

Are you prepared to look like a fool for the sake of God's calling inside you, which, in the end, is the only path that will bring you peace and lasting joy?

Chapter 5

Begin With the End in Mind!

One of the things my athletes regularly hear me bark at them is that when they are in my weightroom they are *not* to think. I do the thinking. I only want them to *do*.

"If you want to fail or have mediocre results," I tell them, "do what *you* think is best. If you want to succeed, do exactly what I tell you and nothing else. Obey me, and you will succeed! Think for yourself and you will fail!"

Needless to say, the freshmen always think I'm nuts, arrogant, or just plain ridiculous. They, of course, are convinced they know better than I do, and when I am not looking they will often adjust their weights and sets to what they think is best.

What they soon discover is that the older lifters who have been around longer are making far greater gains than they are. They soon see that the upperclassmen have greater intensity, longer-lasting energy, and much greater strength. What they also soon discover is that all of the lifters who have been with me a longer time always do exactly what I tell them, nothing more, nothing less. And, before long, the youngsters fall in line and do precisely as I tell them to.

Why? The results speak for themselves. I may be a dictator in the weightroom and when conditioning my athletes, but I have been in the lifting world over 25 years. I started lifting when I was 13, and was competing by the time I was 16. I certainly don't know everything, not by any stretch. But I know when an athlete should push harder, when he should rest, when she should do 12 reps, when she should do 2. I know who is slacking and who is far exceeding her potential. I know who has 2 'burners' or 'suicides' left in him, even though he has already done 3. I know how to get more out of an athlete by expecting less, and how to use peer pressure rather than overt influence. Essentially, while there are plenty of things I don't know in life, plenty of things I cannot do, and plenty of types of people I don't understand, there are a few things in life I do very well, one of which is to get the most out of athletes, even when they're convinced they know better.

They may not always love me, but they respect me. They have goals and they know that I know how to get them there. As they age and get a feel for how life and sports work at the college level, they begin to realize that it behooves them to just shut up and obey. It sounds hard core and it is. But welcome to the world of competitive athletics!

Normal folks don't get it. But intense athletes do. Do you want mediocre, or do you want to be the best? Achieving greatness is never accomplished by niceness and hand-holding. It is done through grit, intensity, focus, and being pushed way beyond oneself. As Jim Collins so succinctly states in his book, *Good to Great*,

"Good is the enemy of great."

Time and time again in the Bible

There's that story of Jonah and the whale in the Bible. You know it. God calls Jonah to go to Ninevah and tell the people they're being bad and that they better change their ways and ask God's forgiveness.

Well, Jonah doesn't want to go, because he hates the Ninevites. So, he ignores God's call, and jumps on a ship going the exact opposite direction. As he falls asleep in the hull of the ship, a big storm comes up on the waters. The sailors are spooked. They awaken him. He says that God is pissed at him and that's why there's a storm.

"Throw me overboard and the storm will stop," he says, obviously quite sick of life and ready to cash in. They do. The storm stops. And Jonah sinks down in the sea, only to be swallowed by a whale. He lives in the belly of the whale for 3 days and nights where he repents and tells God he's sorry. The whale then spits him out on shore. With a change of heart (induced by some 'whale' of an external force), Jonah goes in the direction he was told to go, preaches to the Ninevites, and they repent. God is happy, and ultimately Jonah finds peace, knowing he did what God asked of him.

Now, whether you think that story literally and factually happened isn't the point. The point is that it is the perfect parable for life. And the truth is that there are a hundred other stories/parables in the Bible of God calling individuals to a task or to a life they might rather not do or live. They are called to obey, but they don't want to, or they have other plans.

The Bible is loaded with stories of people who wanted to do their own thing when God called 'em to do something radically different:

> Noah was called to build an ark to prepare for a flood. Job was called to be faithful to God even though he had lost nearly everything. Deborah was called to defeat the enemy armies even though she was a country judge and knew nothing about warfare. Moses was called to lead God's chosen people out of slavery in Egypt, even though he had been quite content to herd sheep. Mary was called to carry the baby Jesus in her womb, even though she knew it would mean snide comments, social ostracism, and possible death. Paul was called to tell people about Jesus, even though he had spent a good portion of the previous years joyfully hunting and killing Christians.[5] All of the apostles were called on Pentecost to bring the good news of Jesus' life and teachings to the world, even though they knew it would bring them certain death.

Even Jesus was reluctant, at times. He says to God in the Garden of Gethsemane, right before he's about to be taken captive and crucified,

"Father, if you are willing, please don't make me do this..."
(Matthew 26:39).

[5] Totally unrelated, yet very funny: One of the best t-shirts I have ever seen said, "So many Christians, so few lions." Oh come on, considering how offensive the Christian Church can be at times, it's at least a little bit funny!

He does go on to say that if it is God's will, he will, indeed, follow through and do what is expected of him. Yet, even later, at the very end, he feels he cannot go through the suffering, and thinks this unbearable pain cannot be God's path. As he is on the cross suffering he cries out,

"My God, my God, why have you turned your back on me?"
(Mark 15:34).

We spend so much time in life trying to assert our own will, trying to do what we think we want, believing we know what is best. Or, worse yet, we let culture or people around us tell us what we should do with our lives. And we often spend years ignoring the calling of God in our hearts. We often pack away that voice that's trying to tell us what would feel just right for our lives or bring us joy. We let ourselves go numb. We get medicated. We do anything to stop feeling….especially stop feeling the pain of how unfulfilled we are. We do like Jonah did. We deny that calling and go instead in the opposite direction.

And when we go away from the calling of our hearts life's storms rise up to greet us. We think that we are living and sleeping in peace, just as Jonah did in the hull of the ship, but the storms of life rage around us. Life starts to fall apart when we're not going in the direction of that call in our hearts.

Like Jonah, our lives often plunge into storms. Our lives go down: Down into the bottom of a ship; down into the deep, dark bottom of the ocean; and down so deep as if into the belly of a whale. When we are not following the call of God for our lives, our lives go down, to the point where it's like we've been swallowed by a whale! When we are not trusting that God knows life far better than we do, when we think that we know what is best for ourselves, when we are not following the call of God inside us, when we refuse to just shut up and obey the call, our lives go dark. Our lives go numb. We become walking shells.

Thus, the only question in life is whether or not you will settle for mediocrity by ignoring the voice or have the courage to shut up, stop thinking, and obey God's call rising up from within you!

Waterskiing

When my children were youngsters and I was teaching them how to ride a bicycle or water-ski, I absolutely required them to scream at the top of their lungs the whole time, "I CAN DO IT! I CAN DO IT! I CAN DO IT! I CAN DO IT! I CAN DO IT!" And they were not allowed to stop during the entire process.

You would see a cute, helmeted toe-head on his little bike, tooling down the street shouting, "I CAN DO IT! I CAN DO IT! I CAN DO IT!" as loud as he could, while his little legs churned round and round. It was so beautiful and cutely funny…but it worked! Before long I was hearing, "I CAN DO IT! I CAN DO IT! Papa, I'm doing it! I'm doing it!!"

My theory was A) The shouting of positive words kept his mind from slipping, even for a moment, into negative thoughts of "I can't do it," which are inevitably followed by failure; but also, B) It kept his mind from thinking about all the different elements of riding a bike; from pedaling, steering, and traffic, to papa's instructions, and so on. By occupying his mind with one solitary requirement (to shout), his mind basically shut off so that it wasn't over-thinking the whole process (which will always kill a good effort). Instead, by shutting off his critical and fear-filled mind, learning to ride a bike just sort of happened!

Same way with the waterskiing. There are so many elements that go into getting up and staying up on skis that it is easy for a little girl's mind to become overwhelmed by any small thing, and then have that small problem become a big problem. Whereas, if the tyke doesn't think about it, or isn't allowed to think about it (cuz she's shouting "I CAN DO IT!" a million times) the subconscious will sometimes just naturally correct it, rather than allow the girl to take a dive. But, once she starts 'thinking,' she will inevitably wipe out. So, the goal with my daughter was to keep her occupied with screaming, "I CAN DO IT!" as the wind and spray blinded her vision and caused her, after a few miscues, to be shocked that she actually was 'up' and scooting across the Wisconsin lake on two skis.

This is almost the exact same practice I use with some of my athletes, particularly when maxing on different lifts. With certain lifters who are prone to getting stuck (which is almost always a sign of a lifter whose mind doesn't believe he or she can lift the weight) I expect them to not only envision and feel the end result before they attempt the weight, but have a mantra in their heads to be recited from the moment they begin belting and wrapping, through stepping onto the platform, through every single rep or max.

In previous workouts I have worked with them to find the area in each lift that is their greatest deficiency. For instance, in working with one of my lifters, a hockey player, on his power cleans, he finally expressed that the reason he often missed weights he should be getting was because of his fear of 'snapping under' the heavier weights.

There is that point on power cleans where the weight has been pulled up to its highest point and time almost freezes. As if in slow motion, the lifter has a moment – just a moment – where there is actually time to make a decision about whether or not he/she is going to 'snap under it' and catch it, or quit and drop the weight.

From start to finish I made him incessantly mutter, "Snap under it." By filling his mind with 'Snap under it' and only 'Snap under it,' there was no room for him to make a decision at that decision point. There was no over-thinking; no thinking, at all, because there was no hesitation. The decision had already been made before the lift even started. His head was full of one command: "Snap under it." Now it was just execution, which he already had the strength and skill to accomplish. I knew that. With that mantra embedded in him and being constantly recited (and sometimes being shouted by his lifting partners), he was breaking through glass ceilings and was cleaning over 300 pounds in no time. 300 pounds....a hockey player!

At its essence, the use of a mantra in such situations is nothing more than a decision in advance to finish and finish with success. Because lifting is like sports, in general, when you're working hard there is always that point when your mind steps in and tells you that you are done. The goal of using a mantra is really the same as having a personal trainer or a coach – to find a way past that 'sticking point' or eliminate the 'sticking point' or the pause for decision, altogether.

A dear friend of mine who runs a very successful women's soccer program is constantly telling his players that one of the keys to success is to 'Begin with the end in mind." It is to break through the 'sticking points' by pre-programming yourself to not even hesitate to think at the point where you might normally get stuck. The sticking point is, in fact, eliminated by forcing the mind to not stop until the goal is accomplished.

Condensing the God-mission

The problem of applying this concept to our spiritual lives is that in some ways life is not, at all, like sports. In sports, there are clear goals. Win the championship. Lift the weight. Go undefeated. Etc. But in life there are not always clear goals, *unless you know what God has called you to do with your life!*

The mantra for getting past the sticking point is determined by the goal. And unless you have examined your heart, unless you have quieted your life and slowed it down enough to actually hear your heart, and unless you have found the courage to actually follow that calling from God in your heart, there can be no mantra. The mantra – the decision to finish – is nothing more than a condensed form of the mission. It is to collapse a person's end goal or mission statement into one very tight phrase, so that it is never far from consciousness.

Ultimately, the mantra is not the point. It is just a tool for reaching the finish. It is the way to fully obey the call of God in your heart.

The point, the goal, the finish is the complete execution of the call God has put in your heart, no matter where it leads and no matter when it ends or opens into a new call. To begin the run to the goal, to begin to fulfill God's call for your life absolutely demands hearing and heeding it – listening for the calling of your heart and having the courage to follow, even to the dark places where it sometimes leads.

Now, here's one little quirk about following the call of God in our hearts. Sometimes we are not called to accomplish a goal, but to perform a task. Sometimes we get so wrapped up in what we think the end result should look like that we forget that God simply called us to perform an action. In other words, God's ends and what we think the end result should be are often two very different things. And, for some, the most difficult part of following God's call is not hearing the call or having the courage to heed the call, but is letting go of the need to control the results. Some people so yearn to always be in control that they cannot rest until life is just the way they want it to be.....even though God may have never put it in their heart to make it look so, but only to do the work and leave the results to God.

To be the person God has created you to be and to do the things God has created you to do demand quieting your life. They demand turning off your inclinations to do your own thing, thinking your head knows better than the calling of your heart. To achieve your greatness and deep fulfillment demands feeeeeling what feels right; listening for God's nudges, and then, once heard, running with that mission a hundred miles an hour with your hair on fire, until that call runs out and you are given a new individual command or call for your life. And, in the end, it means letting go of the results and trusting that God was in the calling. For, you can never know God's full plan. You can only know and do what you feel called to do, and trust that God is in control of the rest.

Are you trusting God's program for your life, or exerting your own will in your life?

What is God calling you to?

Do you have the end constantly in mind, or are you easily distracted by cannots, questions, and worries?

When will you finally let go and trust the Master Coach?

Chapter 6

Creation Is Invariably Preceded by Destruction

Most of the people I work with in any gym are unaware of how exactly muscle is built in the body.

I can explain the exercises, the program, and all that is expected of them. But until they really understand basically what is happening in the muscle at the cellular or molecular level (even a simple understanding), they never get the big picture and never seem to fully 'click' in their workouts and total fitness lifestyles.

When an athlete enters the gym and goes through her program, doing her exercises and adding weight to the bar or machine, she is not building muscle, per se. In fact, what she is doing is tearing down her muscle. During the exercise it feels like her muscles are getting 'pumped up,' but that is actually not the growth of the muscle. That pumped feeling is the increased flow of blood, lactic acid, and ammonia into the muscle area. Because the muscle is being exercised, it is initially being flooded with body fluids to assist the lift (by carrying oxygen to the region, for instance), but also to eventually shut down the muscle as a protective mechanism designed to keep the body from overexertion. (Thus, the feeling of fatigue is not an indicator that the body cannot do more, but that it is trying to trick you from continuing to do more; again, as a protective mechanism to keep you from potential injury from doing too much.)

Thus, the reason doctors recommend a constant intake of water before, during, and after workouts, and the reason trainers and coaches make proper breathing such a high priority during workouts, is because both air and blood provide the oxygen the muscles need for continued functioning and endurance. In contrast, the flow of lactic acid and ammonia into the muscle has the effect of essentially suffocating the muscle, depriving it of that necessary oxygen. (In that vein, in the past few years, researchers have come out with supplements designed to inhibit the flow of ammonia and lactic acid to the muscle region, thereby allowing the lifter to go heavier and longer.) Again, what is happening is that the muscle is being broken down, during the lifting, not built up.

Muscle growth occurs in the period of rest following a workout. Whether it is a day, three days, or a week – depending upon the intensity of the workout – muscle groups that have been worked demand recovery time. And it is in this recovery time that the body begins to drain the ammonia and lactic acid, and process proteins and water to create muscle growth and increase strength.

However, while rest is critical, it is helpful only when in balance with lifting, or muscle destruction, so to speak. Muscle growth cannot occur until the muscle has first been torn down and suffocated. Creation of new muscle is preceded by destruction. It is a physiological impossibility to grow muscle without first taxing or tearing it down. It simply cannot happen.

And, to a very large degree, the harder the muscle is worked, the greater the eventual growth, assuming the workouts are augmented by proper diet requirements (especially protein and an adequate amount of carbohydrates), adequate water intake, and ample rest.

The Mental Game

The mental game – of sports and life – is no different. We get mentally tougher by having to pass through constantly harder challenges. We become poised and confident on the field, the mat, the court, or the rink by pushing harder and harder through new challenges off the field, mat, court, or rink.

(As an aside: It has been my experience that just as lack of rest decreases muscle growth, excessive *mental* taxation [worry, anxiety, and stress] has the same effect of not allowing the body and mind to physically rest, thus depriving the mind of proper recovery, thereby inhibiting growth and breeding illness.)

At one Division 3 college I worked at, I had a sophomore starting quarterback who had transferred in from a Division 2 school and started for us right off the bat. While he did quite well for just learning a totally new offense, he clearly was going to have to be mentally tougher and a stronger leader if he was going to take this team places in the following years. He was successful, even in that first year, but he made too many dumb mental mistakes – throwing into coverage, throwing under heavy rush, eating it when he should have gotten rid of it, not going through his check-offs, and folding under game pressure.

Thus, after the season ended and I had half the team in for their weekly squat workout, I made sure his 3-man lifting group was one of the last to be in a squat rack. In fact, I made sure that every group's workouts were concluded as his group was wrapping up squatting. Then, when his group was done, I put him in the rack for one last burnout set.

I dropped him 50 pounds from where he had done his final high-weight set, and asked him to do as many as he could. He ground out about 15 reps.

I had two boys pull off 30 more pounds from his bar, then told the quarterback to do 20 more reps immediately. Sweating and completely fatigued from a full workout, he stepped right back into the rack and banged-out his below-parallel squats one at a time, slowly. Racking the weight, he was glad to be done. By this time, his entire team had noticed that coach was busting his balls, and they had gathered around to push him and encourage him as he went one-on-one against me. They cheered him as he finished.

But he wasn't done. In fact, he wasn't even close. He wasn't to be done for another 42 reps at continually lower weights. Eventually, he had gone so far on so many sets and reps that he simply 'took a dive' with the weight into the safety rack, even though I still wanted 8 more reps from him in that set.

Upon seeing his inability to finish his final set, one of his offensive linemen stepped into the rack, nodded to his QB, and finished the 8 reps for his quarterback, plus one more rep as a way of saying, "F--- you, coach!" The team swarmed the QB and congratulated him as he lay there. Wiped out, he peeled himself up off the platform and dragged himself out of the rack, utterly fatigued and near-completely incapacitated. Someone said they later saw him dry-heaving.

I pushed that young quarterback. I ate him alive. I broke him. And I guarantee he was hating me that night and for the next several days. Further, I guarantee his teammates thought I was an SOB that day (causing them to feel compassion for and loyalty to their QB). But I also guarantee his stature among his teammates rose about 30 pegs that day when they saw him fight for his survival as I almost cruelly, and quite literally, ran him into the ground. Even though he failed in the end, in their eyes he had beaten me, surviving my test through roughly 100 reps…at the end of an already long workout. By letting myself look like the bad guy, they now had their leader, and they respected him.

Most importantly, however, he got a whole lot mentally tougher that day. He was taken so far beyond what he ever thought he was capable of (and far beyond anything he could have pushed himself to do) that his mind was stretched and challenged. (I guarantee his next squat workout, though hard, was a breeze compared to that one.)

And he had to focus, rise to the challenge, and make his mind overcome his body. His mind had to not quit when everything in him was telling him to quit. He had to keep his mind focused. And *that* is what he needed to succeed on the field later – the ability to stay focused, not quit, and keep pushing, driving, and killing, even when the situations seemed hopeless.

Now, was that workout enough to make him mentally tough enough to successfully lead a team to a championship? Not even close. It was just one piece of the puzzle. Nor is that the sort of thing I did to him or any other player every single workout. It is the exception. But it is always a possibility. And so, my athletes always know that they have to be on their A-game when they are in the weightroom. Further, that quarterback knew that I had it in for him to be the best; and from that day forward my staff knew that he was to be pushed harder than anyone else on the team. If he was to lead, he had to work harder, be mentally tougher, earn the respect of his teammates, and simply go places mentally that he had never gone before.

Thus, by breaking him down, I began a shift in his mentality that was to continue for some time. By destroying the old, complacent, so-so mindset, I began to create in him the mind and passion of a leader. But that new creation was only possible through the destruction of the old.

The following season that same quarterback led the conference in passing yardage, set a school record for passing yardage, and had one of his receivers, "Da CEO," (see Chapter 20) set a Division III record for receptions in a game and later become a two-time All-American! Something had shifted in this young leader/quarterback, but it took breaking him down, first.

God the Creator and Destroyer

It is fascinating to note that this same theme resounds throughout the Bible. Everywhere through Scripture, creation of new is always preceded by destruction of the old, the familiar, the evil, and/or chaos. New does not burst forth in the lives of the Biblical people until the old is busted open, torn down, or eliminated altogether.

In Genesis (as in the Creation stories of nearly all other world religions), darkness and chaos are destroyed. Firmament, sky, and light are created in their place. In the story of Noah, the world is destroyed again, so that new life might be re-begun. In the story of Jacob and Esau, the old pecking order of brothers is destroyed so that the blessing of God to Abraham might be carried on through Jacob and to his future 12 sons, who were to become the 12 Tribes of Israel, who in turn were crushed under Egyptian oppression and slavery so that a new nation of Israel might be birthed under Moses and eventually rise to greatness under David.

Moses had to have the courage to fight and destroy the old Hebrew mindset that all the Hebrews would ever be is slaves. He had to destroy the Pharaoh's belief in his own omnipotence, and had to lead the Hebrews out of Egypt. Then, while the Hebrews were living in the desert for 40 years, he had to daily destroy the bickering, ungrateful, and unfaithful mindset of his people toward God, so that they might trust in God's providence and God's timetable. The creation of the 10 Commandments and the 600+ Laws of Moses were preceded by chaos and criminality among the Hebrews, which had to be destroyed or greatly reduced. Eventually, Moses, via Joshua, led them into the land that God had promised to Abraham, and it was done by destroying or assimilating their enemies who occupied the land. And there God created a new and abundant life for them.

Job's life was destroyed in almost every way so that God might prove to Satan how faithful Job was (Job 1: 6-12). But also, the destruction of Job's life as he knew it was followed by Job's wealth becoming double what it had been before the destruction.

Imagine the humiliation that Mary experienced when it was discovered in her town that she was pregnant. According to the story, she and Joseph knew the child was not conceived by Joseph, but no one else did. Imagine how she was treated, how low she was made to feel. Imagine how she suffered and the destruction of her character. But this only gave birth to enormous joy when the child was born and grew into the marvel he grew into. Destruction gave rise to new creation.

The Apostle Paul had to go through the painful process of leaving behind his former life as a Jewish leader and persecutor of Christians. He had to, no doubt, leave behind his friends, his community status, and the wealth he had likely acquired. He had to watch and endure the destruction of Stephen, the Christian martyr. The old Paul had to be destroyed before a new creation could come to life in him and through his efforts.

Seen through the lens of destruction leading to the creation of new life and new abundance, the Bible opens up as a rich history of God's faithfulness to humanity.

The central story of the Christian Bible, itself – the Jesus story – is one of destruction preceding creation. Jesus came to destroy the belief that humanity needed to keep making sacrifices to God. Jesus came to destroy the belief that humanity needed priests to stand before God for them, and that people could not go to God themselves. Jesus came to destroy the belief that God is an unforgiving and merciless God. Jesus came to destroy the belief that God is outside us and not inside us, too.

Jesus was sent to earth with the express purpose of suffering and being destroyed so that his teachings of 'Love God and Love Neighbor' might live on throughout all of history. It was God's specific plan that Jesus would be destroyed, so that we might begin to understand, offer, and receive forgiving love in this lifetime. Jesus knew that he had to be destroyed physically (even while he wasn't a big fan of the idea) in order for his spirit and teachings to live on. The creation of a new world order absolutely demanded his destruction, first.

He also knew that Judas was the linchpin to making this happen. No Judas = no crucifixion. Jesus knew it had to happen! This is what's behind Jesus at the Last Supper saying to Judas,

"What you must do, do quickly"
(John 13:27).

Judas was the very instrument of Jesus' destruction. Jesus had to be destroyed. It is the very fulcrum on which the entire Christian story turns.

Jesus' Point: Destruction Forces Dependence on God

The nobility of Jesus' destruction and death is the very barometer humanity has used since his time to gauge the caliber of a man's existence. Jesus came to destroy old ways of thinking so that humanity might know new abundance, new joy, new freedom, and new love by God, for God, and for one's neighbors in need.

And all the while the critical element of creation – not only the element that makes creation, but the element that opens us to and enables us to enjoy creation – is human trust that God is at work, *even in destruction, loss, suffering, and sorrow.*

That is, in the end, what faith actually is. Faith is the confidence that even in destruction God is at work….*especially in destruction, loss, suffering, and sorrow, actually!* We must trust that God's plan is bigger than our plan, and bigger than our ability to always understand. To quote Robert K. Hudnut in his book, *Church Growth is Not the Point*,

"Everything is ultimately positive,
no matter how proximately negative."

The athlete must trust in the wisdom and 'destruction' from the coach. The athlete must trust that the pain, hardship, sweat, destruction of the muscles, and destruction of her old mental limitations will break forth into a new and glorious creation of a stronger body, a more beautiful body, a more disciplined mind, a more disciplined body, a more confident mind, and a more joyous spirit. The athlete must understand that there can be no better body or better mind unless the athlete first suffers at the hands of cast iron, or suffers long hours running on asphalt, or suffers by miles through the pool waters, or suffers hours upon days upon years of training.

Right relationship with God is similar to right relationship with a trainer or coach – you must trust that God knows what the heck He is doing and you must follow Jesus' prescription for abundant life (namely Love of God and Love of Neighbor), just as you must trust and rigorously follow the guidance of a coach if you want the abundance the coach promises in the form of wins.

So often in life, God offers hints and clues as to what He would have us do, where He would have us go, or what He would have us become. It's those gut-hunches, strong feeeeelings, brief insights, and inner callings. But we are so stuck in past patterns. We so cling to the security of how we have always lived and worked out, so to speak. We fear change. We fear letting go of past lifestyles, even when we know, at times, that these habits no longer work. And so we ignore the smaller clues God sends, and we go on clinging to who we have always been.

We are so poor at quieting our lives and hearing God's whisperings to us that God is constantly upping the volume of His voice, trying desperately to get us to change and get onto and into the life He has designed for us, the life of our great abundance and adventure. Eventually, if need be, God is shouting at us, just as God was shouting at Jonah in the raging storm, the falling into the deep, dark of the ocean, and the consumption by the whale and days in dark of the whale's belly.

God eventually makes His voice heard by increasing the intensity or severity of life's difficulties. A nudge or hunch to look for a new job, if not heeded, eventually becomes discontent with the present job and potentially even loathing for one's boss and even the general state of one's life. God goes from a whisper to a talking voice to a yell.

An impulse to start working out and eating less is followed by a growing lethargy, often followed by increased food bills, and eventually potential outright obesity. God goes from a whisper to a talking voice to a yell.

A desire to take a vacation from too much work and chaotic life and start spending more time with the kids, if unheeded, can be followed by a string of bad decisions and losses where there were only gains in the past. Eventually one's mate or child is nagging incessantly for more time. If continued failure to 'listen' to the voice persists, stress can overrun one's life, relationships can start breaking down, and life becomes riddled with anxiety. God goes from a whisper to a talking voice to a yell.

Eventually, desiring to bring us abundant life and quite unwilling to let us cling to a lesser form of existence, God tries to talk to us quietly through the "still, small voice" inside. If unsuccessful, God ain't afraid to send suffering and destruction so that we will release that lesser life which we have been clinging to so tightly. God shouts so that we might hear.

Some people don't like this notion. They want God to be always nice, always happy, always sweet, and always kind. But God is far more interested in bringing us to abundance than in always being nice.

A great coach knows and can see when his athletes have greater potential than they are living up to. A great coach can tell when athletes are too dependent upon their own ideas, their own past workout habits, and their own limited mentalities. A great coach can see when a player does not fully buy into his program and is doing her own thing. And a great coach is not afraid to bust the athlete down, punish the athlete's mind and body, or give the athlete a far greater burden as a way to bleed the athlete of his belief that he is king of the world.

God is the Ultimate Badass Coach! Abundant life can never be fully embraced unless you trust that God knows what He is doing, even in times of suffering.

God is just always trying to lead us to higher ground and more abundant life. It's like driving up the side of a mountain where there are lots of switchbacks and scenic overlooks. As you begin your ascent up the mountain you stop for the first sign that says "Scenic Overlook" and are amazed by the great view you see. As you continue your progress up the hard climb of the mountain, perhaps you skip the next scenic overlook or two. But then on your next potty break you stop for another scenic overlook and realize the view is ten times better than that lower one, even when you thought there was no way anything could have been better than that view you first saw. But as you keep pushing up the mountainside you eventually reach the top; and you realize the view far outstrips any of the lower overlooks. But you never could have had that great view if you hadn't pushed through the nerve-wracking hardship of the climb; and you never knew such a view even existed. God is constantly leading us to higher ground, even though we want to hang on to lesser levels of fulfillment. God wants to strip us of our clinging to security, 'cuz He knows how great the view and the abundance are further up ahead. And sometimes the only way He can get us to let go of our mad clinging is to send some suffering to break us. We don't listen to his still, small whispers. We don't listen to his gentle nudges. We don't listen when God uses his 'inside voice.' Often, we don't even listen when God is shouting at us through a life that is falling apart around us. Far too often, God has to send some serious suffering before we finally wake up, break down, let go, and open up to His leading and movement in our lives.

Unless you can find the creation and the learning amid the destruction, you will only see misery. Once you start looking for all that God is trying to teach you, even in the middle of your misery, your suffering takes on a whole new context. It changes from 'suffering that must be run from' to 'destruction that has a purpose and is only a part of life.' If you actively seek the learning, even in destruction, you will be moved to higher ground of greater fulfillment and mastery.

The people in life who survive hardship, seemingly unscathed, and are still able to know peace and joy in life (not fake happiness, but a deeper power, purpose, and inner peace), are the people who most fully trust that even in the dung heap of life God is at work. The people whose spirits are richest and fullest are those who know that in **all** things God is at work for good. In all suffering, hardship, and destruction God sends jewels of learning, waterfalls of insight, and gems of opportunities for new growth and wisdom.

A great many Christians believe that God only 'redeems' bad things, but does not send them. But I don't buy it, 'cuz I know that the greatest coaches 'send' hardship and suffering to the athletes they love and want to turn into the best.

"Whom God loves, God chastises"
(Proverbs 3:12)

Great coaches do not fear hardship for their athletes, but know how to wield it as a powerful tool in the development of the athlete. Just because the athlete doesn't 'feel good' when getting broken down by a great coach, doesn't mean the suffering has no purpose. The great coach knows exactly what he or she is doing and isn't afraid to do the dirty deed of sending suffering to bring about the totally actualized and fulfilled athlete.

Invariably in life, destruction and suffering end up being life's greatest blessing.

Our only tasks are to trust that God has a plan in it all, and to actively seek all that God is trying to teach us in everything that God sends our way. Our task is to find the creation amid the destruction. For there are found joy and new life!

Do you hear the "still, small voice" of God speaking in your life deep inside of you.....or does God usually have to shout before you listen? Does the pain of life have to get bad before you finally change or even considering making a change?

What is God destroying in your life? What new life is breaking through?

Are you able to walk joyfully amid the sorrows of life, knowing that God is in it all, at work, teaching you and growing you?

What is God's answer when you ask, "Lord, what are you trying to teach me in all of this? What am I not getting? What higher ground are you leading me to? Please teach me, Lord. Teach me through this suffering? What am I to learn? What am I to become?"

Can you pray this prayer, and live this prayer: "Lord, please help me to more and more fully trust your will for my life, even though I cannot always see it and do not always understand it. Lord, show me what I am to learn in all this."

Have you yet reached the advanced spiritual state of being able to hear God's quiet whispers and nudges? Can you begin to weed out all the ridiculous "responsibilities" and distractions in your life, so that you can hear God speaking?

Chapter 7

OVERCOMING PLATEAUS

One of the most frequent complaints I hear from athletes is that they are plateau-ing. They are continuing to work hard, perhaps even harder than before, but they haven't been making any gains in many days or even weeks. "Coach, I don't get it. The harder I work, the fewer gains I make. It's so frustrating."

For the serious athlete bent on continual increases in strength or muscle growth this can be an enormously frustrating occurrence. Yet, every athlete has experienced it, at one time or another. And, among extremely competitive athletes this phenomenon can be quite common and quite exasperating.

I have a pretty basic formula regarding muscle growth. Assuming you are engaging in regular workouts, your muscles need primarily only protein, water, and rest in order to grow, as well as a strong dose of carbohydrates to fuel the actual exercise process. Thus, when lifters have hit a plateau it is, almost without exception, the result of lack of rest. That means not just sleep, but sitting on their butt to read a book or watch NASCAR, or whatever it is they do to totally disengage both body and mind for an extended period of time.

The one thing the plateau-ing serious athlete most needs is the one thing he or she is least capable of or least likely to do: Stopping! Or at least slowing down.

It is so easy for the intense athlete to delude himself into thinking that if a lot of working out is good, then an insane amount of ceaseless working out is great. But it just ain't entirely so. And every intense athlete has learned this the hard way, at one time or another. A lot of working out is great. It pushes the body to continually new heights, new challenges, and new levels of excellence. But if extreme challenge and hard work are not balanced with rest they become counterproductive. There is just a natural ebb and flow to the rhythms and energies of the body. It simply cannot always be 'on.' Inadequate rest equals short-circuited growth.

The plateau is often overcome by first taking a few days off, perhaps skipping a workout or even two. After achieving some measure of rest, the plateau-ing hardcore athlete can then adjust the workout by tweaking the workout routine. Rather than two heavy leg days each week, perhaps the routine becomes one heavy day and one light leg day each week. Or, perhaps every other week the second leg workout of the week is skipped entirely to allow for rest and growth. Or, maybe it is time to go down to only one workout per week on legs.

It is an interesting phenomenon that for hardcore athletes who train exceedingly hard an unanticipated week or even two off from relentless lifting (perhaps because a family emergency came up or a vacation at a location that didn't have the necessary equipment) can have the unexpected result of not killing growth, but actually *increasing* performance, strength, and endurance upon return. Every serious athlete who has been at it for awhile knows the truth of this. Sometimes, on occasion, less work means greater gains!

Jesus and His Little Getaways

Relationships with God and life are no different from the over-training athlete. Beyond just the obvious fact that the 10 Commandments call for a day of rest for this very purpose of regenerating the body and rejuvenating the spirit, we see in Jesus' life that he is constantly pulling away from the crowd and pulling away from his disciples, even. He is constantly taking time away to rest, rejuvenate, and re-find the source of his strength.

"In the morning, a great while before day, Jesus departed and went to a lonely place and prayed" (Luke 4:42).

"...And great multitudes gathered to hear and to be healed of their infirmities. But he withdrew to the wilderness and prayed" (Luke 5:15-16).

"Then he made his disciples get into the boat and go before him to the other side, while he dismissed the crowds. And after he had dismissed the crowds, he went up into the hills by himself to pray" (Matthew 14:22-23).

"Jesus withdrew with his disciples to the sea, and a great multitude from Galilee followed....And he told his disciples to have a boat ready for him because of the crowd, lest they should crush him [with their needs]" (Mark 3:7-9).

It is not enough to constantly be in the gut-busting mode. Spiritually, it is not enough to constantly be in the giving or serving mode. It is not enough to constantly be in the action and movement mode. Life demands rest (again, not just sleep, but rest!). Life demands regeneration. Life demands attention to those things, activities, and people who in fact give something to us or breathe life into us, not just those who need something or depend on us. Burnout and plateau-ing are inevitable in life without this constant attention to rest and regeneration.

Simply put, if your own personal gas tank is low, you're no good to anyone else. The more love, the more joy, the more peace you have, the more it naturally spills out of you to others. It's a pretty simple formula.

Note: While I am referencing (above) Jesus' tendency to pull away from life and just go pray, we must not confuse Jesus' prayer with what we typically think of as prayer. We so often think of prayer as begging, begging, begging God to give us stuff or pull us out of a jam. But so often that type of prayer is a choked-up and choked-off type of thing.

The prayer Jesus often engaged in and the 'prayer' that yields the most fruit is the one that flows from peace; where we simply turn our minds off or let them run until they settle down until eventually peace comes over us and new insights, creative ideas, and an inner knowing all rise up from within us.[6] THAT is the voice of God!

This is one area where Buddhism is so much closer to the mark than are traditional Christian practices found in churches. For it is common Buddhist practice to engage in a stilling of the mind and a re-finding of one's center. This practice is also quite common in monastic Christian traditions (if not in churches), as well as among those who have made spiritual disciplines a serious part of their daily lives. Authentic prayer is far less begging, and more of a meditation, a quieting of ourselves until we hear the voice of God rising up from within. And that act of 'quieting' oneself can take many different forms.

Most serious know this practice, as well, at least those versed in the mental side of athletics. Hockey goalies and baseball pitchers are notorious for the time many of them spend in meditative states going through their game ahead of time, visualizing what is to come.

An Obscure Bible Text

Regarding this notion of rest, rejuvenation, and breathing life back into our tired bodies and spirits, there is this fascinating little verse from the Old Testament (Deuteronomy 25:4) that says:

"Do not muzzle the ox while he is treading the grain."

To the person who wants to interpret everything in the Bible literally this verse has no use, unless he or she has a plot of farmland but no tractor. However, the Apostle Paul breaks this verse open for us (and simultaneously blasts the Christian proclivity for incessant literal inter-

[6] Many intense athletes and intense spiritual folks often share a common thread of incessant journaling. Particularly on the deliberate spiritual path, the act of writing everyday to flush out the anxiety and excess thoughts that clutter the mind can be an extremely powerful tool in facilitating this settling of the mind.

pretation), giving us a new understanding of plateaus in life and the need for rejuvenation and joy. Paul growls,

> "Is it for oxen that God is concerned? Does he not speak entirely for our sake? It was written for our sake, because the plowman should plow in hope and the thresher in hope of a share of the crop" (1Corinthians 9:9-10).

Paul is instructing us that just as the ox needs to be able to eat of the grain as he works (in other words, without a muzzle), so that he might work harder, so also do we need that which feeds our soul and rejuvenates us, so that we might work harder and with more vigor.

We need the joy and fulfillment of the end goal being accomplished. But until that comes, we need the daily and weekly successes. The little victories. We need the sense of fulfillment that comes from simply a great day of hard work.

But just as importantly, we also need rest, down time, and that which re-fills our souls with energy, joy, and peace.

For many, this includes prayer, meditation, or solitude. For many, this includes going to church, reading their Bible, or engaging in morning/evening devotions. For many others, it has nothing to do with anything religious. Perhaps it is a slow walk along a beach, a stroll through the forest, or time with their hands in the dirt while working their garden. True rejuvenation, true tapping into the voice of God within comes from solitude and whatever it is in life that puts you at peace and makes you most feel like you are truly alive and full of the presence of God (whatever God is) within you.

My own personal regeneration generally comes in two forms. *Regenerating my physical body* after excessive hard work often comes by sitting on my butt, watching a few TV shows that have really great writing, or taking an afternoon to watch an old Fred Astaire movie or a football game. I'm not even that much into professional sports anymore. After a lifetime playing, ref-ing, and coaching sports, my interests off the field and outside the weightroom have branched into other directions. But surfing back and forth during 3 sporting events on TV can be good just to help me tune out and shut down for awhile. So also, I love going to live theatre and movies, as well as just reading the New York Times on the bench outside the coffee shop.

To rejuvenate my spirit and soul I often put on my iPod, get on my mountain bike and rip through the streets of the city. Hours of alone time while surrounded by the bustle and madness of the city are regenerative for my spirit's need to kick ass. Most people love to bike in the country or on paths, I prefer the madness of the city as a way to unleash and unwind. It's really a bit odd, I know, but it works for me; breathing new life back into my spirit.

The rejuvenation of "prayer" can take many forms for me: mowing the lawn, washing dishes (no lie), heavy labor outdoors perhaps doing landscaping, even seeing a movie alone, or raucous conversation over a great meal with friends. That which is "prayer," that which renews my energy and re-inspires me rarely comes from getting on my knees and "talking to God." Far more often, I am able to hear God speaking (rather than my own incessant chatter to God) when I am engaged in something else.

Another thing that I do every day *to rejuvenate my creative energy* is what the great Rev. Howard Thurman used to call 'simmering.' When I awaken in the morning (or sometimes before bed at night) I do not always jump right out and get on with the day. Instead, I may lay for a half hour or even two hours, when time allows, and simply in that state of rested peace allow my mind to run or simply be. This time in the morning is often my most creative time. All external stimuli are eliminated; body and mind are at peace. Countless books, speeches, articles, sermons, lectures, and coaching ideas have been constructed on pads of paper while under the comfort of my electric blanket in my darkened bedroom in the very early morning hours.

Our capacity to tap into our infinite potential is only maximized when we can hear the voice of God in our lives, and when we have enough energy and motivation to carry out that calling. Rest is absolutely and unequivocally integral to that process. Unless you have physical and mental peace, you will not hear God speaking in his quiet voice inside. He will have to shout. And when God shouts it generally ain't pretty.

Excessive and unceasing activity drowns out the voice of the Creator speaking new visions, new creativity, new ideas, new paths, and new callings. Without rest there simply is no way to access that energy and vigor, and thereby become the fullest expression of who we are. Instead, we plateau or even begin to slide into ineffectiveness, fatigue, frustration, and depression in life.

> "One day he got into a boat with his disciples, and he said to them, 'Let us go across to the other side of the lake.' So they set out, and as they sailed **he fell asleep**" (Luke 8:22-23). When do we ever hear of Jesus actually sleeping?! He needed rest, too!
>
> "In these days he went out to the mountain to pray; and all night he continued in prayer to God" (Luke 6:12). Immediately following that time of rejuvenation and getting back into his focus, he chose his 12 apostles and then preached the famous Sermon on the Mount.

For most normal folks the notion of getting rest is not a difficult concept to grasp. If anything, most regular folks get too much rest, too much sitting around, or too much unfocused, anxiety-driven activity. This is why we have become a fat, lazy, mentally weak society, in many respects.

But for the intense, serious athlete the problem is precisely the opposite. Excess mental focus can be inordinately draining, and demands – *demands*! – regular down time for regeneration. High levels of physical taxation demand ample scheduled time for rest and rejuvenation. For those who are hell-bent on the extreme life there must, must, must be adequate rest, or burnout is certain to follow.

When we slow down our mad lives, when we take time to do nothing, when we 'Zen-out' and simply allow life to breathe itself back into our pores, we find new strength, new capacity for joy, and new zest for life. But to do so takes the wisdom to know that God is in the quiet and in the storm, in the rest and in the flurry, in the leisure and in the ferocity of work. It demands understanding that God is within us, far more than God is outside us.

Caffeine and the Inability to Slow Down

When I was living and writing in Los Angeles I worked days and evenings in high-end catering and restaurants, but earned my health insurance by working mornings at a Starbucks coffee shop. What should have been just another part time job turned out to teach me many insights about life as an athlete, coach, and writer.

One of the most interesting observations I had was on the powerful effects of caffeine. Caffeine is a very strong energy source, which is why most people drink it. It's powerful hooch.

As with everything else in my life, I began to experiment with it and control all the other variables to attempt to determine the exact effects of this energy source, at least on me. I also observed it closely in the lives of my everyday customers, many of whom I got to know quite well. What I discovered was the overwhelming negative effect it could have on my writing! Yes, *negative* effect. Many writers thrive on it. My writing was generally obstructed by it.

A portion of my writing process involves being on a mad tear and feverishly writing as fast as I can to push out of me the inspirations inside me. In these instances some measure of caffeine can be a huge contributor. But too much caffeine became a detractor. Too much makes me jittery and unable to focus.

Yet, most of my writing involves the need for strong mental focus, especially when I move into the process of going back and editing my work with a fine-tooth comb. Thus, what I found was that most any measure of caffeine heightened my physical energy as well as my mental energy. Thus, it became next to impossible to even sit still for an hour or four, not to mention completely tune out distractions for a long stretch of, say, 8-10 hours of writing and editing. If I had the wrong mix or too much caffeine I would be fidgety or up and walking around, or my mind would be thinking about a hundred things at once, none of which had anything to do with the subject of my writing.

The challenge for effective writing, I discovered, was to perk up my mental energy but *decrease my physical energy.* It is precisely the opposite of effective performance on the field, the court, or the rink of competitive sports. In sports we tune in our minds *in practice* to learn, learn, learn. But, when *game time* comes in many sports the goal is to almost not think but simply react in the ways you have trained all week, month, or year. The goal of game performance is, to a large degree, to heighten the physical energy and, to some degree, turn off the conscious mind, so that you're operating on instinct and highly-conditioned reaction. Muscle memory and highly trained instincts are the backbone of inspired play, creating what has been called 'subconscious competence' or 'hypnotic' activity.

The difference between 'thinking' when performing versus being in a subconscious or hypnotic state and simply reacting while performing can be understood by considering driving your car. If you are going to a destination in the city where you have never been, your mind has to be totally keyed in, monitoring street names, and perhaps regularly consulting and thinking about map directions. However, if you are driving somewhere you have driven a thousand times, such as home from work, or if you are driving a long trip down a 400 mile stretch of highway, there is no need for conscious thought. You subconsciously drive the route without much, if any, conscious thought, simply reacting to situations without much thought. Subconscious competence.

While others have had different results, in my own life I discovered that caffeine is great for increasing physical energy, which is great for sports. But caffeine (or a bit too much of it) detracted from any work that demanded quieting the body and turning up the mind, from writing to working 9-5 in an office. Unless I am in a state of subconscious competence or hypnotic writing (what most writers know as a flurry of inspiration), I need to be able to focus my mind without physical distractions.

My point in bringing up caffeine is not to outright denounce it. I still enjoy a Monster or two as a quick high for workouts or the occasional Mocha for some inspired, fast-paced writing. The whole point in this context is simply that it is next to impossible to have caffeine in your system (creating an excess of physical energy), and then slow your life down enough that you can hear that Divine creative voice inside.

Being solitary, being still, and being in a receptive mode demand a silencing of both the body and the mind. And if you already have your

Venti Coffee in your system for the day, you're screwed; at least as far as hearing God's still, small voice is concerned.

If you're tossing and turning, staring at the ceiling in the middle of the night, it's probably due to the wicked mix of caffeine and stress (which, again, can be offset by the incorporation of journaling into one's daily discipline). Caffeine stays in the body for as long as 10 hours. Plus, some people find that it has a cumulative effect – even if they didn't have coffee today, they're still in a general state of high because they normally drink so much of it every other day.

The problem with all of this for the spiritual life is that if your mind is racing 100 mph, you'll never hear that voice inside. You'll spin and spin and spin, and never hear a thing. Your mind will be constantly running with the stresses, strains, and problems of the day.

But also, if you have a heavy reliance on caffeine, you'll likely never have that feeling of being totally rested and rejuvenated. Why? If you can't fully come down from the caffeine to have some relaxation, not to mention a solid night of sleep, you'll never get the rest and replenishment your body needs. In fact, for serious users of caffeine sleep is often easy. But true rest is a different story. The 'ability' (an odd word to use when referring to rest) to be awake and in a relaxed and restful state is no small feat for some people. Some are so used to incessant frenetic activity that true downtime is unheard of.

It is no different from the plateau-ing intense athlete. The mind, like the athlete's body, is simply over-taxed. Stress and anxiety have created precisely the same effect as over-training. They sap the body, eventually sending it into a spiral dive.

Again, it's not that caffeine is innately a bad thing. It is mentioned here to state the strong effect it can have in derailing the spiritual process, because it is such a powerful energy source. Added energy can be a very useful instrument in enhanced performance in any avenue of life. But, generally, when it comes to the deliberate spiritual path it inhibits regular and strong connection to one's spiritual center – the creative voice of God deep within. And fundamentally, any life that is disconnected from its spiritual source is one that is distracted, disjoint, and going in a million directions while accomplishing nothing.

True energy and natural motivation come not from stimulants but from knowing what you love to do, doing it, and using it to change the world and/or breathe life into others.

Hearing God's Call from Within Us

The goal of alone time and down time is not only to rejuvenate us and keep us going when we are on the path. Initially, the purpose of stilling our lives is so that we can actually hear what God is trying to say to us.

We are good at living crazy, frenetic lives and so ridiculously bad at genuinely knowing what it is deep in our souls that we most want to do and feeeeel called to do and be. This is because the only way to know the depths of our soul – hear God's call in our lives – is to shut our lives down for an hour each day or a few hours twice a week, and just do nothing!

There is no prayer in the world that has greater life-changing power than simply doing nothing. It's so un-American, so un-capitalist, so un-consumerist, so un-action-oriented, so not-right. Yet, 'doing nothing' can be incredibly powerful at bleeding the mind of its incessant chatter, and allowing the voice of God to rise up from within.[7] In fact, nothing is more powerful than, at times, doing nothing.

Some people are re-energized by the solitude of a massive cathedral. Some by being alone at a campsite in the woods. Some by laying flat on the floor in deep silence and openness. Some on their knees with hands folded.

The point is that you must find the ways in which you are most receptive to and most able to hear God's voice in your life. If there is action and commotion, you'll likely never hear it.

If part of faith is being able to say 'yes' to the hard calling God has laid before you and say 'no' to the things that would distract you from

---

[7] For a fuller and richer explanation of this, read Lynn Grabhorn's book, *Excuse Me, Your Life is Waiting.* Hampton Roads Publishing Co. Inc., 2000. pp155-176.

that path or calling, then another part of faith is simply being able to listen for *what that calling is*. You cannot show hard work in faith, you cannot diligently follow God's path for your life, unless you know what that path is. And you cannot know that path unless you deliberately create space in your life for you to hear the voice of God speaking to you from deep within.

That is your Energy Source. That is Living Water. That is your spiritual diet. That ability to open yourself and eventually hear God's voice is the spiritual version of controlling one's diet or 'intake' in the kitchen. It is doing that which you need to do to take in the spiritual nutrients necessary for you to do the work God has put before you.

Jesus went away from everyone else to be alone because he needed to. He needed to be told his path. He needed to hear God's voice. He needed new energy to go out and do what he had been called to do. This is never seen more poignantly than immediately before he was taken to be judged and crucified. Here, in his quiet moment, Jesus had his ultimate path confirmed and was steeled for the hard hours that were ahead.

> "Then Jesus went with them to a place called Gethsemane, and he said to his disciples, 'Sit here, while I go over there and pray.' And taking with him Peter and the two sons of Zebedee, he began to be sorrowful and troubled. Then he said to them, 'My soul is very sorrowful, even to death; remain here and watch with me.' And going a little farther he fell on his face and prayed, 'My father, if it is possible, let this cup pass from me; nevertheless, not as I will, but as thou will.' … Again for the second time, he went away and prayed, 'My father, if this cannot pass unless I drink it, thy will be done.' …So, leaving them again, he went away and prayed for the third time, saying the same words. Then he came to the disciples and said to them, 'Are you still sleeping and taking your rest? Behold, the hour is at hand, and the Son of man is betrayed into the hands of sinners. Rise, let us be going; see, my betrayer is at hand" (Matthew 26:36-46).

It is in prayer, solitude, 'doing nothing,' and openness that we receive the calling from God for where we are to go and what we are to face. It is there that we receive the proper spiritual nourishment and energy to go out and face that which God would have us do. There can be no success, no greatness, no massive intensity, no passion, no ferociousness of effort, unless there is first solitude and stillness to re-find, re-energize, rejuvenate, and remind you of who you are and what is before you.

The three critical steps to effectively living God's call for your life begin with this absolutely necessary first step of simply quieting your life to hear the call. The full process is:

1. Create the quiet in your life to hear the call.
2. Have the courage to heed the call, even though your knees may be trembling.
3. Let go of the results, trusting that your call was to engage the action you were called to engage, not create a particular set of results.

But it all begins with simply hearing the call.

Are you able to clearly hear God's voice inside; or is your life too crazy to hear anything?

Are you in need of rest? Is that the piece missing from your physical and spiritual discipline – not just time of 'prayer' and not just sleep, but time for just plain rest and inactivity?

What are the things in life that most rejuvenate you and enable you to hear God's inspiring voice rising up from within?

Are you due for some time alone?

Chapter 8

Competitive vs. Participatory Athletics

My son just completed his senior year on an extremely successful 5A high school football team in Minnesota. (5A schools are the big ones in Minnesota, unlike some other states.) His school has more combined State Championships in all sports than any other school in Minnesota. An elite public school well-known for its hockey, tennis, and soccer, this school has only in the last few years worked its way back into prominence as a football powerhouse in Minnesota, last year going undefeated until losing to the eventual State Championship Team in sectionals.

This year, as a senior, he was a starter and had a top-flight season. However, last year during that undefeated season, one of the hardest things for some parents to watch each Friday night (myself included, at times) was the points we piled up on other teams as some of our own boys sat on the sideline. Only the seniors and the handful of very best juniors ever saw action. As a junior, my son got on the field a few times, but more often than not I cursed the coach as I watched and hoped that my boy would get in and make me proud. It's every sport-parent's desire – to see the boy/girl excel – right? Right. That's how we sometimes feed our own egos. And every sport-parent's challenge is to sit there while the boy/girl rides the bench, right? Right.

But we all knew that frustration was coming and were duly told that it would be so. The head coach, who had a history of creating State Championship caliber teams in another state and who was brought in specifically to take our school to that level, made it abundantly clear at the beginning of every season that he only played the best players, period. He played to win. Participation was not the point. Winning was.

He had been hired to create a winning 5A varsity football program built on excellence, not create a mediocre program where everyone gets to play. And he would spare no player and no parent's feelings in order to accomplish that mission with which he had been entrusted.

We parents bought it and got excited at the beginning of the season by the coach's commitment to excellence. After all, the last few years since he had come to our school had proven that his formula worked. Our teams had gotten better and better each year, beating State Champion teams from previous years and moving our team into the higher echelons. But it is an altogether harder challenge to believe in the wisdom of that way when you're a parent in the stands and your boy is on the sideline. The knot in the stomach and the sense of frustration make it very difficult to keep from pissing and moaning about the coach, even when the team is winning.

If I hadn't been a former coach, I would have been utterly disgusted and driven into fits of rage, not to mention engaged in a cabal to undermine or oust our coach. My own ill-placed need to have my son make me proud would have driven me to be one of those parents that annoy us all.

Having seen coaching from the other side – i.e. as a coach – I not only understood but was able to explain to other upset parents that competitive athletics are entirely different from participative athletics. I worked under and with great coaches of many sports in my days. I saw their neurotic, day-and-night obsession with combing every inch of their programs, constantly, to find what could be improved, removed, and added. I saw them obsess in their own homes with their wives or husbands. I saw the fear in their eyes as another losing season came to a close. I saw them win National Championships…only to go right back to work the next week in preparing for next year. I listened to them consider other career options as their coaching careers were threatened by multiple losing seasons. I saw them count pennies (both in their program and in their own checkbooks), even as they tried to relax and enjoy life. I witnessed that severe stress, fatigue, and almost depression that a bad season can have on their off-seasons, not only in their work and recruiting but in their personal lives, too.

I had one head coach that I worked with who utterly obsessed over his high-budget football team. It near-totally affected his sanity and life, to the point of losing sleep and in daytime often walking about in utter despondency. And this was a coach who had had quite a bit of success in his life and coaching career. But I learned more about coaching simply by observing him than I ever did as an athlete. (For the record, he turned his team radically around in wins and losses in just a few seasons.)

Specifically, I began to realize the difference between competitive and participatory athletics. Sports cease to be about participation when we start paying coaches.

Whether it is at the middle school, high school, or college level, or whether it is on club teams, winning – specifically the hard decisions winning demands – is totally justified once the coach's livelihood depends on whether or not the team wins. Once food on a family's table depends on the win-loss record of a team, the coach is justified in playing or benching whomever she feels necessary to achieve success. Mortgage payments, car payments, medical insurance, family vacations, and so forth all depend on that coach's job, which is directly tied, in most cases, to his or her win-loss record. It is hardly fair to then ask that coach to not do whatever is necessary (within the law) to increase wins and keep his or her paycheck.

Unless the coach is specifically hired to just create a participation program where winning doesn't matter (a rare occurrence), the coach's wife/husband, kids, and 'life demands' are dependent upon the paycheck winning affords. And in that case, the coach is justified in benching my son or any other player that isn't quite good enough to start. (Now, I'd like to believe that playing underclassmen when you're running up the score will give them valuable on-field experience that will pay dividends in terms of depth later in the season or when they become upperclassmen. But that is a separate issue.)

Greater success demands greater buy-in, greater price, greater sacrifice, more tears, more disappointment, and more trust in the leader. Winning and everyone making nice-nice seldom go hand in hand.

Welcome to the world of competitive athletics!

Participatory athletics and competitive athletics are two radically different things. Confusing the two is a big mistake.

When my stomach was churning in the stands or when I heard other parents bad-mouth the coach I had to bring this up. When a coach's family depends on his or her income, he has every right to do what must be done (again, without breaking the law) to win.

Of course, this is much harder on the average parent than it is on the average athlete. When athletes know the price, the sacrifices, the goals, and the rules up front they do not get or stay disappointed when the rules are not broken just to make them happy. Instead, they buy in. Unless the athlete is a whiner or a *prima donna* with only mediocre talent, he or she understands that in order to win the coach must field the best team.

But even when their kids are in middle and high school athletics, most parents are thinking and acting like their kids are still in participatory athletic programs of peewees, squirts, pony, Pop Warner, bantams, and every other level of participatory programs. Many parents only accept kicking and screaming the categorically different nature of winning-driven sports. But winning and the pride that accompanies it are only won at high price, at great sacrifice, and after many tears and broken hearts by many people. Competitive athletics is a brutal world, but it's also one great laboratory for learning the very essence of life.

Welcome to the world of competitive athletics! Success demands sacrifice. The greater the success, the greater the price.

Jesus and Total Buy-in

Ultimately, it boils down to how much of a badass you truly are. We all know that there are levels of badass. It's true in sports. It's true in business. It's true in assessing a person's character. And it's true in faith. This is not to say that one person's faith is better than another's. That's a completely different assertion.

Being a badass in faith is just one element of faith. It is the level of commitment and buy-in. It is the dedication and the willingness to sacrifice for this thing called faith and trust in God. If badass-ness refers to intensity and level of commitment, it is worth noting that there are other elements to faith, such as depth, clarity, gentleness, and so forth. Being a badass in faith refers simply to the level of commitment and severity one attaches to faith and one lives by in one's faith life.

Jesus was constantly pushing his disciples as well as his detractors to greater levels of buy-in and badass-ness:

> "And someone came up to him, saying, 'Teacher, what good deed must I do to have eternal life?' And Jesus said to him, '...If you would enter life, keep the commandments.' ...The young man said to him, 'All these [commandments] I have observed; what do I still lack?' Jesus said to him, 'If you would be perfect, go, sell what you possess and give it to the poor, and you will have treasure in heaven; and come follow me.' When the young man heard this he went away sorrowful; for he had great possessions" (Mt 19:16-22; cf. Mt 10:17-22 and Lk 18:18-23). Ostensibly, being a spiritual badass wasn't his gig. Too high a price.
>
> "If anyone comes to me and doesn't [love my teachings more than] his own father and mother and wife and children and brothers and sisters, and even his own life, he cannot be my disciple" (Lk 14:26; the actual Greek uses the word 'hate' for the portion in brackets). He's basically saying, "Are you in or not? I mean, *really* in?"
>
> "Whoever does not bear his own cross and come after me, cannot be my disciple. For which of you, desiring to build a tower, does not first sit down and count the cost, whether he has enough to complete it? ...So therefore, whoever of you does not renounce all that he has cannot be my disciple" (Lk 14:27-28, 33). Talk about a badass call.
>
> "But Jesus called them to him and said, 'You know the rulers of the Gentiles lord it over them, and their great men exercise au-

> thority over them. It shall not be so among you, but whoever would be great among you must be your servant, and whoever would be first among you must be your slave, even as the Son of man came not to be served but to serve, and to give his life as a ransom for many" (Mt 20:25-28).
>
> "He who is faithful in a very little is faithful also in much; and he who is dishonest in a very little is dishonest also in much. If then you have not been faithful in the unrighteous money, who will entrust to you the true riches? And if you have not been faithful in that which is another's, who will give you that which is your own? No servant can serve two masters; for either he will hate the one and love the other, or he will be devoted to the one and despise the other. You cannot serve God and money" (Lk 16:10-13).

Constantly, Jesus was pushing his disciples to greater and greater levels of intensity, greater and greater levels of commitment, greater and greater levels of self-sacrifice and badass living.

It is no different today. We are constantly pushed by the teachings of Jesus to greater and greater levels of intensity in faith, and greater and greater levels of commitment. We are pushed to, more and more, shut our damn mouths and just trust the Great Coach and Master Teacher – Jesus.

And, while average people shy away from this call for greater ferocity and passion in faith, the intense athlete relishes it, even craves it. Intense athletes, intense artists, intense salespeople, intense soldiers, intense personalities live for and excel in life situations that demand more and more commitment, focus, fire, and sacrifice. In fact, without that call for greater commitment and passion, the intense personality quickly grows bored and loses respect for the path, whatever the life endeavor might be.

The intense character seeks out those experiences in life that constantly pull him, thrash him, choke him, and simultaneously breathe life into him. He seeks the exhilaration of potential failure as much as the dream of success. He experiences God most vividly in the intense experience focused on others.

Total buy-in means living on the edge of life, knowing that success is not assured and security is an illusion. It is living for something far greater than you and yours. It is buying into a vision, a plan, a dream, a way of life that promises nothing but the rush of being fully alive and doing so in service of something far bigger than just the next toy you can buy, the next restaurant you can dine at, the next vacation you can take, and the next bump in salary you can get.

The Malaise of the Christian Church

This is why so much of the Christian church has gone to crap. We have lost these type of leaders who live the passionate Christian life, not because of the income and not to stroke their otherwise frail egos, but because they seek the exhilaration of possible failure and living for something and someone(s) (whose needs are) greater than themselves.

The Church used to attract the best and the brightest to its leadership ranks. When my father, now 82, was a kid in his rural community all the kids aspired to be either a banker, a doctor, or a pastor, because those three professions were the most respected in the community. And so, the best and the brightest kids gravitated to those professions.

Today, we have lost the best and brightest to a cultural mentality of self-service and getting high off the purchases and experiences of consumerism. We have grown so utterly self-indulgent, both as a culture and as a religion, that we cringe at intense personalities, driving them from our midst…and simultaneously siphoning the church's very life-blood from it. It is always those with greater and greater intensity and passion that have led it. People of fire draw others to them. But we have so lost the fire.

What is needed are the intense ones who live for Jesus' message of love and extreme servanthood above all else. What is needed are the people of fire who live not for themselves and their own, but to be other-centered instruments of God's love in a self-centered world.

Why FCA Often Doesn't Work

I might make a few enemies in conservative Christian circles by saying this: While I know that FCA (Fellowship of Christian Athletes) has done a lot of good for a lot of people over a long period of time, and while I do respect their successes, I am rather convinced that, nowadays, in many college settings FCA is, generally speaking, not successful in reaching the best athletes, instead usually attracting a far lower caliber athlete and very, very rarely the most respected athlete-leaders.

Why?

Most FCA groups are far more C than A – far more "Christian" than "Athlete". That is, they far more often embody the mistaken Christian identity trait of weakness than the identity of the most successful athletes, that of ferocious intensity. It has been my experience, through the years from playing to coaching, that often FCA becomes a gathering of mediocre athletes, sub-mediocre, and *even non-athletes*, despite the name – Fellowship of Christian *Athletes.*

The deleterious effect of this mixing of abilities is the driving away of the best and most intense, who are innately turned off by mediocrity and the inability of the mediocre to understand the life of fire, not to mention the fact that the mediocre have chosen a lesser athletic existence, one not committed to excellence.

And when FCA is led by a mediocre athlete or a non-intense athlete, or, worse yet, a *non-athlete*, it is death to the serious athlete. The serious athlete generally finds it impossible to respect the faith or life of an athlete if that athlete is of lesser caliber.

It gets back to the notion of highly-competitive athletics and athletes versus participatory athletics and athletes. Two totally different worlds.

Hyper-focused, intense, and extreme athletes have little desire to be around the mediocre because mediocrity bleeds energy from greatness, pulling it down. That, in and of itself, would be tolerable if the excellent athlete were out engaged in ministry of some sort. But FCA is, by definition, supposed to be a regenerative and renewing experience for the athlete. But if the high-caliber, driven athlete is being drained by the experience of being led by or being among non-serious athletes it can hardly be considered regenerative.

The reason many athletes don't become Christian is because the lone representation they see of Christianity is the member of FCA, someone the most intense, most driven, and most successful athlete cannot respect, and therefore cannot follow.

As Robert Maxwell writes in his brilliant book, *The 21 Irrefutable Laws of Leadership*, people will only follow someone who is stronger than them. He calls it the Law of Respect. And he is not referring to physical strength (unless the area of leadership is physical strength-related). He is speaking in regard to the given field of interaction. Musicians only respect and follow other musicians who are stronger, more capable musicians. Business people only respect and follow others who are stronger or more successful, business-wise.

One reason many athletes do not become Christian is because the other athletes who are FCA-type Christians are simply not persons who are stronger than them, either athletically or character-wise.

My purpose in noting the problem many athletes have with FCA is to highlight that the problem is not that serious athletes don't want God. They often simply don't respect the people who follow God (or who are trying to lead people to God), for one reason or another. God is the unfortunate recipient of guilt by association.

FCA is a microcosm of the Christian Church, in general. The reason so many men (and women) have stopped going to church over the last 40 years is because there are so few leaders worth following. There are so few leaders who are spiritually stronger than the person wandering into the church, seeking answers or guidance.

Clergy like to think of themselves as strong and capable spiritual leaders. But, quite simply, they're not. Sure, a very small few here and there are, but they are an inordinately small percentage of the cleric population.

Instead, the church is riddled with overweight leaders, weak leaders, or 'slick' leaders, none of whom the intense personality (or even most normal folks) is innately inclined to follow. Or, a much stickier problem, many denominations are led by women leaders, some of whom are good, but men generally don't innately follow women – confer the book, *Why Men Hate Going to Church.* They will if the woman has rank or power, but seldom if it is voluntary. It ain't politically correct to say so, but it is often quite true among men, particularly intense personalities.

The church is so, so, so in need of leaders of fire, passion, intensity, and strength of character.

BMOC

I had one of these intense types on one of my teams. He was the big man on campus (BMOC). Handsome as hell, smart, humble, likeable, serious partier, ladies' man, and a killer athlete. Every gal wanted to be with him. Every guy wanted to be him.

And he was hungry, sports-wise and life-wise. He was just hungry. He wanted it. Wanted life. Wanted success. Wanted to live at the edge of life. Wanted the intense experience. Wanted fire. He had the hunger for more. The desire for something to buy into. Midway through his senior of college he was seriously considering entering the Marines. Thought he wasn't fully able to articulate it, the passionate life of the military, and fighting for something bigger than himself, very much appealed to him.

He was also considering going into business, because he had an uncle who was offering him a sales position that would definitely yield a solid income. Unfortunately, this path, while intense, didn't fill his need to be a part of something bigger.

Going into church work or ministry wasn't even a blip on the radar, because, in his words, he saw all pastors as 'pussies,' incapable of being looked up to. This 22 year-old kid longed for someone to look up to, someone to follow, a life that called him beyond himself to a life of greatness in self-sacrifice – a life on the edge. He wanted to be a badass among badasses.

After many long conversations it became apparent that, despite his loathing of Christian leaders, he had a close relationship with God that he had long ago buried when he couldn't find any leaders who really brought it out of him. He had generally stopped going to church, because there were no leaders in the church who inspired him.

During these conversations I also began to plant the seed in him that it is precisely because of the church's lack of intense leaders that the church needed men of fire and intensity, such as him. Of course, I also told him that the same Christianity that needed him also had no awareness that it needed him, and it would therefore do everything in its power to crucify him and allow him nowhere near leadership.

I allowed him to harbor no illusions of grandeur or ease. In fact, I impressed upon him that if he were going to do it and do it right he absolutely had to take the high, hard path. He and I both knew that he sought and ached for a life of noble purpose. He longed for the most powerful and fulfilling existence he could possibly live, and he and I both knew that could only be one path – Jesus' path of utter self-sacrifice and other-service, bringing others into relationship with God and with the Great Teacher, Jesus.

But I also informed him of what he already knew: For an extremely intense and focused person, such as himself, there would be no peace in his soul until he was on the path of noblest purpose. There would be no joy in his young life without sacrifice. There would be no vigor without the fires of life's hardships. There would be no fulfillment in his longing heart without following the call that yanked him out of his own small existence. There would be, in the end, no mad zeal without choosing the most intense life he could possibly choose.

He knew it. I knew it.

And he chose it.

Within six months he was in seminary, and coaching on the side. I so believed in his power to change the church and the world that I pushed my Athletic Director to give him my job as Head Strength and Conditioning Coach, so that the kid could help pay for seminary and have a release from the suffocating environment of Christian seminary on his ferocious personality. I went on to other things, and so did he. Within a year of that, he had transferred to an inner-city seminary in Chicago for an even more intense seminary and life experience.

Most interestingly, in that final six months before graduation, after this BMOC had decided to go to seminary, many of the other ducklings began to fall in line. Two other graduating seniors from the football team committed to seminary in the following year or two, and several other athletes began to look more seriously at their own faith. Inspired by the BMOC, one of my female bodybuilders began going back to Mass. Guys on his rugby club team – a personality type notorious for hard living – began to, all of a sudden, rethink God stuff, only because he could drink, swear, sing, and get seriously wild with them. And countless others began to consider God conversations possible and even cool.

This only fired the BMOC more, helping him to see that his life could indeed have an impact. He had originally thought that a partier and wildman such as himself would never fit in and never be accepted as a God guy. And he was right. He would never 'fit in.'

But what I helped him to realize and what these later commitments of others to God/church helped him to see is that it is precisely because he is a partier, a swearer, and a regular guy that makes him such an odd juxtaposition as a Christian, specifically a Christian leader. His job as a true leader is not to 'fit in' but to *lead*! His job was to create a new box, a new mold, a new mentality, rather than trying to fit into some old one. A Christian who is a good boy or good girl is a cliché. But this kid who was known for vigorous living as well as having a great and generous spirit was sorta the last one anyone would pick to become a Christian leader, which is precisely why his decision to do so had such a powerful affect on those around him and those who followed him, especially when there was no expectation that he now had to become a 'good boy' and stop his wild ways. It was precisely because he continued to be a wildman at heart and in action that drew other wildmen and intense personalities to him! If he had 'stopped sinning,' so to speak, it would not have had the same effect that just continuing to be normal (for his age and life situation) had on those around him. It was precisely because he stayed real that his path appealed to and inspired others to draw closer to God.

In other words, the church is not experiencing a shortage of people. The Christian church is experiencing a shortage of passionate, fiery, intense people who buy in with all their heart, mind and soul, and who, in so doing, draw in all the people who look up to them, follow them, and are inspired by the vigor and spirit they bring to life!

Competitors! Not participants.

Your Buy-in

The question is, what are you waiting for?

You know you want to buy into something bigger than yourself. You know you are holding onto yourself and your security…at the expense of yourself, your fullest experience of God, and the mad, intense life you crave. You are standing in your own way.

Whether it is a mate, an income, a career, a something or another, there is some element (or perhaps many) of your life that you are holding onto as more precious than following the call of the good Lord with all the vigor and force of your personality and character.

And so, Jesus is up in your grill asking you, "How bad do you want it? How bad do you want the rush of intimate and powerful experience of God? How fierce and noble a life do you want to live? Are you ready to step out of your own stupid-ass, petty life and truly come alive? You ready to light it up?"

What you got?

Chapter 9

The Most Annoying Person in the Weightroom

It was the mid-1980s. I had been a cadet at the Air Force Academy for not even a year. The football season was done. Our team had beaten the University of Texas Longhorns in a major bowl game and had ended the year ranked 5th in the country. We were all pumped to get back into the gym and start knocking out some heavy weight in preparation for spring ball and next year's season.

It was about this time that I picked up a nickname in the weightroom among some of the freshman big men (offensive and defensive linemen). They started calling me 'Darrell Grayson;' or 'Darrell,' for short.

Darrell Grayson[8] was one of the upperclassmen O-linemen. He was a big southern boy who had gotten a reputation in the weightroom for often telling other guys what they were doing wrong and how they should improve their lifts. Everybody hated his condescending crapola, including me. His assumption that he knew better than everyone else and was ordained to tell everyone so was very annoying.

This meant I only hated my new nickname even more. For, I had gotten into the very stupid practice in the weightroom of doing exactly the same thing. Sure, I did know a bit about lifting, having been a competitive lifter in high school. But so did many of these other guys. I'm sure many of them knew far more than me. Possessing any knowledge I had,

---

[8] Not his real name.

in and of itself, was no crime. But I would tell other guys how to lift, *without them ever asking me.* I was going around offering unsolicited advice.

Prior to that experience at the Academy, I had always been one of the strongest guys in my high school weightroom and in some other gyms in which I worked out. But here I was at a Division I school among many athletes far superior to me, and I had forgotten to check my arrogance at the door.

In response, whenever I was in the weightroom the guys would say, "Hey Darrell, could you give me a spot?" Or, "Darrell, are you done with this rack and these weights?" Or, "Darrell, Schwarzeneggar just called for you. He needs some training tips." It drove me nuts! I hated it.

I tell you what, though. That was one of the best lessons I ever learned in a weightroom. Humiliating, but important! In fact, over the years, I began to realize that is one of the most important rules of the weightroom: *Never tell another person how to lift*, unless they ask you or unless you are their trainer/coach.

The reason is pretty obvious. It is inherently arrogant and condescending. It basically assumes that the other person is stupid and you are smart. It assumes that the other person is ignorant and needs your advice.

To make matters worse – much worse – not only was I giving unsolicited advice, I was giving it to some guys who were both bigger and stronger than me! It was such a stupid thing to do that one of the guys turned to me one day and said, "Darrell, if you know so damn much, how come you're not stronger than us?"

Oh hell!

He was totally right, and there was nothing I could say. I realized then and there that I had become the most annoying person in the weightroom. Further, I realized it made no sense to give unsolicited advice in the weightroom, especially to someone bigger than me.

To this day, I am extremely reluctant, even when I was working as a strength coach, to give advice to someone who is not one of my athletes.

I consider it disrespectful, and will therefore only do it in the cases of grossly obvious dangerous practices. And if I have an athlete who is stronger than me in a given area, I will sometimes defer to their existing plan, because they obviously are making it work well. And it would be insulting to their work ethic and program.

The weightroom is a place of respect. And, unless I'm in a weightroom at a college where I'm the boss, I do everything I can to respect guys bigger or stronger than me by keeping my mouth shut!

People know this about me, and have sometimes asked why I insist on almost never giving advice to someone bigger or stronger than me. My response is simply this, "Would you take investment advice from someone who is poorer than you?"[9]

The weightroom is not a democracy or a place where fakery lasts. Either you're big, strong, and fast, or you're not. And people generally know it right away by looking at you. It is a place of brutal reality and hard-earned respect. It is a true meritocracy, one of the last remaining places in our society where hard work and Alpha-males rule, and that's that.

Either you earn respect by hard work and being big and strong, or you are smaller. The weightroom is still one of the few places in the world where might makes right, or at least creates a clear pecking order. (And, most serious lifters and athletes are up on the latest medical sports information and are quite knowledgeable, despite the myth of the dumb jock or the ignorant weightroom grunts.) Normal people hate it and try to bring their pretend knowledge into the weightroom, but it's all show. For, the weightroom is about size, speed, and strength, and either you got it or you don't.

Yet, what's most interesting and very ironic is that in most gyms the biggest and strongest guys are often the most docile and the nicest guys around, and especially so in my weightroom. They aren't bossy. They defer machines and weights to others. And they are genuinely respectful of people littler than them, because they know it can be in-

[9] Unless the person had been wealthy, lost all, and had learned great lessons.

timidating to be in a weightroom. So, while big men have the might to be obnoxious, often, they simply respect anyone who has the guts to get in and grind it out. Except for the rare jerk, most big guys in the weightroom don't flaunt their stuff by getting in other people's faces. They don't have to. Everybody knows and everybody respects their ability…or should.

In that regard, I can recall one time when I had my own two children with me for the full day, and I had to get an hour workout in. I was going to be out of town for a few days on business and wouldn't have access to equipment. I wasn't in a coaching job. So I was a member at a suburban Gold's. My kids were pre-teens or so, at the time. It was a sunny day. So, I had them wait on the lawn outside the gym and read their books while I went in and got a quick one in.

They were a bit taken aback when I came out of the fitness center rip-snortin' mad. I told them I wasn't mad at them, but I had a lesson I needed to teach them right there, right then, especially my daughter.

My daughter was sitting in the front passenger seat and I looked her square in the eye so that she would never forget. I explained to her, while my son listened from the back seat, what had happened in the gym.

The gym had been pretty quiet at this time of morning with only 15-20 people in it. And, as you often do when you're in a gym, you observe who is where and doing what; who is with whom; and what is going on. It's a way of killing time between sets. Well, there were only three or four other people in my area working out, and it was obvious that none of them knew each other. But…

At one point a guy in probably his early 30s walked up to a pretty woman who was about the same age. She was working out on a machine. Between sets she would sit on her bench, resting. During one of those rests he came up, stood over her, and told her what she was doing wrong on that machine and what she needed to do to improve.

Now, I had noticed her lifting earlier and she looked fine to me. No danger of falling weights. No gross stupidity. No nothing. Just a grown woman minding her own business, working hard. But this guy walked up and started telling her what to do. My skin began to crawl. It was obvious they didn't know each other (because he later introduced himself to her). But he felt the need to tell her what to do.

I told this to my daughter, and then I said this, "If some guy ever comes up to you in a weightroom and starts telling you what to do without you asking, it is pretty obvious that he is interested in you, is trying to hit on you, and wants to ask you out on a date. 99 times out of 100, there is no other possible explanation. But what makes it so incredibly, stupidly wrong is that by telling you what you're doing wrong on that machine he is basically trying to win you by putting you down! It's like my saying, 'I really like you. So I'm going to tell you how stupid you are and how smart I am. Wanna go on a date with me?' Would you like someone who said that to you?"

"No way!" she responded.

"That's right," I continued. "Sweetheart, it is so unbelievably wrong for someone to do that. I get so annoyed when people do that that I am going to teach you right now how I want you to deal with that. Okay?"

"Sure, Papa."

I went on, "If a guy you don't know *ever* comes up to you in a gym and starts telling you what to do, I want you to raise your middle finger and say 'F--- you!'"

My daughter was a bit taken aback and started to giggle a little bit.

"No, I'm serious. I want you to do it right now. Pretend that I have just walked up to you out of the blue and started telling you what to do and basically how stupid you are. What are you going to do? Put up your middle finger and say it."

There she was, my tough little daughter, and she did it. She stuck up her middle finger at me and said, "F--- you!"[10] I told her that was perfect

---

[10] For the record, I believe in teaching children how to use power, not withholding power from them. For this reason I taught my children all of the swear words at a very young age, including explanations of why these words can be so powerful. As they aged I would then grant them permission to use certain words, starting with heck and darn, and progressing by middle school to the most severe words. I taught them that it's not

and that I wanted her to do it again. And then one more time, for good measure. She did. She was laughing almost hysterically, but she did it. She just thought it was the funniest thing in the world that her papa was teaching her to swear in a certain situation. But she did it, God bless her.

I then ended the lesson by looking her square in the eye and telling her, "Don't ever let any man assume you are stupid. Having a boy interested in you is great. But, if he's so lame that he can't figure out some way to start a conversation, other than treating you like an idiot, then you need to tell him to go f--- himself. And then go back to being the positive person you are. Now, we might treat the situation differently in a different setting, perhaps a little more gracefully. Like if you were at a store or in a park. But in the weightroom you gotta be right up front. Don't *ever* let someone in any situation treat you like an idiot. Are we clear?"

"Yes, Papa."

I knew that by sheer observation my son would get the point, as well, that he ought never be that guy. To his credit, he has never been anything like the jerk-off that I was in college and that that gentleman was at Gold's.

The three of us then went on to have a great, beautiful and brilliant day. But that was a core lesson that needed to be firmly embedded in them. For it was not just a weightroom-learning, but a life-learning that truly enables us each to be sources of joy, inspiration, and love in the lives of others. Sometimes we increase the joy coming into our lives by forcing the junk or negativity out.

A bit of an extreme way of teaching a lesson? Yep. But I know for fact that my daughter has never forgotten that lesson. And I know for fact that she will not let anyone treat her disrespectfully, especially if she is ever working out. Yet, more importantly, she and my son will not treat others disrespectfully, but will strive to be sources of inspiration, support, and love to others!

---

okay to swear around old people, small children, strangers, or their mother. But they could use the allowed words around their friends if they desired and around me. I knew they would likely learn and use swear words anyway, at some point. So, I felt it far better to learn them in a controlled setting and learn to use them responsibly.

This Cardinal rule of the weightroom is also one of the Cardinal rules of life:

Don't ever tell someone how to live their life.

It's offensive. It's arrogant. It's rude. For it's based on the assumption, "You're stupid and I'm smart." It's based on the assumption, "I know your life better than you do" which is preposterous. And no one wants to listen to someone who is going to treat them like that. No one likes bossy or arrogant people.

Instead, we thrive and most enjoy being around people who find the good in us! Every person naturally enjoys talking with and befriending people who are supportive, positive, upbeat, and always capable of focusing on the good in any situation.

What Jesus Really Wants from Us

Jesus had a thing or two to say about that when he spoke with the Pharisees and the Sadducees. Referring to these religious leaders who were supposedly leading the people when they, themselvcs, were spiritually messed-up, Jesus said:

> "Let the religious leaders alone; they are blind guides. And if a blind man leads a blind man, both will fall into a pit" (Matthew 15: 14).

> "The Scribes and the Pharisees sit on Moses' seat … but do not do what they do; for they preach, but do not practice" (Matthew 23:2-3).

Jesus goes on in many other places with this exact same thought. The entire 23rd chapter of Matthew is devoted to Jesus' denunciation of those who would presume to tell others how to live their spiritual lives when they, themselves, were in no position to tell others so. The point, Jesus says, is not, not, not to be focused on the problems, failings, mistakes, and blunders of either yourself or others. The point is to find the good in yourself and others, and strive to stay focused on that good!

Sure, our own failings can and should be tremendous sources of learning and growth. But, ultimately, the emphasis in life must be on the good in us and around us, and especially in others!

Jesus taught love, positivity, joy, hope, and peace. By his example and his teachings, Jesus calls us to be supportive of others and to build others up, not tear them down, put them down, or constantly find the bad or the negative in what they do. Love is not negative. Love finds the good, and strives to offer it to others. Just as God sends the rain and the sun on both the evil and the good, we are to be sources of love and positive energy in our own lives and in the lives of all others. Jesus kept coming back to these things as the goals for which we are to strive.

How much more luck might that guy in the weightroom have had picking up that female lifter if he had come over and complimented her, or found something positive about her or about the gym, or about the day, or about life, or about anything? How much more likely are we to attract others with positivity than with negativity?

How much more success might I have had if I had not been condescending in the weightroom at the Academy? How many fewer headaches might I have had if I had been supportive, encouraging, or just curious about how others did their thing, rather than coming off as a pompous know-it-all?

The Christian Problems

Part of the problem is that many branches of Christianity have spent decades selling the idea that the most important thing in Christianity is 'making disciples' and bringing other people to Jesus. So, many Christians have gone around telling people how right the Christian religion is (or how their version of Christianity is more right than another's) and how wrong everyone else is, sorta like I used to do in the weightroom, before they started calling me 'Darrell.'

Unfortunately, the same is true of the Christian version of Hell. Oftentimes, Christianity has pushed, pushed, pushed the whole notion of Hell and your being bad as a way to make you supposedly need Jesus. If you scare people enough, then they'll really want your Jesus to help them stop being scared. If you put people down enough, then you can make 'em really want the salve you're selling.

What a horrible way to love God! What a depressing way to live! Further, what an absolutely wrong way to understand Jesus' teachings. Does Jesus mention hell and sin? Yes, of course. But his obsession was not on the bad. He basically said to stop focusing on the flaws of others. He said to stop obsessing about some afterlife, because ultimately it's up to God, anyway. Instead, spend your life NOW doing as much good as you can for those in need. The goal is to bring love!

One of the most interesting things about Christianity and Jesus' teachings is that Jesus never said that making people into Christians, per se, is the ***main*** *goal of being a Christian.*

Instead, it's about buying into and living Jesus' primary teachings, specifically his first and second greatest commands. And this is very different from turning people into Christians. In fact, Jesus said several times (and other people in the Bible say it or write it approximately 30 times) that the goal of being a follower of his is to follow and live by two simple commands:

> "And one of them, a lawyer, asked [Jesus] a question to test him, 'Teacher, which is the great commandment in the law?' And [Jesus] said to him, 'You shall love the Lord your God with all your heart, and with all your soul, and with all your mind. This is the first and greatest commandment. And a second like it, You shall love your neighbor as yourself. On these two commandments depend all the law and the prophets" (Matthew 22:35-40).

Jesus' greatest commandments are 'Love God' and 'Love Neighbor.' These are the very goals of life! If they're good enough for Jesus, perhaps they're good enough for us, too. And we certainly don't love someone by treating them as if they are stupid, ignorant, or don't have the 'right' religion. We don't show someone love by treating them with arrogance and condescension.

Chapter 3 of this book dealt primarily with the first command, 'Love God.' But this one is about 'Love neighbor' and about how that is a way to love God.

We show love by offering respect and graciousness. We show love by deferring and stepping out of the way for others, both in the weightroom and in our everyday lives. We show love by building up, not tearing down.

We show love by being instruments of grace, generosity, and kindness, just as Jesus taught. We show love by being sources of positive-ness, joy, laughter, and peace in the world. We show love not by telling people who or what they should be and do, but by coming up under them and supporting them, *and helping them to find and follow the call of God in their lives, individual as that call is!* We show love for others by giving them the courage to practice following the call of God in their lives in little things, so that they then have the courage to follow God's call in the big things.

We show love for others by using our own gifts, abilities, and talents as means for serving them, attending their needs, and being a source of life and inspiration in the world. We show love for neighbor by using God's call inside us as a means to serve those who are most in need.

It's not enough to be self-centered, anymore. It's not enough to live in the dominant American mentality of self-service, incessant consumerism, and living at the center of the universe. It's not enough to live such a lesser life. It's not enough.

Truth is, it doesn't feed your soul. Truth is, you long for more. You long for a greater, nobler, fuller life. You long for something greater than yourself. You long for a life of noble purpose.

And that is precisely what Jesus was in the business of offering: A life greater than yourself. Ultimately, he wasn't selling some after-death heaven, some forgiveness of sins, or some anything. Fundamentally, he was selling love and a way out of the misery and un-fulfillment of today.

Ultimately, all the other stuff will take care of itself (or be taken care of by God). Ultimately, the only life worthy of respect and great honor, and the only life that brings overflowing and abundant fulfillment is the life of doing what you love to do *in service of others and in service of humanity.* The *fun* is doing what you love to do and are good at. AND, the *deep and unsurpassed fulfillment* comes from using those great abilities to serve humanity.

The proof is in the pudding. Plenty of people get rich. Plenty of people have all the 'things' they want in life. And those same plenty are, more often than not, quite unfulfilled. The people who tap the joy and abundance of life are invariably those who have found a way out of the center of the universe, found a way to use their gifts, their abilities, their wealth, or anything they have to be instruments of love in the world.

To love neighbor is to pull ourselves out of the center of the universe, and place there those who are in need. It is a goal we can never fully attain and may often fall short of. But we strive toward it, knowing there is no higher goal to which we can orient our lives!

Are you living a life of nobility?

Are you the most annoying person in the room?

Are you a bearer of other-centered love in the world?

In what ways can you expand yourself to bring greater positive energy and love to the world?

Chapter 10

HITTING THE ZONE

I have a pretty simple formula for getting people stronger. Over the years as I have developed this program, I have never once had even one person who has not gotten significantly stronger when they have closely followed it. Concomitantly, people on the program lose the weight they wish to lose, sculpt the bodies they desire, and find a zest for life they had long been missing.

It's not that I'm some genius. I've just put together into a very successful formula all the winning ideas from all the lifters, coaches, and teachers I've had over the years.

My program is rooted in one very simple principle: Always add weight if you hit the 'Zone.' It's also known as lifting by constantly progressive weight.

Understanding the Zone

The workout goes in two week cycles.

For two weeks you lift between 8 and 10 repetitions in all sets on all exercises. 8-10 is the 'Zone.' The target number is 10 reps, but if you hit between 8 and 10 reps, you add weight, say ten pounds, to your bar or machine for your next set, whether you want to or not, and whether you think you can hit it or not.

Then, if you hit between 8 and 10 on your next set, you add that same amount of weight – ten pounds, in this case – for your third set. But, if you hit, say, 7 reps, you would then *drop* by ten pounds. Every lift should be done in this manner, from bench press to hack squats to cable flys, constantly adding weight when you hit the Zone, and decreasing weight when you fall out of the Zone.

(**Note**: Never, ever do two sets in a row at the same weight. If you didn't hit the Zone the first time, you're 98 times out of 100 not going to hit it the second time. And if you did hit the Zone, there is no point in staying at the same weight; nothing to be gained. You must go up, even if that means dropping out of the Zone on the next set, because doing the same weight two sets in a row does not push you to get stronger. It creates endurance, but not strength.)

Then, after two weeks, the Zone shifts from 8-10 to 6-8 reps per set. So, you increase the starting weight of your opening set by, say, 5 or 10 pounds, and hit 6-8 reps. If you hit in the Zone, add 10 pounds for your second set. If you miss the Zone (which you won't), drop 10 pounds. Third set, if you hit the Zone, go up; if you miss, drop by 10 pounds. Again, do this for all exercises; and never, ever repeat the same weight on consecutive sets.

After two weeks of a 6-8 Zone, shift to a 4-6 Zone. Two weeks later go to a 2-4 Zone. Then, complete it with a two week stint at a Zone of 1-2 repetitions per set.

With each successive two week period of decreasing reps, your opening weight on your starting set should be higher; always higher. Plus, and this is critical, even within a two week period, *you must start your first set weight higher than you did in your last workout (assuming you hit in the Zone on at least half your sets the last time you did this exercise).*

For example, in your last bench press workout you did four sets. You were and still are in your two weeks of 8-10 Zone. Here are what your last workout numbers looked like on bench:

1st Set: 215 lbs x 10 reps
2nd Set: 225 x 9
3rd Set: 235 x 8
4th Set: 245 x 6

So, for this next workout, start at 220 on bench, and continue to go up by 10 pounds when you hit in the Zone. The goal is to hit all of your sets, except perhaps your last set, in the Zone.

(**Note**: I will often, though definitely not always, bring the lifter way down for a final set to 'rep out' or 'burn out' at a much lower weight, generally 10-20 pounds below the weight of the very first set. Here the athlete simply does as many reps as possible.)

(**Note**: As a general rule, when increasing your starting weight from workout to workout go up 5 pounds on upper body exercises, and up by 10 pounds on lower body exercises, because the upper body is often less able to handle larger jumps in weight.)

This is what your Zone should look like then, over the course of two months:

- June 1-14: 8-10 reps/set
- June 15-28: 6-8 reps/set
- June 29-July 12: 4-6 reps/set
- July 13-26: 2-4 reps/set
- July27-Aug 9: 1-2 reps/set

If you are not interested in putting on serious mass, you can start with a Zone of 10-12 reps in June, then work your way down to a Zone of only 4-6 or even 6-8. You will get more 'toned' and look better than you ever have![11]

---

[11] **Myth**: "Doing lots of cardio tones the body." That's a big fat lie, at least in the way most people think of it. Most people who do lots of cardio think that by doing so they can carve off the fat and reveal beautiful muscles underneath, such that when she wears that little black dress, for example, her shoulders, arms, and legs will look terrific. Yes, cardio will carve off fat (though, interestingly, not nearly as effectively as resistance training), but, unless the cardio is accompanied by strength training, all that will be revealed will be flatness. In order to look what most people think of as "toned" you must build the muscle. That doesn't mean becoming some massive bodybuilder, but simply doing the work of building the muscle so that when the cardio pulls away the fat there is something underneath worth looking at.

Starting the Cycle Over, Again

Once you have worked your way down through all the rep Zones, after spending two weeks in each Zone and going up in weight on every exercise when you hit the Zone, you then cycle back up to the top and start the cycle all over, starting again with an 8-10 Zone.

This is when it gets interesting, because you will really begin to see results your second time through the cycle. Nearly all of your numbers will be significantly higher, including, and most importantly, your opening weights on your opening sets.

So, the dates and Zones for your next two months are:

- Aug 10-23: 8-10 reps/set
- Aug 24-Sept 8: 6-8 reps/set
- Sept 9-22: 4-6 reps/set
- Sept 23-Oct 6: 2-4 reps/set
- Oct 7-20 1-2 reps/set

(**Note**: All the way through the cycle your number of sets per exercise remains constant. In other words, if you are doing 5 sets of squat when you are in the 8-10 Zone, you will continue to do 5 sets of squat in all the other Zones, including the 2-4 zone and the 1-2 zone. This enables you to expend a massive amount of energy on higher weight when you are in these lower rep sets. And your strength gains will be nothing short of enormous, if you religiously stick to the program.)

The most startling challenge you will encounter will be moving from the completion of one full cycle into the next full cycle, because it requires you to go from weeks at sets of 1-2 reps all the way back up to sets of 8-10 reps! It is a shock to the system! A massive mental drain, and extremely physically exhausting.

It forces your body to re-master the effort of pumping lots of oxygen to your muscles for an extended length of time. You will likely find it hard to keep your wind when you move back into these high rep sets.

More importantly, you will find it much more difficult to focus mentally when you move from low-rep sets back to high-rep sets. In low-rep sets the mental comes mainly before the set in prepping for the massive exertion of energy. In high-rep sets the mental is necessary through the set.

Yes, you will have to drop your weight significantly from when you were in 1-2 or 2-4 rep/sets in order to get to work back in 8-10 rep/sets. So there will be less weight on the bar. (But your weight will be higher than when you were last in 8-10 reps Zone, 8 weeks ago.) But the notion of going up and down 10 versus 2 times is a jolt to the mind and requires you to up the ante mentally. You will quickly discover how much you miss low-rep sets.

Back to the example above in which you were benching four sets per workout. Let's say you worked all the way through the 5 two-week cycles, from an 8-10 Zone all the way down through the 1-2 Zone. And by the end of the two weeks in a 1-2 rep Zone you were hitting roughly 315-325 for 1-2 reps on your bench press.

Then the question is, at what weight do you start your workouts when you jump back up to sets of 8-10 reps? This is the tricky part. And it is by no means an exact formula. But you must go back to your numbers from the last time you were in the 8-10 Zone. As a general rule, add 15-20 pounds (maybe as much as 25 or 30 pounds on some leg exercises) to your opening weight from the last time you were in the 8-10 Zone.

So, for example, if the bench press workout listed above had been your last bench workout in the 8-10 Zone, then after going through the entire cycle and now coming back to 8-10s, you would start your workout at 225 (or 230) pounds. If you hit in the Zone on your first set, you would go from 225 to 235 for the second set, and so on.[12]

---

[12] It is very important to note that just as your starting weights must constantly be increased, so also must you constantly increase your warm-up weights. If you are benching in the mid to upper-200s for reps, there is no point in taking a warm-up at the standard 135 lbs, or even anything below 200 lbs. For, as your workout weight continues to increase, if you keep doing low-weight warm-ups, you have to do an extra warm-up in between the low weight and the opening set weight. Thus, you are no longer just warming-up, but are actually burning valuable energy you'll need in later sets. (The same also applies to Max Day. If you are maxing high weight, you should be taking

Again, what you will find as you go through the full cycle of decreasing Zones every two weeks is that your numbers blow you away! Within a month or two, you will be lifting weight you never thought possible. But, again, this is only true if you stick with the formula, *even when you don't feel like it!* The program works if you think as little as possible and don't let how you feel on a given day cause you to get too ambitious (the curse of the serious athlete) or too lethargic (the curse of the everyday semi-athlete) in setting your numbers. In other words, just follow the program.

(**Note**: Every lifter has a day every month where they simply have no energy or are really not motivated to lift. In these cases, I take a very different approach from many coaches. With some teams I work with I tell my lifters they get one free day per month where they can just blow off their workout entirely and not even come to the gym, no questions asked. They also get one day per month when, if they are just feeling tired or lazy, they can choose to do 1/3 of their normal workout. As stated at other points in this book, I am a firm believer that the body needs plenty of rest to maximize muscle growth. When we are tired or lifeless it is generally the mind's or the body's way of telling us to rest. And high-caliber athletes are notorious for over-working themselves and not allowing adequate rest.)

What underlies this entire program is the undying desire of the lifter to get bigger, faster, and stronger. But, most lifters just want to rush willy-nilly to strength and size, and have little idea how to maximize their potential. Thus, I constantly tell my lifters that the right to lift greater weight is *earned*! I do not let my lifters just keep throwing on weight with no rhyme or reason, unless they have proven themselves at lower weight – that is, unless they have hit the target number of reps in the Zone. That is one of the hardest thing for lifters in my gym to understand – *you must* ***earn*** *the right to take on greater weight;* and you do so by proving yourself fruitful at lesser weights.

---

minimal warm-up sets, and generally not at low weights.) The goal of warm-ups is to get the blood going, get the joints and muscles prepared to accept heavy weight, and get the mind to start focusing. Think about it, if your max were 245, would you take a warm-up at, say, 95 pounds? Probably not. The only reason people generally use 135 is because it is simple: a bar and two plates.

The Jesus Zone

There is that great parable Jesus taught of a rich ruler who was going away for a long time and called his 3 most trusted servants to come to him, entrusting each of them with a certain amount of his wealth. Simply put, in this *Parable of the Talents* (Matthew 25:13-40) the ruler entrusts to the first servant 10 bags of silver; to the second servant 5 bags of silver; and to the third 1 bag of silver. Each was told to tend the money while the ruler was gone.

After a great long time, the ruler returned and called his servants to him; first, the one who had been given 10 bags of silver to tend. The servant returned the original 10 plus 10 more, which he had gained from investments and commerce. The ruler applauded his efforts, and entrusted to the care of this industrious servant a large portion of his kingdom. Same with the second servant, who returned the original 5 plus 5 more bags of silver. He was commended by his boss, and was given a larger portion of the ruler's kingdom to take care of than he had had before.

Unfortunately, the third servant returned the original 1 bag of silver, but that was all. When asked why he hadn't turned a profit of any sort, he responded that he was fearful of losing the original money; so he did not invest it, but buried it in the ground. The ruler was angry with him for his fear and laziness, and cast him out of his kingdom.

It's a pretty trippy story. But it is loaded with one of the greatest insights into the nature of life and following God's call in life.

The easy and obvious lesson is to say that God gives each one of us gifts, abilities, dreams, and talents in life, and our job is to use those gifts. We are to 'invest' them in life, in others, and especially in those who are in need. For, if we don't we are wasting all that God has given us.

It's like giving a teenager a new computer for Christmas. You certainly would not expect that teen to put the computer in the closet and never use it. In fact, it would be almost insulting if the kid did that. Implicit in being given a gift is the expectation that you will use that gift, even while discarding the gift is fully within the realm of free will, as the gift is now the property of the new owner.

'Use and invest what you have been given' would be the main and obvious point of this story Jesus told, except there is a far more powerful point that is almost always forgotten. Yes, we are to use our gifts, talents and abilities. Yes, we are called by that voice within us to become whom God created us to most fully be.

But the even greater point is what happens when we do 'invest' in others with all the gifts, talents, and abilities God has given us. Notice in the parable that none of the servants received gifts, wealth, or even many accolades for his hard work and wise investments. There was no reward, per se, apart from a verbal 'Well done.' There was no celebration. There was no kickback.

Instead, the 'reward' was greater responsibility! The reward was the opportunity to use their investment and management abilities on an even greater portion of wealth and land. *The 'gift' the ruler gave them was the opportunity to take on even greater responsibility* and test their mettle with greater and greater challenges.

The pat on the back is nice. And even a monetary reward can be nice. But nothing, nothing, nothing satisfies and brings a greater sense of fulfillment than the opportunity to be entrusted with even greater responsibility.

In a way, the 'gift' the ruler gave the two servants was two-fold:

1) The ruler gave each of the two faithful and profitable servants the opportunity to try their wits at an even greater challenge. It's like getting to higher and higher levels of a video game. You *earn* the right to get there. You *earn* the right to have.....*greater challenges.* And that is the thrill of life. That is what keeps life interesting and exhilarating! That is what draws so much more potential and ability out of us – the challenge of greater tasks (not to be equated with *more* tasks of a trivial nature. Greater tasks of significance are great in and of themselves, not because they are bunched together to make a big pile of a to-do list.). There is no true fulfillment in the supposed security of staying static or staying in one place – safe with no great challenges. The only true fulfillment comes from

expanding one's soul and spirit with greater and greater challenges and opportunities to use all the gifts God has given you. Expansion of the Self (which has the end goal of being in service of others) is the goal and the only source of true and lasting joy.

2) The ruler gave each of the two faithful and profitable servants *trust*. There are few rewards more fulfilling in life than to know you are appreciated so much that you are given someone's trust. The successful young stockbroker or investment banker is entrusted with bigger and bigger clients by proving her ability to make money for the smaller accounts. The social worker who is effective at helping people in the daily and the lesser tasks of life is trusted by a family to step in when heavier times of death, loss, and illness come. The athlete, the dolphin trainer, the dancer, the electrician who pays his dues by proving his ability is trusted with greater responsibility by proving himself faithful and fruitful in lesser tasks. That is why a promotion is so powerful. It's not just the money or the title. It's that you have earned greater trust. It is not just a statement through externals such as money. It has a powerful internal effect – it is the granting of greater trust. It is a statement that the boss and the company value YOU!

Hitting the numbers in the Jesus Zone means proving yourself at lesser things. It means investing yourself, your abilities, your dreams, your talents, and your whole life in the causes God has given you to care about. It is only when you have proven yourself that God gives you even greater opportunities to prove yourself, and thereby do even greater good!

Jesus says that you must earn the right to take on greater and greater weight in life. You must earn the right to help more and more people by simply helping those around you. And as you do so, God will put more and more opportunities in your lap to have an even greater impact.

You earn the right to bring greater love, greater joy, greater hope, and greater positive-ness to a greater number of people by bringing enormous love, joy, hope and positive-ness to those you come into contact with every day. By flowing positive energy, joy and love in the small, God naturally places more and greater chances to flow even more to more people.

And *this* is life's greatest fulfillment. *This* is the great abundance Jesus constantly preached about! The abundance Jesus taught is not all the things we get, like pats on the back, monetary rewards, a new title, a new SUV, a new vacation house, or praise by others. Those are nice, but they ain't the nub.

Jesus says it ain't about what comes *to* you, per se, but about the enormity of what flows *through* you! We are called in life not to be cups that collect God's blessings, God's divine inspiration, and God's energy. We are called to be funnels through which God's blessings, love, and energy flow to others. Jesus taught about the boundless abundance of the love of God flowing into you constantly…and flowing out of you. That is abundance!

Why is the Dead Sea dead?

As I mention in my previous books, the reason the Dead Sea (in the Middle East) is 'dead' is not because there is no life flowing into it. Plenty of fresh water and even living organisms flow into it. But they die. And the reason they die is because there is no water *flowing out of it*. No rivers, no tributaries, nothin'. Rather than a constant cycle of death and rebirth, there is only a sedentary pooling of dead or dying water.

Every sculptor, actor, writer, painter, dancer, and artist of any stripe knows the truth of this concept. Unless the artist expresses (the Latin root of the word express: ex=out and press=push; to express means, quite literally, 'to push out') that which is inside him, he begins to rot on the inside.

Every artist knows the feeling. Every artist knows what it is like to decay because he or she has not been pushing out that creative force that is inside him or her. The joy of being an artist is being not a vessel that holds art, but a vehicle or a funnel that allows creativity/art to pass through. The joy is in receiving the inspiration and expressing that inspiration in some form.

The breastfeeding mother knows this same concept. If the baby does not awaken for middle-of-the-night feedings, the mother's breasts become swollen, or 'engorged', and painful from all the milk inside. She must then 'express' (that is literally the medical term) – manually push out – the milk to relieve the pain of her swollen breasts. The joy of breastfeeding for a mother, I am told, is to feel the very food of life growing inside the breasts and then feeling that creative life force being passed to the child who needs that food of life to live and grow.

Every athlete knows the need to 'just get a workout in.' Every athlete knows what it means to miss workouts and just feel sorta stopped up and in need of blowing out the energy. Every athlete knows the need to feel drained, wiped out, or totally spent from a great workout. This is that same 'expressing' or pushing out the strong energy inside.

Isn't that what we all feel with our abilities and with our love? We feel like we have so much to give, so much to bring to the world. We long to be in love with great work. We long to be in love with a great person. We long to have greater jobs of more responsibility. We long to have children. Or we long to have people depend on us. Or we long to be free of 'responsibilities' so as to let out the free spirit that is inside.

We all have so much inside that is waiting to be 'expressed.' And the truth is, we increase the flow of all these things *into* our lives by increasing the flow of these things *out of* our lives. We cannot have more until we make room for more. We cannot receive new until we have cleared out the old by putting it to good use. God gives us so much inspiration, creativity, love, and joy, and basically says we're not getting more until we give away what we've already been given. We must constantly be pushing to new heights. Then, our capacity to flow energy and love out of us increases as God stretches us by giving us even more. By stretching our loving muscles we gain the capacity to take in (and give away) even more love.

It's a pretty simple formula. Push yourself, hit the Zone with the strength and energy you have, and then you earn the right to take on greater weight, responsibility, challenge, and opportunity in life.

How Do You Know God's Will for Your Life?

This leads to another point.

Investing in the true calling of God in your life brings enormous joy and vigor. Investing in something else will eventually only bring dullness, deadness and muting of your vibrancy. That's the simple way to know if what you are doing with your time and life is God's calling or just a burden imposed by others or by culture.

If it breathes life into you and invigorates you, it's God's call! Unequivocally!!!

If it sucks life out of you, in the long term, it's something you are doing for some other reason. It's probably some other burden someone else has put on you (parent, spouse, priest/minister, culture, to name a few), rather than a natural drive that has risen up from inside you. It's a 'should' that someone has dumped on you.

It's that simple. If it dulls you or just bleeds the life out of you, you're wasting your time, cuz you're not on your path; you're not on the path God has planned for you; you're not listening to that brilliant, creative voice of God deep within you. On the other hand, if it invigorates you, feeeels right, inspires you, happens almost effortlessly, and motivates you to drive forward with greater joy and passion, it's from God. *That* is the very energy of God flowing through you. It is something so simple that we, too often, make so difficult.

Believe it! It's just that simple.

Now, don't equate that with quitting when things get a little sticky or when you hit a tough patch. We all have down days or things about our calling that demand intense focus and just plain hard work. But even when things get really tough, there is a joy in knowing that the path, in general, that you are on is the one. When on your God-given path the work feels almost effortless and joyful. If your heart is truly in it, bumps don't derail you.

But if the tough patch persists… Then, Houston, we have a problem.

There are two basic ways to know if the path you're on isn't God's calling for you. Either it is a problem, situation, life, or set of circumstances that just persists, persists, and persists, and doesn't go away. When you see that happening in your life, your task is simple: Walk away.

It's that simple. If all your attempts at finding solutions have yielded nothing, brush the dust off your feet and walk away. Either an inspiration will finally come that brings the resolution or solution you need; or you will find an entirely new path that inspires you and draws you forward.

You must find the good in life. You must release the negative and go in quest of that which breathes life into you!

The other way to tell that your path is the wrong one is if the problems are inside you rather than outside you. If you are on the right path, and know so deep inside, then nothing outside you can pull you off that path. But if things are awry inside you, you'll never be able to keep the course outside you. If you find yourself questioning and questioning and almost incessantly doubting what you're doing with your life, you're not on God's path for your life.

Yes, it's pretty much that simple! If it takes that much internal effort to stay the course, you're not even close to God's call for your life.

When it's God's call and God's path for your life, it just wells up from within you quite naturally. It is, in so many ways, quite effortless. All of the effort is outside you, but there is peace within you. It doesn't take internal effort. Instead, you just 'know' that this is where you gotta be or this what you gotta be doing. There is an internal knowing that this is 'what God put you on this earth to do.'

So often we say, "Oh, if I only knew God's will for my life, I'd go a hundred miles per hour in that direction. I'd give my total life to it. I just want to know what God wants me to do." We say that as if the real challenge is in the knowing.

Well, that's part of the challenge. But more often than not, God's will for your life is pretty clear and obvious.

There's an old Zen proverb that fits well here:

"The truth is obvious."

The real challenge is in having the guts to do what God is calling us to do.

I begged God for literally a decade to show me his will for my life. I lost so much sleep and spent so much anxiety wrestling with that one, as if the answer was somewhere outside of me. Literally, years and years were given to begging God for his will for my life. And in the meantime, I was slowly, blindly, without plan or purpose, writing and writing, because the doors to ordained ministry as a pastor were closed. I was following that which was breathing life into me (by expressing in writing my thoughts, theology, and creativity), but I was convinced God's plan for my life was over there in that direction as an ordained pastor, even while that path continued to throw up roadblocks, frustration, and misery.

Eventually, it dawned on me that maybe God's real path for my life was the thing that was flowing and flowing and flowing into me and out of me – writing. Writing wasn't always easy. I often wrestled with things. I occasionally got stuck. I fumbled my way through trying to edit my own work (train wreck!). But it still kept flowing.

What's weird, though, is that I kinda knew it for years and years. I knew this was the bigger fish God wanted me to fry. But I was so, so, so, so, so, so stuck in my belief that I was called to be an ordained pastor, that I just found it impossible to let go of the old and embrace the new calling at a hundred miles per hour. The very thing I wrote and spoke about was my own greatest problem.

It's not that God doesn't want us to do hard things. But the hard is on the outside, not the inside. When we are on God's path the challenges are almost always external circumstances that can be overcome, *not* internal wrestling with whether or not this is the path. The true path of your God-calling flows effortlessly from within, even as it rises to meet the external challenges.

To be on the path of that voice deep inside you is to be pursuing a path that breathes life into you. It is to be using your gifts at things you love to do.

And when we are allowing the love and energy of God to flow through us – rather than pool in us or be saved just for us – more and more of it flows into our lives. When we become funnels for the love of God to flow through us and be channeled and directed to others, we naturally attract more and more energy, love, hope, joy and peace.

When we push ourselves to hit the Zone, spiritually speaking, we earn the right to move on to more. God rewards our faithfulness and fruitfulness at lesser levels with greater opportunities, greater challenges, and greater trust. And *that* is abundant life!

Are you busting your ass with what you have?

Are you a vehicle for God's energy, power, and love to flow through you?

What are you great at? And/or, what do you LOVE to do?

How can you use that in service of others? Is there an itch – a need somewhere in the world or in the lives of people you know or have heard about – that you just might have the ability to scratch?

What is it in your life right now that is sucking life out of you? Do you have the guts to walk away?

What is it in your life right now that is breathing life into you with joy and excitement? Do you have the guts to more fully embrace this path and take it to the next level?

Chapter 11

'No Glory' Days

Results are the reason people work out.

Fun as workouts can be, invigorating as a great day in the gym can be, there is one main reason people, especially intense athletes, workout: Results.

If there were no visible results or results we could feel or see in our performance, most of us would not work out at all. Further, most people are inspired to work harder or just keep working out because they begin to see results.

In fact, the nature of working out is such that we all want to see results every day. Whether it is a reduction of the fat around our waists, an increase in the size of our arms, an increase in the distance we can run in a half-hour, or a boost in the amount of weight we can lift, every one of us likes to see results and see them regularly. And, generally speaking, results, if not noticeable every day, are possible every week or certainly every month.

Unfortunately, sometimes the problem for lifters, runners, swimmers, and other athletes is focusing on daily results rather than working the program or system for long term results. It's so easy to get sucked into the mad dash for daily bumps in results.

One of the tools most coaches use in charting the strength progress of athletes is to have a 'Max Day' two or three times per year. Using a few basic lifts – such as bench press, squat, power clean, and/or dead lift – the coach charts the maximum amount each athlete can lift, whether as a one-rep lift or a maximum number of reps at a given weight. Then four or five months later, the athlete is tested again to determine the progress and commitment of the athlete. And, if the coach has an effective system and committed athletes, the max numbers of the athletes will increase, sometimes radically.

As mentioned, however, the problem is that many athletes want to see increases every day. Many athletes want to go to failure in every set on every lift as a way to reach max lift weight in every workout. Every day becomes max day for these athletes. I fall prey to this, myself, in some of my own workouts. Unfortunately, when this is done the body never has ample time to rest and recover.

On top of this, wanting to see results every day indicates a lack of faith in the coach's system for increasing size and strength. It is an impatience that comes from lack of knowledge – lack of knowledge and experience in seeing that the system *will* work.

Therefore, at many times in the months between Max Days my lifters hear me barking at them, "This is a 'No Glory Day,' gentlemen. Just do the work. No glory, just the joy of hard work side-by-side with your brothers!" A 'No Glory' day is a day not to see results, but to simply do the work. I constantly bombard them with the message that the gains will come. They need only focus and do the work.

If you're crossing the sea in a rowboat
and you keep looking at the horizon expecting to see land,
you're going to know a whole lot of frustration.

But if you keep your eyes on the water,
you'll see the constant progress that comes with every oar stroke.

The satisfaction on No Glory days comes from just doing the hard work, doing it with your lifting brothers/sisters, knowing you did the hard work, and knowing you accomplished something en route to the larger goal of becoming stronger, faster, and bigger 5 months from now. The satisfaction on No Glory days is not from the ecstasy of major accomplishment, but from the deep inner-knowing that more of the foundation has been laid in the creating of something that takes more than one day, one week, or even one month.

Every intense athlete *knows* this type of satisfaction is deeper and lasts longer than the satisfaction of crossing the finish line or accomplishing some great new max. In fact, time and time again, when I talk to aging athletes who were in their prime a decade or more ago it is the memory of the training more than the gloried successes that fills them with joy, satisfaction, and a sense of accomplishment. They will say such things as, “I was in such great shape back then,” “I was working so hard back then,” or “It was great. The team used to work out together every day. I still remember those morning runs and those afternoon workouts together as a team. I’ve never felt so close to a group of guys, or so focused in my life.”

10-time National Championship **UCLA coaching legend, John Wooden**, when asked which he would choose if he could go back and relive one day of his phenomenally successful coaching career, said that while all the national championships were great, the day he would most love to have over is any one of the thousands of the days he spent on the court in practice with the young men of his teams. It was the daily work, sweat, and shared love of the game that he missed most.

In a February, 2009, article in *Men’s Journal* by Bill Gifford, **World Champion downhill skier Bode Miller** was asked about doping in his sport. In commenting he offered powerful insight into the difference between the ‘joy of the pursuit of the goal’ and the goal itself, which in his sport is Olympic gold.

> “If you’re only trying to win a medal,” [Miller] goes on, “then yeah, doping makes a lot of sense, trying to cheat makes a lot of sense. Why not do a Tonya Harding kind of thing and try to take somebody else out?”
>
> While it may not play well with Bob Costas, *the medals and crystal globes continue to matter far less to [Miller] than the pursuit of them and the quality of that pursuit.*

> "If…you just want that gold medal, go and f-ing buy a gold medal," [Miller] says.
>
> …
>
> Which brings up one last question. When I ask whether he still "skis for fun," Bode looks at me incredulously. "This *is* fun," he says. "It's *why* I do it."

The successes and awards are great, of course. We all love and strive for them. But the deeper joy comes from the months and years of building that success, the prices paid, the hours spent, the sweat and blood sacrificed, and the enormous mental energy and focus needed to make it all happen.

(**Note**: As many professional athletes attest, what makes working hard more difficult later in a career is not the physical taxation but the lack of desire to conjure the mental energy necessary. Most great athletes retire not because the body is unwilling, but because competitive success demands such extreme levels of mental focus. That is the great difficulty of sports, and the primary determinant of success in any venture in life. This is also why it is so much more difficult to repeat as champion than to become champion. Why have so many teams won the Super Bowl, but so few have repeated consecutive years? Maintaining excellence is infinitely more mentally difficult than achieving excellence.)

That high that comes from crossing the finish line, scoring the game-winning goal, or nailing the critical three-pointer is quickly fleeting. It is a happiness that passes as quickly as it came. But, there is a pervading sense of joy that lasts over months or a year as the day by day foundation is laid en route to something greater. It is a joy oddly mixed with peace that does not need the high, even while it is building toward the high. It is the slow satisfaction of crescendo rather than the ecstasy of the high moment.

Mixing this notion with the seminal work of Lynn Grabhorn in her book, *Excuse Me, Your Life is Waiting*,[13] the happiness or high of crossing the finish line is essentially a sense of contentment. But the joy of

[13] Hampton Roads Publishing Company Inc., 2000. p175.

building, creating, and preparation is a sense of passion that is deep, powerful, and invigorating. Contentment feels good, but passion feels great! Passion is fuel to accomplish things.

Yet, our natural inclination is to focus on the high, the happiness, and the sense of contentment. We want to get high every day, rather than have the passion that moves us and transforms our daily lives, no matter what is happening around us.

This, again, is why I have to remind my lifters that most days are No Glory days. Most days are building days – the 'joy of hard work' days – not accomplishment days, Max Days, or happiness and high days. No serious athlete can last long on just a high or some contentment. No athlete will last long if he or she needs big results or highs every day or even every week. Driven athletes live for the sense of passion, power, and purpose that come from *creating* something new, *growing* a dream, and *building* a great accomplishment over time – far more than the actual accomplishment itself.

Heaven Today

Sunday School kids have been taught by their teachers and pastors for decades that heaven is a great party in the sky we go to when we die. But, quite interestingly, one of the constant themes resounding throughout the teachings of Jesus, as well as through the remainder of the New Testament, is this notion that 'heaven' is not just 'later,' but is both 'now' and 'not yet.'

So often when Jesus and others in the Bible speak of heaven *they don't use future tense words*, but present tense words!

> "...The kingdom of heaven **IS** in the midst of you" (Luke 17:21).
>
> "The kingdom of heaven **IS** at hand" (John the Baptist, Matthew 3:2).

"And when Jesus saw that he answered wisely, he said to him, 'You **ARE** not far from the kingdom of heaven'" (Mark 12:34). Jesus said this after a religious leader acknowledged that the only teachings that really matter are 'Love God' and 'Love Neighbor.'

Note the present tense verbs: *is*, *is*, and *are*. It's not *will be*, *is coming*, or *happens after you die*. There is a very real sense that heaven is created *right here and now, everyday*! There is talk of a later heaven, but what is routinely forgotten is the very explicit notion that heaven is *today*!

This community of love and world of love that Jesus sought to create were already happening, and still yet to happen. There were 'No Glory' hard work days. But there was also joy *today* in knowing what was being created. And there was also a joy for what was ahead that motivated Jesus and his followers to keep pressing toward the finish line.

Jesus and the No Glory Life

In that vein, it is interesting to note that in most Biblical translations the words *happy* and *happiness* are never ascribed to Jesus. Accurate translation of the words Jesus spoke notes that Jesus indicates being *fulfilled, blessed,* and having *abundance*, but he is *never* credited with using the words *happy, happiness*, or even a rough equivalent. Odd, isn't it?

Blessed, fulfilled, and *abundance* are very different notions from happiness. The actual word *happiness* comes from the word *hap* which quite simply means *luck*. Things that are happenstance occur by accident or luck, not design.

Happiness has a very similar quality. It is fleeting. The high of happiness is great when it happens, but it comes and it goes, almost inexplicably. It happens less by design and more by the whims and fancies of the day or of life. A person can have the exact same experience twice, yet have a completely different reaction each time – once happy, once unfulfilling.

But joy, peace, and abundance are something else. Jesus said,

> "...These things I speak in the world, that they may have my **joy** fulfilled in themselves" (John 17:13).
>
> "Peace I leave with you; my **peace** I give to you; not as the world gives do I give to you" (John 14:27).
>
> "...Ask, and you will receive, that your **joy** may be full" (John 16:24).
>
> "I came that you might have **life** and have it **abundantly**" (John 10:10).

Jesus did not speak of a happiness or even a feeling that is fleeting, dependent upon luck, or happening by accident. Jesus spoke of an experience that occurs quite by design. It is not something that 'happens,' per se, but is made. Joy and passion are brought into our lives by the understanding that some days are No Glory days – i.e. not every day will bring a high with it. Joy is the experience of crescendo, of building something that can only come with time and hard work.

Jesus had a workout plan. He had a system. If you follow it, he said, you will know lasting joy, deeply penetrating peace, wellsprings of hope, and abundant love. It's not about constantly being high and happy. His workout program was one he stated again and again. He said we will come to know and experience these things in our lives, as well as greatness, when we use the gifts, strengths, and abilities God has given us to bring new life and new hope to those who are in need.

We gain the abundant life Jesus promised by following his program of self-sacrifice and hard work for those who need help most. Of course, we want the high every day, which is why we go shopping, long for our days off, buy a new SUV, eat chocolate every day, over-exercise, become workaholics, and overeat at mealtime. But Jesus said there is nothing in the world that compares to the abundant life that comes from loving and being who God created you to be – Love God – and using your gifts and abilities in service of those most in need – Love Neighbor.

The upside-down, counterintuitive program Jesus taught his athletes was one they had never seen before. He, the ultimate coach, knew his system worked, but his athletes were skeptical. How could such a program ever bring lasting joy, for it seems to bring only the opposite? But Jesus pushed them, just as his program pushes us even today. And what they found and people still find today is that there is no joy like banging it out for those who need it most and by doing the things you most love doing. It is the yin-yang experience of doing the actions you most love doing, but doing so in service of humanity. Thus, the joys are found not just in the accomplishments, but in doing what one loves doing and in serving people who really need what you are good at.

We find it so hard to have No Glory days. But Jesus' workout plan for the badasses will fill us and satisfy us in ways no fleeting high can. Jesus' life workout program will bring us fulfillment, joy, and peace, even on No Glory days.

We simply must trust that the Great Coach knows his plan, knows it works, and knows that we, too, will find the great joy, peace, and abundance he promises.

Are you bucking God or buying into God's plan for your life?

Are you working the program – attending to the work of your calling and using it in service of humanity? Or are you constantly looking for the highs?

Do you get easily frustrated, or are you confident in the path, even when a day offers a setback?

Are you ready for greatness, or are you staying stuck in mediocrity?

Do you have the guts to go for your greatness?

Chapter 12

STRONG CARRY THE WEAK

It was Max Day for my football team at the college. Max Day, as anyone who has lifted with a team knows, is an exciting, adrenaline-filled day, at least for those who have been working hard in the months prior. (For those who haven't been working hard it is a day of excuses and humiliation as their lack of preparation is exposed.)

I had been working with these horses for over a year, and had seen enormous gains in all of their lifts, not to mention a complete transformation in their collective mental focus and work habits. Thus, this was going to be a great day.

Normally, for workouts I would split this team into 2 or 3 large groups (and then multiple small groups within those large groups) working out at 2-3 different times throughout the afternoon and evening, because the weightroom was simply not big enough to accommodate a hundred-plus footballers, all at once, not to mention athletes of other teams. And there was simply no way to control traffic flow and monitor progress with such a large group.

But Max Day was different. The entire energy of the whole team was packed into the weightroom on max day. Because the gym was simply log-jammed, many other athletes and non-athletes who had clearance to use this gym hustled out after an abbreviated workout, so as to stay out of the way of the stampede.

Metallica and *Linkin Park* blasted from the speakers. IPods were tuned into *Infected Mushroom, Cold, Nelly,* and all other manner of blood-pumping music. My very best 'cleaners' were on, and were throwing just stunning weight. All of the platforms were in use. Most of the weight in the gym was scattered about the platforms. The team was packed around the power clean platforms, and was completely jacked as the weights kept getting higher. It was a frickin' beautiful, heart-pounding thing as 300, 350, and 400 pounds were being pulled and cleaned. And, as is necessary with cleans (for safety reasons), the weight was being dropped to the platform from shoulder height after the completed maxes, causing an enormous thundering to punctuate the blasting music. The horses roared, grunted, swore, spit, howled, and bled in a cloud of chalk as they attacked these monstrous weights.

It was in the middle of this electric, testosterone-driven aggressiveness, bordering just this side of madness that a scrawny little kid, no more than 19 years old and weighing little more than, say, 110 lbs, pushed his way through to one of the platforms. He was not a football player and clearly didn't belong. But there he was – as the gym suddenly seemed to go in silent slow motion and many players looked on in shock – bending down next to one of the platforms to pick up two 10-pound weights for the barbell he was using on a bench press nearby.

This goofy little kid with thick glasses had just walked into the lion's den, quite unbothered by it all, and took weights that were obviously in use by the biggest of the big! He was breaking one of my Cardinal rules of the gym ('Never use something that is in use by someone else without asking.'). But it was the most stunning, time-stopping, impressive thing I had seen in a gym in a good long time -- almost Twilight Zone-ish.

There he was. Comfortable. Fine. And, after the initial shock, the football players moved quickly out of his way to let him go by and go about his business.

In that moment of loud intensity and power a scrawny little kid had personified everything I ever wanted a gym to be. In that moment I had achieved one of the greatest victories in my entire sports career.

Lion and lamb working side-by-side, co-existing with mutual respect.

Most Gyms

Any gym or fitness center that has free weights can be an intimidating place for beginners, some women, and smaller guys who generally aren't used to being around free weights and heavy lifting. For people accustomed to cardio equipment, machines, and small weights, there can be a great amount of anxiety in going near the big weights, big men (and some women) and their loud expulsions of air and noise, as well as sweat and spit.

This is why many gyms and fitness centers go out of their way to cater to women and the novice lifter by eliminating or greatly minimizing heavy weight areas, or by imposing many rules upon heavy lifters – no noise, no dropping weights, no spitting, no swearing, etc.[14] In fact, nowadays, it is quite common for gyms to have a 'women only' workout area.

In contrast, some gyms go precisely the opposite direction, catering to the heavy lifters, thereby sometimes driving away the beginners or intermediates seeking general fitness.

In the weightrooms I have run or worked in I have always sought a compromise – a place where the weak and the strong not only co-exist, but understand the needs of the other and bring respect for the other.

I have always coached all of my athletes on the general ethic of most weightrooms, regardless of who the weightroom caters to. Some of the basics include:

- Always ask everyone in the immediate vicinity of a machine or rack before using it, because it is a courtesy, and the person using it may simply be at the water fountain.

[14] I was actually once in a gym that had the rule "No whistling." Talk about the dumbest rule ever, especially for me, since I always whistle and sing when I'm lifting. Yes, I know it's odd. But it's true.

- Never, ever tell someone else how to lift, unless you are their coach or they have asked you, because it is inherently condescending to do so.

- Always defer to others.

Similarly, I have always coached my biggest and strongest male teams that in the weightroom, as in life, strength brings responsibility, not privilege. The strongest have a responsibility for the weak. The big have a responsibility for the small. The vocal have a responsibility for the quiet.

Thus, my big athletes know that they have a responsibility in my weightroom to constantly be on the lookout for smaller people who might need weight, need clamps, need a bar, need a rack, need a spot, or what have you. They must go out of their way to offer these things, even if it means going without them or making uncomfortable adjustments, because smaller people will generally not ask for them. Big and loud people can be intimidating, even if they're not trying in any way to do so. I explain to my male athletes that walking into a weightroom where there are big sweaty men can be intimidating for girls, small guys, and older people. Thus, the big fellas have to go out of their way to make others feel comfortable and respected.[15]

However, it doesn't stop there. Just as I take time to educate my young men on the needs and feelings of my females, non-athletes, and older folks, I also take time to educate my girls and non-athletes on the needs and ways of the big boys. I tell all of my smaller female athletes, many of whom have never been in a serious gym, on their first day in the gym, that many of the exercises we will be using can be uncomfortable, can look stupid, and can make them feel silly. I tell them I understand it can feel uncomfortable to be in the weightroom with the big guys.

---

[15] I know this all may sound sexist to the outsider. But anyone who knows serious athletics and the inside of a serious weightroom knows the truth of it. It's not good, bad, or otherwise; it's simply true. Just as they know that in a weightroom anyone who is busting their butt will gain respect, regardless of gender, size, age, body shape, or what have you. Hard work rules.

But, I tell them, they need to understand that if they are in the weightroom genuinely working, they will be respected. If they are in just horsing around or chatting, they will not be respected. As long as they are working, they are seen as fellow athletes, striving for excellence, and will be treated as such.

I go on to tell the females what I expect of the males. I tell them that I expect them to treat the males (and heavy-lifting females) with respect by understanding the nature of lifting heavy weight (which many of the young women begin to understand more fully as their strength increases). It is impossible to lift heavy weight, impossible to push oneself beyond what one has lifted in the past, impossible to have seriously intense workouts without the adrenaline coursing through the body, without occasionally releasing loud noises upon completion of a set, without lots of sweat being thrown around, and without snot and spit occasionally emitting from the body. It is impossible for good athletes to become great without force, fire, strain, struggle, noise, shouts (of frustration, fatigue, anger, and ecstasy), and controlled aggressiveness.

And the smaller athletes need to understand that they are safe in this environment, that my big boys are looking out for and looking after my small athletes, but my big boys need their space, too, to simply be who they are when they are pushing themselves to greatness.

The point I try to help them see is that we do not bring up the weak by bringing down the strong. We bring up the weak by creating space for the strong to get stronger (and provide for the unusual needs of that process), and then by teaching the strong of their responsibility to lift up and help the weak.

This is the ethic I teach in my weightroom. No matter where I have worked or what athletes I have worked with, male or female, I tell all my lifters that this is the way I expect them to approach life, as well. If you are strong and do not go out of your way to attend the needs of the weak, you are living as a coward who is only in life for himself. If you are rich and do not go out of your way to attend to the needs of the poor, you are living as a self-centered child whom others will ultimately not respect and have no desire to be around. If you are a person who is part of an 'in group' and you do not go out of your way to bring lovingkindness to outcasts, you are simply being selfish.

These are very strong words I use with these young men and women. But my job is not only to unlock and increase their inner strength (and their physical strength), but to teach them the yoke of responsibility that comes with increased power in life.

To live a noble life is to orient yourself to causes higher than your own gain and well-being. It is not about 'being good' or 'looking good,' but about doing good, doing great, and doing outside of your own best interests.

I teach my athletes of all abilities and sexes that the purpose of strength – be it physical strength, fiscal strength, character strength, spiritual strength, or some other – is to engage that strength in service of those who are in need, or not strong enough to help themselves, or who are oppressed by systems that drain the life blood from their spirit. Therein is the responsibility, and therein is the joy!

Jesus and his Badass Call to Nobility

This is precisely the message of Jesus' life. Whether or not you personally believe Jesus was the son of God or not, whether you believe he performed larger-than-life miracles, and whether you believe he was born of a virgin or ascended into heaven after he died, you cannot deny that Jesus was a man of enormous character strength. He had the inner power to walk against the grain of an entire society, and at startling personal price, so that others might know life!

> "And they rose up and put him out of the city, and led him to the brow of the hill on which their city was built, that they might throw him down, headlong. *But **passing through the midst of them** he went away*" (Luke 4:29-30).

Again, whether you believe Jesus to be savior of the universe or not, it is indisputable that Jesus had such enormous personal power that, undaunted, he could pass through the center of an angry mob intent on killing him! (…not much different from that 110-pound kid passing through the big horses on powerclean day, even though, unlike the crowd wanting to kill Jesus, the big boys held no malice toward that youngster.)

Jesus' entire adult life was spent going against society by giving his strength in defense of those who had no strength in the eyes of society – the outcasts, the harlots, the crooks, the dense (think Peter), the occasional leader who did not buy into all of the establishment's thinking but who couldn't risk coming out as an objector (Nicodemus), the salty earthy folks (changing roughly 175 gallons of water into wine so that regular folks might celebrate a wedding; John 2:1-11). He fought not for himself, but for others.

And this is Jesus' calling to each of us. For each of us has strength in different areas of life. That strength we have simultaneously earned and been given by God. Strength brings responsibility, not privilege. And Jesus calls each one of us to use our strength to serve those who need it most and those who can benefit us in no possible way. Jesus calls us to step outside of our zone of strictly looking after ourselves into the areas of life where our strength can be used for the benefit of others.

The great reward of a life of other-centeredness (serving others) is a deep, deep joy and peace that no other path can bring. It takes far too many people 40 or 50 years of life to discover that the real joy in life comes from giving back. But for the serious athlete and intense personality there is very early in life an innate knowing, deep down, that a life of serving a cause greater than oneself is full of passion, intensity, fire, and joy. And there is a desire to choose and live that path.

And so, the question is, are you using your strengths for yourself or for others who need it most? And when will you begin to more fully heed God's call (a call felt deep within; a call seen in a need somewhere around you) to greater service?

For when you begin to give more of your strength, your strength increases, your joy increases, and you begin to taste the power of life flowing through you. You begin to truly 'get' the power and depth of Jesus' teachings. You begin to tap into the power of God flowing through you.

Who are the weak or defenseless, the outcast or oppressed, and the needy or alone who need the strength you bring?

What is the noble path to which you are being called?

Chapter 13

Focus, Focus, Focus!!!

In all the years I have been in sports, in the coaching business, and in the lifting world, two of my very favorite lifters are twin sisters, one of whom attended the college where I was working; the other attended another college nearby. They approached me one summer, asking if I would train them to compete in bodybuilding competitions. They had never done this before, but knew I had experience training lifters for competition.

I had known one of the sisters because she was a regular in my weightroom. I'd had conversations with her before about my respect for her lifting ability and, most importantly, her intensity and ability to focus. Thus, I knew these girls were, indeed, serious, as well as capable of the passion and focus necessary to compete in bodybuilding.

I agreed to take them under my wing and within months had them banging out some serious weight. In fact, when working with the football and hockey teams I would often call over one of the twins to humiliate, and thereby motivate, some of the heavy hitters by the amount of weight these girls were able to lift. When the freshman football and hockey players came into training camp and I had them in the gym on leg days doing leg extensions (back when athletes still did leg extensions) I brought one of the twins over to show the boys how it is done. The boys, fresh out of high school, some of whom were lifting maybe 150 lbs or 180 pounds for 2 reps, were shocked and humbled when one of the twins would do the stack for 4-6 reps!! The stack was 250 pounds!

What made it even more humiliating and motivating for these male athletes was that these girls were no East German Shot-putters. Both of these twins were slender, ridiculously pretty, and friendly as all heck, often flirting with the footballers, baseball players, and hockey players while kicking their asses!

Or, when I was teaching a team about the effectiveness of Straight-leg Dead Lifts in really nailing the hamstrings and lower back, I brought the other twin over to demonstrate. She was a natural at this lift – perfect form, terribly strong, and a pleasure to watch as a lifter. The boys loved having the pretty girls around, and the twin loved both being the center of attention and sorta sticking it to the boys, showing them that she not only knew this lift and many of them didn't, but also that she could hit some serious weight. As would happen most days in the weightroom after that, rivalry, sexuality, and respect were bouncing around a bit to create an electric gym where serious work was getting done!

These two girls, as with a few lifters on my female teams, brought a level of intensity normally only seen in the gym among the most intense guys. I know that's not politically correct to say, but it is simply true. As it turns out, the twins had been lifting since they were very young. Their father, a successful businessman and serious lifter himself, had raised his girls on hunting, fishing, weightlifting, digging wells and ditches, and all other things he would have taught his sons if he had any. As a result, these girls possessed a level of focus that was nearly unrivaled. It was remarkable, really. And I loved working with them.

I don't know their father's name, but I do know they always referred to him as 'Teddy.' When they were young they called him their Teddy Bear, and the nickname stuck. This guy was gentle with his daughters, but pushed 'em hard and taught them the importance of focus and intensity. For, once you know which way your heart is calling you, it is only by focus and intensity that the dream gets accomplished in this lifetime. Teddy had taught the twins at a very young age that focus and hard work are king, and it was obvious in everything the girls did – from lifting to studies, and from work to playing musical instruments.

All of my lifters knew that this was the one thing I harped on more than anything else – focus! For, lifting, as with life, is fundamentally not a physical exercise! Lifting, really, is all mental! It is the mind controlling the body. It is the mind that decides to keep pushing when the body wants to quit. It is the mind that decides, in advance, to complete the max. It is the mind that tunes out all distractions and channels all of the body's energy. It is the mind that determines success. Only the mind!

If you want to be a successful parent, I would explain to my athletes, you need to have the ability to leave work at work and be fully present when putting together a puzzle with your daughter or listening to your son's recounting of school that day. If you want to be a successful spouse, you need to have the ability to tune out the distractions of other men or women trying to get your attention and potentially ruin your marriage. If you want to be a successful artist, you have to tune out the distractions of all that would keep you from your work. If you want to be a doctor, you have to be able to focus your mind through years of med school, sifting through the boring and the profound. If you want to successfully run a non-profit, you have to focus on the goal of constantly raising funds, as well as providing top-flight services.

Inspired by the Weakest Link

Often in sports the analogy of a chain is used to describe what makes a team succeed or fail.

"A chain is only as strong as its weakest link,"
coaches often say.

We had a weakest link on one of the teams at the college. This kid, Jeff, was on the football team for three years and had never been in the game. He was at times treated nicely by the other players and at times, at least in his early years, with disdain. But he was clearly seen by them as the weakest link on the team, at least until his senior year.

After being hired by that college, I gave my opening speech to his team in the winter before the weakest link's senior season. And I happened to mention in my speech that I loved having lifters who were math majors. I then asked for a show of hands of who on the team was a math major. Only one kid raised his hand....the weakest link. Some of the other players snickered...until they heard what I had to say.

I went on to tell the team that the one advantage that math majors have – in sports and in life – that most other majors don't have is that math is one of the few academic studies that, even at the most basic levels in junior high, demands daily study – every day! – if the student is going to be successful. Math majors, I told them, are used to sitting their butts down and doing the work, *even when they don't want to.* Math demands daily attention. Math majors have the ability to focus their minds, on demand, and zone into a project, because they are used to doing it every day. (The reason most people hate math is 'cuz it simply demands daily attention, focus, and work. And when you're in junior high – the age most people develop a math-aversion – attention, focus, and work are in rather short supply.)

I told them that the purpose of the weightroom is not to make them stronger or to get them into better shape physically. A monkey can do that. Physical strength is simply the residue of accomplishing the real work.

The real work is the long, slow struggle of training not our bodies, but our minds. Lifting is like math; it teaches you how to focus your mind.

(**Note**: I believe very strongly that there are two things in athletics that have the power to make you infinitely stronger mentally – asphalt and cast iron. Both of them force you to overcome gravity, day in and day out. Both of them, whether it be by running [on asphalt...or grass or turf] or lifting cast iron weights, force you to be alone; force you to overcome yourself when you want to quit; and force you to, ultimately, make your mind stronger than your body. It could be argued that similar things have the same effect, such as laps in a pool or ascending a sheer rock face.)

When your body wants to quit – which, when beginning a new program, comes very quickly in the workout – your mind must push the body to overcome itself by overcoming the weights. By teaching your mind how to overcome your body once, you teach your mind how to overcome your body again; and then again; and then again. Eventually, the body is doing far more than your mind could have imagined.

And this is the key to success in life in any venture, I told my athletes. There is no success in any area of life, unless you have the ability to focus your mind and channel all of your physical energy in the direction of your mind. There is no success in any venture in life unless you have the ability to focus all of your energy on whatever task is in front you.

I would tell my athletes that when they have kids some day it will be all too easy to be thinking about work when they are teaching the child how to bait a hook. When they are at work it will be all too easy to be thinking about going to pick up their new boat. When they are out with their girlfriends it is easy to start thinking about (and hence talking about) themselves, and not giving energy and attention to her.

The challenge in life is to learn how to focus our minds. By doing so, we acquire the cornerstone for success in any venture.

Jeff, the weakest link, ended up putting his math focus to good use. six months after I got my hands on him, he was squatting 400 pounds, roughly double what he had been lifting prior to my arrival. His power clean improved radically and so did his bench press.

A chain is only as strong as its weakest link. And, after only six months, he had strengthened the team chain, because he was no longer the weakest link. Instead, his increased numbers were humiliating others and thereby pushing them to work harder. Further, he had won the respect of his teammates through his tireless dedication and the intensity of his workouts!

Without the focus that Jeff brought, that Teddy taught, and the twins lived, without the extreme focus that intense lifters know, without the capacity to channel all of your energy in the direction of your mind, you will never, ever know the greatness and the deep joy that Jesus promised is ours to have. You will never live the fierce and exciting existence God put you on this earth to live.

Instead, life will be a series of missteps, stumblings, half-accomplishments, and only surface fulfillment. Without the ability to focus your mind and your life's energies on that which you feel called to do, you will find yourself stuck in mediocrity, unfulfilled, and constantly yearning for more.

For there is no success in life without focus.

Jesus and the Big Ugly-ass 'S' Word

Sin.

Sin is one of the biggest, nastiest, and most beat-up words in all of Christianity. Truth is, most folks hate the word. Don't want to talk about it. Definitely don't want to hear about it from somebody else. And don't really care even one bit about any discussion of sin.

And, given how we have normally thought about it or had it rammed down our throats in churches in the past, that response is totally understandable. In my last book, *The 7 Evangelical Myths*, I explained how old-school Christianity basically had to make you feel bad before they could sell you their version of Jesus. They 'created a need' for their savior-product by selling sin and your crummy nature, life, and future. Is it any wonder people lost interest in discussion of sin, not to mention church, as a whole? Who wants to hear that stuff? Who will long tolerate being told they're scum?

But what I am proposing is an understanding of sin that is radically different from the 'be a good boy, do good things, and don't do bad things' version of sin that we have always been taught. I am proposing a version of sin that is much more in alignment with Jesus' notion of 'Love God and Love Neighbor' and his instruction to each of us to find and follow the call of God within. I am proposing an understanding of sin that can only be understood in light of our discussion of focus in this chapter.

As mentioned in previous chapters, the true and only mission in life is to follow the call of God in your life that is speaking to you from within you (the 'computer chip,' so to speak, that was implanted in you when you were created). The only calling and the only joy come from reading the 'chip' and living it – being whom God created you to be, doing what God created you to do, using the skills and dreams God gave specifically to you; and doing so in service of humanity.

It is fascinating to note that Jesus rarely laid out lists of things we should **not** do, as if creating some moral agenda. In fact, it is interesting to note that the book of Matthew devotes Chapters 5-7 strictly to Jesus' Sermon on the Mount, one of the most popular and most quoted Jesus pieces in the Bible. Yet, a thorough reading of the Sermon on the Mount indicates that the bulk of Jesus' message is not spent on what not to do, per se, but on the good that men and women can do, *and every single thing he says is simply some form of expressing love toward your fellow men and women!* Here is a slice:

- Blessed are the meek, for they shall inherit the earth…
- Blessed are those who show mercy, for they shall obtain mercy…
- Blessed are the peacemakers, for they shall be called sons of God…
- You are the light of the world…
- Let your light so shine before me that they may see your good works and give glory to God.
- You have heard it was said, 'You shall love your neighbor and hate your enemy.' But I say to you, Love your enemies and pray for those who persecute you, so that you may be sons of God…
- For he makes the sun rise on the evil and on the good, and sends rain on the just and on the unjust. (Matthew 5:1-16, 43-45)

Even when Jesus does discuss what we should not do, it is replaced with a command for what we can do instead. Hence, life is not about trying to avoid missteps and screw-ups. Life is not about trying to avoid the negative, but going after the boldest, most positive course of action. For example:

- Therefore, I tell you, do not be anxious about your life, what you shall eat or what you shall drink, nor about your body, or what you shall put on. Is not life more than food, and the body more than clothing?

- Look at the birds of the air: they neither sow nor reap nor gather into barns, and yet God feeds them…
- *Instead, seek first to create God's world of love and to follow my commands* [love God and love neighbor].
- Do not be anxious about tomorrow, for tomorrow will be anxious for itself.
- Let today's own trouble be sufficient for today. (Matthew 6:25-34)

At points in his ministry Jesus clearly condemns divorce, hypocrisy, and hurting others in any way. And all three of these things fall under his primary message of creating and showing love to others.

The point Jesus keeps coming back to
and keeps coming back to
is to stay focused on doing as much good for others
as you possibly can.
Therein will you find your greatness and your greatest joy!

The whole notion of faith itself is staying focused on the power and possibility of God at work in our lives. That's what faith is! Lack of faith is failing to trust in God and God's activity. It is taking the focus off God's actions and getting caught up in the anxiety of thinking you have to do it all yourself!

So, if 'Love God and Love Neighbor' is Jesus' command to us, if this is what Jesus says will bring us true fulfillment and abundance deep in our souls, then sin is simply that which pulls our focus from that mission. Sin is not the opposite of 'being good' but the opposite of faith, the opposite of trusting God. For, it is the opposite of focusing on God's power, ability, actions, and desire to bring us abundance. Sin is the absence of faith, the absence of focus. Sin is forcing life and trying to make it happen on your own rather than trusting in inspired action, trusting that the Lord provides.

Sin is nothing more than that which distracts us from doing what Jesus has commanded us to do (Love God and Love Neighbor). Sin is that which distracts us from most fully being who God created us to be and doing what God created us to dream and accomplish. Sin is that which pulls our focus from fulfilling our souls, finding our abundance, and being sources of rich love in the world.

Sin, at its core, is not some devil or some evil in you. Sin is not even about morality or immorality. Sin is not about being a bad boy or bad girl.

Sin is distraction. Nothing more, nothing less. It takes many forms, but it is ultimately only that which pulls you off the mark, off the goal, off your focus, which is God, God's will for your life, and God's desire for you to have total abundance and greatness.

If Jesus' greatest commands are to love God and love neighbor, then anything you do that is not loving of God and who God created you to most fully be, OR is not loving of or respectful of your neighbor/humanity is a distraction from that call.

Anything that distracts you from maximizing your potential is sin. Anything that pulls your focus from following God's voice inside and doing so in service of humanity is sin. It is a violation of God's creation in you and God's will for your life.

With that in mind, the general character of sin takes on a much different look and flavor from what we have always been told. If sin is distraction, then life is not about following a list of do's and don'ts. It is about honestly assessing what it is you allow in your life, looking for things that might pull you down from that which you are called to do.

And what are the biggest sins?

- **Fear**. Fear is always the biggest! There is nothing that has greater power to pull our focus off the mark. It keeps us from following and doing that which we know we most want to accomplish – that which is written on the very DNA of our being. Fear obstructs our courage and keeps us in lower energy and lesser joy. It sucks the life right out of us. And rather than passing through it, lack of focus and strength cause us to cower in the face of fear and never reach our fullest potential.

- **Commotion**. Often it is not our willingness to follow God's call that is the problem, but our inability to simply hear it. We let our lives spin with so much activity, commotion, and anxiety that we cannot even hear God's call in our lives. TV, kids, appointments, incidental crap, planning for this or that, work stuff, grocery shopping, and all sorts of petty stuff are effective at keeping us distracted and off-focus. If you are constantly busy, you cannot hear God's voice speaking from within. If you can't hear the call, you will never be able to follow God's voice; and you will be a bundle of anxiety running frantically in a million directions.

- **Comfort**. One of the biggest distractions in life is the desire for security and comfort. Security is a lower existence. It is the farthest thing from a life passionately lived on the edge, fully alive. If our lives are safe, secure, and semi-happy today, why change? Why pursue some fool inner-calling when I have reasonable happiness and comfort today? This is also known as the inability to let go. We cling to the safer, lesser existence rather than follow God's leading to higher ground, because we like our safety and comfort. (Of course, this is just fear in disguise.)[16]

- **Control**. One big God-killer in this world is the innate human belief that I must understand the results. So often we think that if the results don't look like what I imagined in advance then it is failure; then it is contrary to God's will. Rather than simply following the call and trusting that God's plan may look very different from what I have planned (and then moving on when it feels like I've fulfilled the call and am called to something new), we try to force the results and get offended when the ends look nothing like we originally imagined. We so desperately lust for control of everything in life that we utterly block God out of the equation.

  - Do you think Stephen liked where his life went? Here he was, faithfully following the call and speaking of Jesus, just a decade or so after Jesus' death, when he was seized and stoned to death. He followed the call of his heart…and it led to his

[16] In *Rescuing God from Christianity* I discuss the work of psychologist Abraham Maslow and his Hierarchy of Human Needs. Maslow said that one of the most basic of all human needs is a sense of security. However, by staying stuck in holding on to this lesser need, at nearly all costs, we limit our ability to meet our higher needs, such as the need for deep fulfillment of the soul, not to mention our true greatness.

death, which was likely not his first choice or his goal for a life of following Jesus. But, it was precisely this event of his stoning that impacted Saul, who would become Paul, who would end up being the greatest evangelist in the history of Christianity! Sin is thinking that the results I want are the results God wants. Sin is distraction from what I am called to do, no matter where it leads.

- **Cool.** A huge killer of the will and killer of the passion to follow God's call inside is the desire to avoid anything that might make me look foolish. We are so self-conscious that the notion of looking foolish is anathema to existence in America. Where Paul said he was a 'fool for Christ,' it is written on our very character that we won't do anything that makes us look even semi-stupid. And so, we live in this safe, sheltered life of religion, quite apart from true, alive spirituality that not only changes our lives but changes the world. The fear of looking foolish is a faith killer as sure as anything is.

- **Fear**. Did I mention the power of fear?

Fundamentally, all sin boils down to three things:

1. Inability or unwillingness to listen to God's voice speaking from within (or ignorance that the voice even exists and is valid!);
2. Fear of following the call; and
3. Thinking the results should be the way I want them to be.

These are the three things that pull our focus from following the call and thereby finding deep fulfillment of the soul.

Three Caveats

One:

Focus is incredibly important. Avoiding distraction is critical to following the call and accomplishing one's greatness.

However, this is not to say that we are constantly to be driving, driving, driving relentlessly toward our dreams and goals. Yes, we are to drive, drive, drive, but (as explained in Chapter 7) not without rest and that which also fills us up. We are supposed to be on fire for that which we feel called to do. But we do also need to refill our tanks and recharge our batteries.

Also, when you are on the path of your life's calling, the drive, drive, drive is effortless. What would have been work is now just joy and terribly exciting! There are down days, but on the whole it is a great ride. We have all heard people say, "I love my work" and "I get paid to do this?" and "I am so lucky. I'd do this for free!" Those are the words of someone who is on a killer great drive doing what they know they are called to do in their heart!

So, the defining question of sin is "Does whatever you are considering take you off your path and onto a new path that doesn't sit right with your inner calling? Or is this action in sync with your path? Or perhaps, is it just a necessary pit stop on the journey, intended to give you energy to continue down the path of your calling? Bottom line, does this new path feeeeel right inside?"

Two:

This is not to say we are not to change paths. Very often what makes God's call so difficult is that it usually demands a very different path from the one we are on. Further, it demands changing courses more than once, which is anathema to old-school mentalities that think life is one decision, one path, one career, one life, etc.

It's not a sin to switch paths. In fact, if you really are following God's call from within, you *will* switch paths, perhaps several times in life. God has a lot for you to accomplish. Most of it you will not be able to see in advance. Further, God's not into boredom, except as a way to teach you what you really don't want. Further, God gave you a lot of gifts when you were born, and there is so much more you can do if you have the joy of using a whole new skill set you didn't even know you had.

Switching paths is no sin. It's a sin to get off track once you know what God's call in your life is, once you know what God's path for your life is! It's a sin to stay on a path because it is safe, even though that path no longer breathes life into you and even though you know you're supposed to be doing something else (even if you don't fully know what that something else is).

That is sin – distraction from that which you know you gotta do with your life! It's a sin to basically not do what God is calling you – from within – to do.

Three:

For the record, and this is a very important point, no one – AND I MEAN NO ONE! – can tell you what *your* calling is! Others can help you discover your skills, uncover your dreams, and engage your vision for what would bring you joy and what joy you can bring to others. But, ultimately, only you know what God is calling you to do, be, and become!

Therefore, the purpose of pastors, priests, ministers, and spiritual/religious leaders is *not* to put something into you, for the most part, but to help draw something out of you. Their purpose is to help you quiet your life so you can read your chip, then help you find the courage to attack the mission. It is to draw out of you what God has written on your heart. The great religious leaders are the ones who encourage you and help you to become the great person God has created you to be and accomplish the great tasks God has put in you to accomplish!

There is no success in life in any venture, especially following God's call for your life, without the capacity to focus your mind and focus your life! The only path to true fulfillment and a compelling sense of purpose is through hearing God's call from within, focus, hard work, and elimination of all those things that would pull you from your calling.

What is distracting you?

When do you most find yourself thinking about something else?

What do you need to do to better focus on the task at hand?

Are you ready to move up to the next level of success by increasing your mental focus?

What is the calling of your heart?

Chapter 14

INSPIRING OTHERS

When I first started coaching the strength and conditioning program at one college, I was charged, primarily, with strengthening the football team. NCAA rules required that I include all other sports and non-athletes, and, at this college, that included working with faculty and staff, as well. And, as I began, the fitness center at this college was just another sleepy gym at just another college.

But as I focused more and more energy on educating and strengthening my primary charges – football players – we began to see greater changes. Working out now as a team, rather than individually, which they had always done in the past, the football team, in very short order, began to catch a spark. And they began to get noticeably stronger. Within two months, nearly every player was lifting more weight than they had ever lifted in their lives.

With those significant increases in strength came increases in muscle size, which is a huge priority for most 20 year-old males I come into contact with. And, as size and strength took off so did enthusiasm for the program and for the weightroom, as a whole. The football team, which was upbeat and well-liked at this college, even thought it hadn't had a winning record in a few years, was energized to a whole new level. There was a buzz. Athletes and the people they hung out with were talking about what was happening in the weightroom.

Coaches and players were telling me, "We've never seen this many people in the weightroom before." After I completed my first full semester at the college many came up and said, "There is a totally different energy in the gym. It's like a spark has been lit in the athletic department and at the college for fitness, strength, and off-season training."

A sense of energy and community were developing. More people began showing up to work out. Kids we had never seen in the fitness center before were coming in to get in on the action. Within six weeks, I went from coaching one team to four teams. And, over the next several months I would be hands-on with players of nine different teams, as well as countless non-athletes, faculty, and staff.

Just a year later, every coach in the athletic department became much more deliberate about using the strength and conditioning facilities for his or her athletes. They weren't all using me, but they were buying into the shared energy and spark that was happening in the weightroom and training facilities. And sports at the college began to change, seeing both more winning and a higher level of mental commitment.

I have been around athletics long enough to know that there is no way any one element can be solely attributed to a team's or a college's success. It's not just the off-season strength and conditioning; nor is it just the head coaches; nor is it just finding good recruits; nor is it just the caliber of the athletic facilities; nor, important as it may be, is it just the support of the administration in budgeting for excellence, or the alumni in donating funds. Any coach knows that in the best programs all these elements work together to create a whole that is far greater than the sum of its parts.

But it is also true in sports that a spark can be lit in one of these areas that then catches on and spreads like wildfire, creating light, heat, and energy in all the other areas. A great head coach can come in and transform a program seemingly overnight. A college president or athletic director who sees the long-term value of a top-flight competitive sports program can infuse a tired athletic department with new blood and new energy. Similarly, an enthusiastic and experienced strength and conditioning coach can light a fire inside athletes, particularly in the off-season, that drives them to new heights and begins to spread to others. The power of the spark cannot be underestimated.

With that spark inside, my football players began to push themselves like they had never pushed before. We began to talk more about mental focus, tuning out distractions, and bringing more intensity and passion to their in-season and off-season work. We began to see more athletes fighting through pain and fatigue, and climbing to new levels of success. Soon other teams were doing so, as well.

Many of the athletes began to change who they were outside the weightroom, too. We began to talk more about becoming strong for a reason – besides just doing great in sports – such as using our strength to help the weak, and using our ability to focus as a way to give energy and attention to others when it would be so easy to grab attention for ourselves. We began to see more athletes in more sports pushing themselves harder, growing, yearning to do more, and fighting to become impact players on the field and in life; as well as becoming involved in leadership, community work, and personal lives of sacrifice and other-service.

But it all started with the spark. It all started with the desire to build a fire among a small group of young men. And it quickly spread.

No Guts, No Glory

This is precisely what Jesus meant when he said in Matthew 5:14-16:

> "You are the light of the world. A city set on a hill cannot be hid. Nor do men light a lamp and put it under a bushel basket, but on a stand, and it gives light to the entire house. Let your light so shine before others, that they may see your good works and give glory to God."
>
> "Jesus spoke to them, 'I am the light of the world; he who follows my teachings will not walk in darkness, but will have the light of life" (John 8:12).

The energy of the spark and light changes people! People become inspired when someone they like or respect is inspired. My lifters inspired others with their dedication, their hard work, and their new-found zeal for strength and putting their strength to good use on the field and in the world.

Jesus calls each one of us to live on fire. Jesus calls each one of us to be a spark, to be a light, to be an energy source for others, particularly to those who need it most.

(As an aside, it ain't always the poor and hungry that need a spiritual spark the most. Often those most in need of the light are those whom you'd think would have the least reason to be so. Often the most dead inside are those who have the most outside.)

Intensely spiritual people are called to bring the fire of passion, strength, and new life to those who are the most dead inside and whose souls ache for something to believe in and something to live for and get excited about.

But, it ain't as pretty as it sounds. See, fire comes at a price. Light is not free, so to speak. Something has to be burned up. Something has to be lost to create that heat and energy. The spark in my lifters came at the price of exceptionally hard work together in the weightroom.

As the WWII concentration camp survivor and great writer, Viktor Frankl, once stated,

"That which is to give light
must endure burning."

The only way a candle can throw light is if the wick and the wax burn. Something must be burned up or burned out. Thomas Edison sought, and eventually found, a substance that can simultaneously burn and produce a glow but not immediately burn out – coiled carbon filament in an oxygen-free bulb.

We are called to be a source of energy, warmth, strength, and vision for others. We are called to be a light to all nations and all people. Yet, *that which is to give light must endure burning.*

Just as getting physically stronger requires tearing down the muscles in the weightroom so that they grow back stronger in the period of rest following the workout, our capacity to be spiritually stronger only comes from our own failures and life challenges. Our strengthened spirits come only from having our spirits broken, our hearts broken, our plans broken, our designs for life broken, and the opportunity created for God to break into our lives. Being able to carry others spiritually – as sort of Spiritual Marines! – requires having strong shoulders and back that have been hardened through a life of hardship and taking the steeper path.

To stand up as a light for others means you will be beaten down, often by those who claim to love you most. You will get burned. You will be undercut, betrayed, lied to, minimized, demonized, and walked away from. Something must burn for something else to have light. It's just an ugly-ass truth of life.

The Call of Jesus: You Burn So That Others Might Have Light

Jesus knew about suffering and about giving light to others. He never said the path would be always easy. In fact, he and his disciples knew it would be hard. The path of graciousness and truth is always the highest and hardest.

When in the history of humanity has truth or change been greeted with open arms? When has the speaker of truth not been beaten down, kicked around, or cast out? Normally, truth is met with resistance. It is denounced, and so is its messenger.

But Jesus also knew there is no path in life that provides greater fulfillment than this high, hard path. He said,

"I have come that you might have life and have it abundantly"
(John 10:10)

But we mistake the world's definition of abundant life with Jesus' definition, even though they are near-polar opposites. TV, Madison Avenue's advertisements, Hollywood, and so many other sources have convinced us that more money, more toys, more vacations, and more stuff are what will fill that emptiness we all have inside.

To that, Jesus states a resounding “Hell no!” For that life is, indeed, hell on earth. It is a life of constantly trying to fill ourselves with things and stuff that will never fill us. Jesus teaches us that the only way to be filled is to strengthen ourselves and find our joy, and then give ourselves in loving service to others and to humanity. And, while Jesus’ path of other-service will bring hardship and burning, it will also bring enormous joy, deep satisfaction, powerful sense of purpose, and wellsprings of love and hope for things to come.

We are called to be candles of light to the world. And while Jesus knows we will be burned as we seek to bring light, he also taught that we will find true joy and find the greatness that God put inside us – the greatness of being the brightest and clearest possible light we can be. Jesus calls us to the greatness of drawing others to us, so that they might be strengthened, warmed, re-energized, and given new vision for life!

Are you a spark? How?

Can you amp it up to a higher level?

In what ways are you most capable of bringing the spark and zeal of life to others?

Are you giving light to those in need? And in what ways are you being burned?

Who is a light-bearer in your life? Who brings spark, energy, and new life to you? And in what ways do you bring burning to other light-bearers?

Chapter 15

Bad Fear and Good Fear: Trust, Part I

As mentioned in the last chapter, in a very short time I began to see changes and great improvement in the workouts at that sleepy little college. Athletes began to work harder. Athletes began to work in groups. Athletes began to feed off each other. Athletes began to see results.

What caused the change?

Besides the impact of the 'spark' mentioned in the last chapter, there was another factor at play in turning that program around.

I've worked with teams that were perennial national champions and perennial losers, as well teams that had climbed from the bottom to being championship contenders, and teams that were beginning their climb and developing momentum. I've worked with individual athletes from junior high level through Division I and professional, from Olympic hockey players to ultimate fighters. I have also counseled countless people in their personal lives. From all of this I have come to discover several very core truths about life. One core truth is:

Ultimately,
there are only two things that ever cause lasting change in life:
pain and love.

I came into a school where there was no real all-sport lifting program, no sense of commitment, and no love for the weightroom. I brought with me a solid plan for working out and gaining strength.

But what really made the difference was my own high energy, love for working out, and love for the kids, coupled with, dumb as it sounds, the fact that I was 6’4” and 255 pounds of mostly muscle. In other words, my own success in this sport (lifting) was obvious by my sheer physical size, but it was joined with a high intensity level (which they saw in my own personal workouts and my character), high expectations, and a genuine love for the kids and their best interests, as well as a love for lifting and thorough knowledge of it.

I generally do not like talking about myself like this, but on this topic it is necessary as a means to understand motivating people who have no reason to get motivated. At this school the lack of motivation for off-season training and lifting was obvious. But I changed that simply with my strong attitude and my refusal to accept anything less. I won the kids respect by being excellent at what I do and by being a fierce coach with high standards, who also occasionally let the love come through with a kind word or a statement of what the athlete was doing right!

What happened is that they basically grew to respect me very quickly. And, as is so often the case, respect and love began to grow together. I appreciated them, and they began to appreciate my love for hard work and for them.

Before long, *their motivation became simply the fear of disappointing someone they greatly respected and even loved.* They knew that a disapproving word from me about their failure to work hard would sting. And I never let them get away with slacking. Without turning into a nag, I was on them at every turn. In the beginning it was my job to use my energy to keep them on focus and moving forward with increasing levels of intensity.

Their discipline was to lift weight. My discipline was to keep them on task. It’s the same way I taught my children good manners. Every single time they forgot a ‘please’ or a ‘thank you’ I filled it in or asked them to fill it in. I didn’t have to scold. I just constantly, constantly, constantly reminded. It was a discipline in the exact same way that getting up to go running every morning at 6am is a discipline. You just do it, and do it, and do it. Eventually it becomes a life pattern.

Discipline means *to disciple. To disciple* means *to teach.* Just as the athlete is disciplining/teaching her body, her circadian rhythm, and her muscles to run at 6am, I was teaching my own children good manners constantly, and I taught my athletes to stay focused and stay on task. To this day, my children have great manners and my lifters are highly focused.

Eventually, I was able to transfer their fear of disappointing away from me and onto their teammates. They would see their teammates working hard and getting praise from me. Then, the less motivated players would begin to not only want praise from me and want to stay away from my scolding, but also want praise and respect from their teammates. They also began to fear being looked down upon by their teammates. Positive peer pressure and punishing peer pressure. Carrot and stick.

Ultimately, there was yet another transfer. The goal in teaching winning work habits to college kids, or even teens or young adults, is to teach them to find the fear and love not in a coach or teammates, but within themselves. The key to the highest levels of success and motivation in any sport and in any venture in life is to find the passion inside yourself. It is to want it and work for it because *you* want it! That is the goal of life.

It is, first, knowing who you are and what you want. Then, it's the fear of disappointing yourself and the high standards you have set for you. Fear of developing a crummy body. Fear of the long term effect of unhealthy eating habits. Etc. It's these fears coupled with the things you love for you. Love of looking good. Love of accomplishing dreams. Love of the energy that comes from intense and passionate living. Etc.

But for an athlete who has no motivation success starts by trying to please someone she loves and not disappoint someone whose critical word she fears.

It's crazy that so often in our society we hear about fear being a bad thing. And it can be. Fear can be a powerfully crippling thing. But fear can also be a powerfully positive motivator. Quite simply, there is both good fear and bad fear.

Breaking Through Barriers Using Fear

At that same D3 school, I had 4 lifters who, after a few months, began to approach the 500-pound mark in their squats. Prior to my arrival, these boys had never even conceived of doing a 500-pound squat. All of them were right around 430 and had been for a year or two. Yet, here I was telling them on the first day I spoke to them that they should be doing 700-pound squats, because that's what D1 and D2 guys their same size were doing.

They thought I was a Martian! Totally nuts! Why? They couldn't even imagine a number bigger than 500. They had no idea what they were truly capable of, but they were *utterly convinced* they could never, never, never put up such numbers.

After a month with them, I could see that to them a 500-pound squat was goal enough, and an unattainable one at that. 500 was just such a big, round, impressive number. Just the sound of it was intimidating. It's half of 1000, for Pete's sake!

So, as their numbers began to climb in those first months they would talk about 500 at lunch and in their dorms. All they could think about was 500. As they obsessed over this amount, seeing it both as a goal and as an unthinkable amount, they began to create a mental block, a glass ceiling, an obstacle in their own minds that no amount of work, it seemed, was ever going to overcome.

Fear of 500 had set in. And that kind of fear is bad fear. There is fear that motivates us to positive action (such as fear of disappointing those we respect) and fear that cripples us into inaction and failure (such as fear of 500). And these guys had become absorbed with fear-filled tentativeness and inaction.

After a couple of months, they would several times get up to 500 in their workouts, load up the bar, squat it down, and fail. They had plenty of energy to succeed, and if they didn't have the mental block, they would have already been doing 500 for multiple reps. Time and time again these guys would try it and fail. It became very annoying for me as a coach, because I knew these guys would soon be way past this, and 500 would be nothing but a dot in their rearview mirrors. But they were stuck here now because of the weakness and fear in their own minds.

Everything is mental.

So, I did a few things. First, as will be discussed more fully in the next chapter, I kept acclimating them to higher weight. If their third set was at 485 and they were going to put on 500 for the fourth set, I would have them put on 505 or 510, or even 515, essentially forcing them to look beyond their mental obstacle.

One of my athletes, an NCAA National Champion sprinter and Olympic hopeful, told me that when running the 100-meter she always, always, always finds a spot well past the finish line that she focuses on from the split-second she comes out of the blocks. She disciplines herself to look beyond the finish line, forcing herself to run through her goal rather than slow-up or come up short.

In the weightroom this method is highly effective, as well, which is why I had the boys load up weights beyond 500. But the 500 obstacle was too great. It wasn't just another weight for these boys. It was an intimidator. It was half of 1000 lbs! So, even though this is an incredibly effective method 99% of the time, when it wasn't working for these fellas I took a bit more aggressive approach.

In a few workouts I made them start their weight on their first set higher (say 450) than previous workouts (when they might have previously opened at 430 or 440) and then jump by 15 or 20 pounds with each set. However, I never allowed them to put 500 on the bar or any weight higher than 500. Eventually, I would make them simply start getting more and more reps at 475, 485, and 495, until they were doing a rather silly and unnecessary amount of sets and reps at 495. One kid was doing 2 sets of 3 reps each at 495! But I knew that if I put on 500, he'd still fail at it, 'cuz his mind was intimidated.

But I still refused, for weeks in a row, to let them put 500 on the bar.

They grew frustrated that I made them do so many reps at such high weight without letting them move forward to higher weight. By building up so much momentum at 490 and 495 they began to realize that it was ridiculous that they couldn't just smash through the 500. In other words, the 500 obstacle became overwhelmingly illogical and just plain dumb. And so, they got mad that I wouldn't let them even try it. The subconscious barrier was coming down quickly by the force of sheer foolishness and a growing anger at their coach.

Lastly, I drove the dagger through their fear-filled hearts by really making them mad. As mentioned, I had about four guys who were close to that 500 mark. In that group there was a definite pecking order as far as who was the Alpha Male and who were second and third in the chain, as well as who was the least respected lifter of the four.

Well, the least respected lifter was so for a reason, at least on squats. Great guy otherwise (who ended up being one of my dear friends from that team), but on squats he tended to sometimes not go low enough for the reps to count. So, as I did with inadequate lifts from any lifter, I would regularly take reps away from him in workouts, informing him they didn't count because he was coming up short.

It's frustrating and tiresome to work hard and not have reps count. It can also be humiliating if this is an ongoing occurrence for a lifter. Hence, it is a powerful instructional tool for lifters who are doing what they're supposed to be doing.

In the case of these four guys and all my lifters I had strong reasons for insisting on solid depth for the squat. I am a former powerlifter and football player, and believe in deep squats for three reasons:

1 When you're on the field or rink in a game your legs go through an entire range of motion, including deep squat position, especially for football linemen. Thus, it makes sense to strengthen the muscles and joints through the entire range of motion, so that they are prepared and less prone to injury. By forcing all parts of the muscle to fire and be strengthened in the off-season the athlete is infinitely more prepared, come the season.
2 By going extra low on lighter weight the lifter has some leeway to cheat a bit on higher weight, but still have his femur at parallel or below so that his maxes count.

3 They're just harder. If you want to make yourself tougher, mentally and physically, you want to make your workouts as hard as possible (without inducing injury). And deep squats are as hard as it gets, but are still quite safe. Plus, they're just a sign of power. To be able to do them well is a huge confidence booster, because they are so damn hard.

His buddies knew it was a constant hassle to get him to go low enough. And they always questioned any rep he ever got. Consequently, they always looked down their noses at his successes and muttered their discontent.

So, as the final element to piss these boys off and break this group through the glass ceiling barrier, after they had all completed their back-breaking work at 490 and 495, I let this #4 guy load 505 onto his bar and break through the barrier. Without telling why, I made him do fewer reps on previous sets so that I knew he would have plenty of energy to blow through 500 when we got there.

When he had burned through 495 I gave him a shot at 505. He not only did it, but came out of the squat rack beaming! Most importantly, I made sure his depth was just deep enough that it could have been regulation depth, but, as always, it was just close enough to shallow that the other guys would say it was not deep enough. I gave it to him, proclaiming it as regulation depth, which it was!

The other guys were *enraged* – absolutely livid! – at me for what they thought was letting him get away with murder. I could see the anger and envy in their faces. Yet, they were enraged at not only me but themselves for being one-upped by what they saw as the lesser man.

But, they could do nothing with this rage, because I run a tight ship and tolerate no lip from anyone. Plus, the #4 guy was the last lifter in the group that day, and I refused to let any of them back in the squat rack. So, these boys had to stew in their anger and rage for a week until the next heavy squat workout.

Well, you can pretty much guess what happened the following Monday on heavy squat day. I turned the boys loose and they just blew the living heck out of 500. By the end of the day all of them were past 500 *for reps* – at 505, 510, 515, and I think one was even at 525.

500 had been bled of its power. From there on out, for these boys, for the rest of that team, and for the entire athletic department, as a whole, 500 was just another number. Over the next few months these boys and others charged ever higher. 5 months later I had 1 kid shooting for 660, 1 just under 600, and 5-6 others who were maxing in the mid-500s.

The bad, debilitating fear of 500 had been crushed by hard work, to be sure. But good fear drove the hard work. It was the mind driving the body. What drove the hard work was fear of disappointing their a-hole coach whom they respected, fear of being last in their group of 4 heavy squatters, fear of being showed-up by a supposedly lesser man, and fear of looking weak to the smaller guys. These boys were known as the strongest, and to look stuck or intimidated was humiliating. They hated it.

They were also driven by illogic and the 'negative' emotions of envy, anger, and rage (at injustice). These three emotions are actually just fear in disguise – versions of 'fear of being screwed' and 'fear of not getting a fair shake.' Thus, these emotions we generally think of as 'bad' were turned against a greater fear – the crippling fear that causes inertia and failure. They were used to accomplish the good of overcoming negative fear.

(For the record, I did later continue to insist that the #4 guy continue to go sub-parallel, even as he moved further above 500. Also, I later told the boys that I knew they were angry with me and that I was able to use their anger at me to overcome their fear, which had created a mental block at 500. I helped them see that anger can be a good thing if used well.)

An Interesting Look at Fear in the Bible

If you ever get a chance, go through the Bible and look up all the times the word 'fear' is used.

What's most interesting is not how often 'fear' is in there, but the pattern that you begin to see. Though it doesn't use these exact words, the Bible basically speaks of two kinds of fear – good fear and bad fear. Good fear is fear of God. Bad fear is fear of anything or anyone on earth. Good fear (of God) motivates us to do great things. Bad fear (of little stuff on earth or of uncertainty about what is ahead) causes us to cower in inaction and not accomplish what God wants us to accomplish with our lives.

For some people, fearing God means fearing God's punishment, either here on earth or in a hell after death. However, what I assert is that one of the ways God speaks to us is through that quiet voice deep inside us; and to fear God is to fear having that 'voice' be one of condemnation or disappointment – to simply let down your own potential. It is to know you have let yourself down. It is to come up short of what you know you are capable of and what you know God has put you on this earth to do.

For others who think of God as being outside them and in heaven, fearing God means disappointing God and the potential of incurring his wrath; kinda like the lifters who wanted the approval of their new strength coach and did not want to disappoint him or hear his critical word. And so, these sorts think that winning God's favor (and getting into heaven) demands being good. Morality, for these people, mistakenly becomes the point of religion.

Yet, when the voice of God speaks from within the wrath is one's own disappointment at not meeting one's goals, dreams, and potential.

However you think of 'fearing God,' this type of fear is a powerful motivator. It has the capacity to jumpstart your life each day and keep your life moving forward into new successes and new challenges.

The other fear the Bible speaks of is essentially fear of things on earth – people, situations, things. It is the fear that cripples us. We erect glass ceilings. We obsess over obstacles we think we'll never overcome. We overthink and overthink, giving even more energy to these obstacles. Eventually, without the right catalyst, we end up trying and failing many times, or simply never trying, at all. When bad fear dominates us the power of the earthly exceeds the power of the Great Unseen – God.

But Jesus tells us that the only way out of this nasty mess is to fear God and not fear humanity or man-made obstacles. It is to fear not being all we have been created to be, not because wrath will come but simply because we'll live a smaller existence.

The goal, he says, is to recognize that God has created a universe that gives us far more power to tap into than any 'obstacle' on earth. This is the very definition of 'faith.' By tapping into the power of God's voice inside and power of the universe God created we can blow through our obstacles here on earth to accomplish great things on God's behalf.

But this raises the question, how do you tap into the power of God that overcomes fear? It's not easy, but it is simple: Trust.

You must simply trust that all of the power of the universe is marshaled on your behalf to blow you through to greater heights than you can imagine. You trust God's power *not* because you know for sure that this power is greater than your own power (at least not yet), but because you've heard it from others, especially some folks you respect; and because you're sick of the crappy half-filled life your own efforts have gotten you. So you *choose* to trust.

The core reason the boys were able to move past 500, the core reason I was able to conjure emotions strong enough to blast through their immobilizing fear was that they chose to trust me and trust the program for success I brought with me. They could have snuck into the weightroom when I wasn't around and tried 500 on their own that evening. But, instead, they made the choice to trust me, in large part because they respected me. They saw that I was physically huge and had a track record of success, so they figured my program *must* work. It sounds so simple, so plain, but it is very true. They trusted the program because they saw the results.

They followed me not because they had to, but because they wanted to and they believed in me and my program for success. Remember, this was still D3. They weren't on scholarship. They could have flipped me off and walked away. But they didn't. Their trust and respect for my program and me enabled me to use fear as a tool to move them. Their trust in me enabled me to push them very hard and even make them angry. But that anger moved them past their fear.

Interestingly, by trusting me in all things related to their lifting and diet, they overcame 500, *which only caused them to trust my system and me even more.*

The parallel is that trusting God and fearing God are at the very core of life. And trusting God and the power of the universe God created are the drivers to overcoming the ridiculous glass ceilings we create in our lives. The reason we come up short, the reason we fail to maximize our potential is because we choose to not trust in the power of God and the universe God created. Far too regularly, we choose, instead, to live in fear. Rather than believe we're going to be okay, we choose to worry and stew about the future; and this too often leads to forced action and inevitable failure.

Can God be Trusted?

What's really interesting is that the greatest obstacle to faith is not anything except your own belief that God cannot be trusted. You can go through the motions and supposedly believe the beliefs, but really relying on God is something altogether different. The reason people choose to not trust God is because they believe at their core that *God cannot be trusted.* They believe their fears are bigger than God. They sorta believe in God, but not enough to really lean on God.

Further, sometimes the people who have gone through the God-program, so to speak – the Christians – aren't always the best indicators of the successfulness of the program. It's hard to trust the Great Coach of the Universe and his kickass program for radically transforming lives, because it's hard to find people who have really done great things with that program – things even a non-Christian can respect. So, we are inclined to dip a toe or two into the water of trusting that God will provide, rather than hurling ourselves into total trust of him.

That's why most people have to have their lives fall apart before they trust God. They just refuse to believe that trusting God is a viable formula for life. They refuse to believe that God can do it better than they can. So they spin and spin and spin their lives, until all their frantic motion creates a heap of nothing and they are utterly spent in the process, and sigh with a heavy heart, "I give up! You do it, God. I suck at this."

But it doesn't have to come to that. While getting steamrolled by life is a powerful motivator toward the God-centered life, there are ways to engage the power God brings to life without hitting rock bottom.

The simplest way to overcome our own inclination to not trust and overcome bad fear in our lives is by challenging ourselves to trust God a little more and a little more each day and each month. It is to choose God anyway. It is to live "as if" God can be trusted. It is to "fake it 'til you make it." It is to make the deliberate choice to do just the opposite of what we think is best. Our fear causes us to not move forward with boldness. But Jesus says 'Fear not' the things of this earth; instead 'Trust in God.'

So, when we trust God anyway, even when we are afraid, we are acting counterintuitively. We are choosing to trust God above ourselves.

What we discover is that the more we let go and trust God, the more God can be trusted. God's program for life is like a great lifting program. It works. We discover that the power and potential of the universe God created is so much more enormous and full of force and power than we can even begin to imagine.

But you gotta trust the 'program' of the Great Coach and the power of the universe he created. You gotta just keep working Jesus' program for life. And what is Jesus' program? It's the one he comes back to time and again – "If you really want abundant life, love God and love neighbor, particularly those most in need." The only way to overcome earthly fear is to trust God and trust Jesus' program of never-ending love.

In the night before he was brutally murdered, Jesus was praying in the Garden of Gethsemane. He knew he was going to be killed, and he prayed that God would take it away and not make him go through it. God's plan for Jesus' life was not what Jesus wanted. Jesus did NOT want the suffering. But, Jesus' love for people was so great, his trust in God was so utterly complete, and Jesus was such an overwhelming badass that his prayer morphed into, "...but your will be done, Father." Ultimately, it was Jesus' love for God and love for people that drove him to give up his own will and submit to the calling that was laid upon his heart.

Our inclination is to not let go and trust God, because our fear of failure and humiliation is so great, our fear of pain is so compelling, and because our glass ceilings look so real. But the only way through the fear is trust, either inch by inch or all at once. Only then will we know the overwhelming sense of abundance and fulfillment Jesus taught!

For, once that love is flowing out of us we begin to attract and magnetize more and more of it back into our lives. It is just the great truth of life. The more love and positive energy we flow out of us, the more it is attracted right back to us. There is simply no higher joy and no greater fulfillment. Jesus states it, and all the great spiritual masters of every religion confirm it. If you desire total spiritual fulfillment and deep peace and joy in your soul, then Love God and Love Neighbor. And trust God's call for how to carry out that love.

Which do you fear more, an unfulfilled life or the contempt of others?

In what areas of life can you trust God and the power of his universe more?

What fears motivate you?

Chapter 16

CONSTANTLY ACCLIMATING TO HIGHER WEIGHT: TRUST, PART II

There is one more point to learn from the notion of overcoming obstacles and glass ceilings discussed in the last chapter. To better understand it, I'll focus in on one of those lifters mentioned.

One of the big horses who had broken through the 500-pound glass ceiling was a kid named Mark. Mark was a 220-pound All-American linebacker with a neck the size of a coffee can. When I first got him in my program Mark had a one-rep max on his squats at about 430 pounds – okay for a D3 linebacker, but nowhere near where I knew this kid could go. After getting him past his 500-pound glass ceiling and in the subsequent months he was hot on the trail of nailing a max over 600 pounds.

This kid was the epitome of the ultra-intense athlete. He had so mastered mental focus that his mind had him lifting weight far beyond what his body should have ever been capable of. After shattering the 500 glass ceiling he began to fast approach the strength of the upper echelons of competitive natural powerlifters in the country!

As an aside, Mark couldn't step into the squat rack without blowing a gasket. In every heavy set his nose would start spitting blood! It had happened so many times over his years of wrestling that doctors couldn't even cauterize it anymore. It was funny and inspiring at the same time. We were constantly cleaning up the squat area. With enormous respect, the team even developed a motto after him: "You ain't really lifting unless you're bleeding." (See Chapter 4 for the team motto that came after this one.)

During one workout he had worked through his fourth set, from an opening set of 520 pounds up to 575 pounds. I knew he was fried after that rep at 575. He had nothing left in him, except for me to bring him down to maybe 475 for a burnout set. But instead, as I had done when he was trying to bust the 500-pound glass ceiling, I took him over the desired amount. I threw 605 on his bar.

I normally never allow my lifters to take anything more than a 20 pound jump on squats. And, it would generally be considered completely fruitless to attempt a weight well beyond anything you've ever maxed, especially to do so when your goose is already cooked. But I had a reason.

My lifters have heard me say a million times, "Constantly acclimating to higher weight!" And I wanted this rock star to feel the weight when he had no chance of getting it, so that when he missed it it would be no big loss, because it wasn't a fair shot anyway because he didn't have all his energy. *But*, after missing it, Mark would have the benefit of having simply had the weight on his back. He would *know what the weight felt like*, how it balanced, how it came of the rack, and so forth. Before he ever had a chance to give 600 pounds a real fighting chance, he would already know it well and simply know how it feels.

Mark did precisely as I expected. He attempted the 605 and took a dive into the safety bars. Utter failure. But, as I knew it would, this failure pissed him off. The minute he failed he wanted to try again, cuz he felt cheated. All he could talk about for the next week was how he didn't have his full energy when he had tried it, and how he couldn't wait for the following week to get back in and give it another shot.

A mere two weeks later, Mark crushed the 600-pound mark. During Max Week, Mark banged out a killer 640 regulation-depth squat. He even went for 660, just barely missing it! But, for a guy who weighed only 220 pounds it was a sensational sight, as his nose started spurting blood and roars went up from around the weightroom! He was an inspiration to everyone, including his coach.

Zero Sets and Constantly Acclimating to Higher Weight

When dealing with athletes who are trying to get much stronger or who are trying to radically sharpen their mental focus and intensity, one effective tool is to constantly add weight to the bar on nearly all of their lifts, as I did with Mark and as explained in Chapter 10 ("Hitting the Zone"). I have seen far too many athletes undershoot their potential simply because they, like most people, are incapable of pushing themselves beyond their limits.

(**Note**: This is why personal trainers can be so effective. A personal trainer or strength coach can push most lifters far more than they can push themselves.)

Hence, whenever possible within NCAA guidelines or when working with people I am personally training, I control my athletes' lifting amounts, as far as how much weight they will lift in each set. I set all of their weights on their workout cards before every workout.[17] By controlling their weight and by insisting that they continually add weight (with occasional relenting when I see they need it), they are pulled well beyond what they ever thought possible, expanding both their physical and their mental strength. Even more so, it expands the strength of their spirit. They grow in confidence, and they begin to see the power that is inside them, quite apart from simply the cast iron that is being moved in opposition to gravity.

My lifters know that if they hit in the Zone (again, see Chapter 10), they are to constantly add weight. But one of my favorite approaches, within a bench workout for example, is to add weight with each subsequent set, even though they have dropped out of the Zone for the day. I don't do this often, but I will employ it occasionally.

As my lifters increase the weight with each set, the number of repetitions naturally decreases. They may do 8 reps in the first set. But with the

---

[17] This is incredibly labor-intensive for me the coach, but I enjoy doing it, and it is simply the very best formula I have found for taking lifters beyond themselves. Though, at some levels the NCAA has implemented regulations prohibiting this practice in the off-season.

increase of weight and the slow setting in of muscle fatigue they may only do 6 reps in the second set. Third set is 5 reps, perhaps. Fourth set 2 reps.

Then I may choose to keep pushing this lifter to do additional sets, if the lifter is a bit gung-ho or if I just want to take them to new heights. Thus, in the fifth set they may get 1 rep. In the sixth, 1 rep again. Then I will take them up even again, knowing full well they have no chance of hitting the weight for any reps (as with Mark). Sure enough, the lifter will crash and hit zero reps at the final weight. I'll then bring him/her back down for a burnout set at a weight well below their original starting weight.

This technique of going up to one-rep sets and eventually a weight at which they fail I call 'going to zero reps' or 'zero setting.' It is the effort to be constantly acclimating to higher weight. It is a physiological impossibility to get stronger without adding weight. Thus, it is pointless to constantly do the same weight in set after set – a common mistake among beginning or recreational users of resistance training.

Further, in this vein of 'constantly acclimating to higher weight' I take them to zero reps because sometimes they just need to get a feel for what that new weight feels like – how it feels in their hands, how it feels coming off the rack, and where it strains their body most.

Also, they now know their limit, and what must be broken past. Lifting is about constantly clearing new hurdles. That initial failure is a big step in clearing the mental hurdle, which soooooo much of weightlifting is. All lifters, even the most experienced, have mental blocks at certain weights in certain lifts. And I have found that one of the only ways to get past the hurdles is to keep failing at these hurdles and keep adding weight.

Failure is at least a getting-used-to what's going to be involved in the next big struggle. And when that next struggle or next weight is finally surmounted the sense of accomplishment for the lifter is enormous. To fail at something and then later succeed at it is uplifting and emboldening!

I believe there is simply no way to achieve goals in life without being pushed well beyond ourselves. Without constantly adding weight, constantly increasing the challenges, and constantly raising the pain-threshold and endurance level, you will never achieve the ultimate success you are truly capable of

God the Badass Coach!

A large percentage of Christian theologians would disagree with me on this, but I am a firm believer that this is how God works in our lives, too. I totally believe that God is like the greatest trainer/coach anyone could ever have. He knows when to rest us, but he is constantly pushing us through greater and greater challenges, because he knows that is the only way to higher ground and more abundant and fulfilled lives.

God *sends* the challenges. *Sends* the hardship. *Sends* the temptations. *Sends* the pain. *Sends* the experiences that break us down and tear us open.

We say we want abundance in our lives (not simply material abundance, but a truly fulfilled heart and soul). But we so want it without pain, without challenge, without hardship, and without suffering. To which God just laughs. For, there is no true fulfillment in life, there is no higher ground in life without the pain that comes from letting go of lower places, lower expectations, lower habits, lower mindsets, lower lives and the sense of security that comes from clinging fiercely to all these lower things.

We so desperately don't want to let go of our lower existence. We cling to what we think is best, believing that we actually 'get' life. We cling to lesser lives, thinking that we know what is best for ourselves. At which God just laughs.

Yet, we cling and cling, pouring all our energy into never letting go of that lesser life. We cling because we so treasure the safety and security of having that which we know, that which is comfortable and that which is sure. The safety of mediocrity is far preferred to the risk of a fuller existence, especially when that fuller life looks like it is not guaranteed!

But God sends challenges, hardship, and setbacks precisely to break us of our clinging to lesser lives, smaller lives, lower lives, and lives lacking fulfillment. God is constantly acclimating us to 'higher weight' or greater challenges. God is the Great Coach who knows *precisely* what we need and precisely what he is doing by sending these greater and greater challenges and hardships.

I absolutely believe and have seen time and time and time again in the lives of people I counsel, speak to, coach, and have befriended that God is constantly acclimating us to higher weight, so to speak. I do not, not, not believe in the old saying 'God never gives us more than we can handle,' because it's just not true! In fact, this saying is one of the greatest lies perpetuated in the name of Christianity.

The Bible is constantly telling us and showing us how very wrong this saying is! We are told frequently how God scolds, punishes, and sends hardship.

> "The ones I love I scold and punish" (-- God, Revelation 3:19).
>
> "Although he was a Son, he learned obedience [to God] through what he suffered" (Hebrews 5:8; referring to Jesus).
>
> "The eyes of the Lord keep watch over knowledge, but he overthrows the words of the faithless" (Proverbs 22:12; the faithless are not the unreligious but simply those who do not trust in God's power in their lives).
>
> "My son, do not regard lightly the discipline of the Lord, nor lose courage when you are punished by him. For the Lord disciplines him whom he loves, and chastises every son whom he receives. It is for discipline that you have to endure" (Hebrews 12:5-7).

Not only does the Bible say it, but life is constantly showing us how wrong the saying is, too. God regularly burdens us, challenges us, and even breaks us in our lives.

For, just like the people of the Bible, until we are broken we continue to live as if we know what is best for life. Until we are steamrolled, we never recognize our deep need for God. Until we are torn asunder by God, we continue to live on our own strength. As long as we are trusting our own abilities we are not trusting God's voice inside us and the power of the universe God has created.

It is precisely because we think we can handle it all that God breaks us and strips us of all that is important to us. Like a great coach who knows exactly what he's doing, God breaks us so that we might finally cling only to God, trusting his providence and program, even if we can't see or understand the plan.

"God never gives us more than we can handle"
is nothing more than a feel-good fantasy
perpetuated by people.

We all suffer in life. We all go through hardships. We all have sorrow befall us. And much of it is stuff that no nice saying of 'just be positive' can abate. Life's hardships are, at times, stuff that can only be slogged through like a rough set of heavy powercleans or military presses. There is no joy, just work.

"Pain is the root of all knowledge."
-- Simone Weil

But in the suffering is truth. By enduring the suffering we find the wisdom. In suffering is the very gift of God, just waiting to be discovered, sent to move us to higher ground. In all suffering is the voice of God speaking higher truth to us. Or sometimes, as in this snippet about Elijah, the voice of God comes after God sends his ferociousness:

> "And the Lord God passed by [Elijah], and a great and strong wind split the mountains, and broke in pieces the rocks before God, but the Lord was not in the wind; and after the wind

> an earthquake, but the Lord was not in the earthquake; and after the earthquake a fire, but the Lord was not in the fire; after the fire a still small voice [and it was the voice of God]" (1Kings 19:11-12).

It is the suffering that prepares us to hear the truth God knows we need to learn. It is the suffering that sets the stage for greater trust in God's inspiration and in-dwelling in us and lesser reliance upon our own abilities.

These times of failure, times of suffering, times of loss, times of hardship, times of feeling awash with problems, and times of feeling like life is sitting its fat butt right on your head are nothing more than a constant acclimating to higher weight. They are God pushing you onto the dead lift platform, forcing you to do more weight or more reps than you have ever done, forcing you to acclimate to something greater, forcing you to fail at something you never thought you could even touch.

The great tragedy of life is to have the experience but miss the meaning. So many of us see suffering as an aberration. We see suffering as an anomaly or not what life should be; something that is just bad. And so we run from it, rather than learn from it.

But, like a great coach who knows what his players are truly capable of, God says, "To heck with that!" when we think we've had enough. God refuses to let us cling to lesser lives. Jesus said:

"I have come that you might have life and have it abundantly"
(John 10:10).

And so, God gets to work, challenging us, pushing us, breaking us of old patterns, weakness, and lower levels. God says we will never know true fulfillment and we will never be able to accomplish all the great things he has in store for us to accomplish, unless we are given greater and greater challenges, and grow stronger, more confident in his program, and more capable of trusting his power.

The Bible is loaded with stories of people given greater and greater challenges, and even at times burdened with excruciatingly painful tasks, all in preparation for the great heights God had planned for them later. Every single one of the great heroes of the Bible had to be broken of faith in self and moved to trust in God's power: From Deborah to David, from Jonah to Job, from Abraham to Andrew, and from Jeremiah to Jesus.

Abraham and Sarah were asked to live nearly their whole lives without children, a curse in their day. Then they were asked to believe, well into old age and beyond Sarah's childbearing age, that they would have a son. Then, years later, after his wife miraculously had a son, Abraham was asked by God to kill his own son as a sign of his total trust in God. Abraham must have thought, "Why, why, why?"

But God knew why. God had a plan, even if Abraham couldn't see it. And God had to make sure Abraham was trained and ready. As a result of his willingness to execute God's plan, he was blessed with great land, many descendants, and a promise of blessing from God. In addition, God went on to make Abraham the father of three of the world's largest religions of all time – Islam, Judaism, and Christianity!

Could a man of weak character and no mental toughness, could a man of little trust in God the Great Coach do all that Abraham had to do? No way! God broke him down and built him up over years, so that he would eventually be able to take on the great responsibility.

Joseph of the Old Testament was beaten up and sold by his older brothers. Abandoned by his family and sold to slave traders who took him far away, Joseph had to have felt broken and alone. God loaded 600 pounds of life onto his little back, so to speak, knowing Joseph had no chance, at all, of lifting such weight. But he survived. And he placed his total trust in God.

As if that wasn't enough, Joseph went on to work his way up in life, but had lies told about him, and was thrown into prison. Another great challenge intended to break him and make his trust in God stronger.

Then, in the type of turn of fortune that only happens when following that inner call, Joseph wins the favor of the king of the land, ends up becoming his most trusted advisor, and eventually becomes the #2 leader in all of Egypt. He even leads the country through seven years of famine, and eventually saves his own family that had originally rejected him!

Jesus, himself, even as a child, was in the temple challenging and being challenged in debate by the leaders and people – slowly growing and being tested and pushed. Many years later, Jesus went through increasing levels of ridicule, scorn, and abuse, eventually culminating in his trials before Pilate, Annas, and Caiaphas – the leaders of the land and people in his day. Everything was preparation for his trial and crucifixion, which demanded his total trust in God's plan.

God knows the formula of life. God knows how to keep pushing you. God knows that he needs to overload you at times. God needs to break you of thinking you know what is going on or what is best. God needs you to depend on his formula for lifting life.

Just as a great coach has a proven winning formula on the rink or on the court for making athletes tougher and far more competitive, God has a proven winning formula for making you stronger in your own life, and thereby more capable of bringing strength, healing, and power to those most in need. And God's life-workout program demands total trust in his formula, even when….no, *especially when* you think you know better or think the pain is meaningless.

Ultimately, relationship with God is *not* about believing such and such set of beliefs or about being good. Instead, life-giving relationship with God is about trusting in him and his formula for life success, even when you have absolutely no clue why he is asking you to do this thing at this exact minute, and even though you have no idea where he is leading you. Just like intense challenges in the gym, in the pool, or on the field, God's challenges always result in strengthening the character, spirit, or soul of the recipient….in preparation for something even bigger.

As long as you believe that God never gives you more than you can handle, you will never fail; you will never risk fully; you will never be fully challenged; and you will live in the boredom of safety, comfort, and security within the limited boundaries of your own present abilities.

We so often think the goal of life is to 'not fail.' But the goal of life is to keep striving for new heights and new successes, even when we do fail. The goal is to keep risking. Every great athlete knows that as long as you fear failing you will never succeed. When you fear failure you are tentative, full of anxiety, and hesitant. When you fearlessly strive for success (accepting that failure happens sometimes, trusting that you'll be okay if it does), your effort is aggressive, driven, and fluid. You are locked in, on fire, and intense.

What is most interesting, however, is that the only athlete who can play without fearing failure *is the athlete who has failed many times before,* recovered just fine, learned something, and gotten back to the business of kicking ass. The only way to live without fear of failure is to have failed many times in the past.

Babe Ruth was not only the home run king, but had a ton of strikeouts. Tiger Woods has lost more Majors than he has won. Lance Armstrong was just another biking champion wannabe until testicular cancer and brain surgery throttled him and utterly changed his life, resulting in unparalleled success. Many experts in cycling believe it was precisely the cancer that turned him into a champion, somehow.

"Sometimes you have to lose major championships
before you can win them.
Losing is a learning experience that's worth a fortune."
-- Tom Watson, golfing great

"I have missed more than 9,000 shots in my career. I have lost almost 300 games. On 26 occasions I have been entrusted to take the game-winning shot…and missed.
I have failed over and over again in life.
And that is why I succeed!"
-- Michael Jordan, basketball legend

Once God unleashes you and breaks down what you think you are capable of, your life explodes before you – explodes with opportunity, explodes with adventure, and explodes with new power, new strength, and new capacity to inspire both yourself and the world.

"Through him we have obtained access to this grace in which we stand, and we rejoice in our hope of sharing the glory of God. *More than that*, **we rejoice in our sufferings**, knowing that suffering produces endurance, and endurance produces character, and character produces hope, and hope does not disappoint us because God's love has been poured into our hearts…" (Romans 5:2-5).

"**Happy is the man whom God scolds**; therefore do not despise the scolding of the Almighty. For [God] wounds, but he binds up; his hands heal the wound inflicted by his blow" (Job 5:17-18).

We so desperately want to believe that God is nice!

But the bottom line truth is that God is loving, but not always nice. God is willing to kick our asses if it will get us to let go of the lower existence we are so clinging to, and if it will lead us to higher ground. God knows that challenges and pain are necessary to take us where God needs us to go, to accomplish what God wants us to accomplish, and to achieve the fulfillment deep in our souls we so desperately crave.

Do not ever think that life with God is intended to be safe or easy. It's not. It is intended to be a constant challenge, a dynamic life of hardship and ecstasy, oppressive pain and exhilarating joy. It is to be badass hard work and the complete rush of accomplishment!

God is constantly acclimating us to higher weight. Life is the constant movement from what we don't want to what we do want and what God wants us to do. And through it all we feel more alive than any other life path could ever make us. Through it all we become fountains of wisdom, channels of energy, and infusions of spirit and soul for those who suffer most in this world.

Are you in a time of being 'broken' spiritually? Or perhaps a time of new growth after being broken?

What new challenges are being presented to you in your life?

Are you too dependent upon yourself, your own efforts, your own anxiety, and your own hustle?

Do you trust – *really trust!* – God's voice in you? Or do you trust the calling only to the degree it is comfortable?

How scary is it for you to trust?

Do you have the courage to trust anyway, despite fear and trembling knees?

Chapter 17

Gym Etiquette

It was a warm California morning. I was getting my own personal workout before working with some athletes. There were roughly 15 people in the fitness center, most of whom were in among the machines and free weight racks, while two women were on the elliptical machines in the cardio area at the far end of the gym. This particular gym had no air conditioning. The gym was warm, but not yet approaching hot.

Thus, it came as a bit of a surprise to several of us in the machine and free weight area when one of the two women in the cardio area got off her elliptical, walked over to the one fan in the whole gym and turned it from facing the middle of the gym to facing just the two of them in the smaller cardio section. We were stunned! For, even though the fan oscillated, she had pointed it so that it would only affect the two of them on cardio.

After this woman got back to her elliptical, one woman from the free weight area walked over to the same fan and turned it back to the center of the room! Oscillating from this position it could obviously create the most circulation for all people.

The woman on the elliptical did not notice her do it, but minutes later she did notice that the fan wasn't on her. So elliptical woman went back over to the fan and turned it on herself and the other cardio woman, and then went back to work on her elliptical.

A guy on a rack near the fan responded by turning the fan back to the center, with a wink to the ten or twelve of us who noticed what was going on and who were sweating just as much as the women on the cardio.

Upon seeing the fan being moved back to center, elliptical woman shouted out, "Hey, I need that fan. Turn it back this way."

"Lady, we all need it," the gentleman pointed out.

"Are you going through hot flashes?" she angrily shot back.

The man was a bit stunned. "No lady, but that's not the point," the man said.

"Yes, that is the point. I *am* going through hot flashes, and that *is* the point, cuz I need the fan," she snorted.

All of us non-cardio people looked at each other in wide-eyed silence. All ears had perked up; stunned by the brazenness of the woman who believed it was all about her. There was electricity in the air.

The gentleman was just about to respond when the lifter woman who had first turned the fan back on us stood up, clearly livid, and growled to the cardio woman, "The *point* is that it's not your fan and it's not your gym. But you're acting like it is. We're all hot in here. Look at these people. We're all sweating hard. We all need maximum circulation. But that's not even the point, really. The point, like he said, is that you just took it. You didn't ask any of us if it'd be okay. You just took it like you are entitled to it. If you had explained the situation, most of us probably would have said 'no problem,' but that you took it sucks! You acted like a child, rather than acting out of respect for everyone else"

Oh wow! There were snickers, raised eyebrows, and muffled laughs throughout the gym. Lifter woman stuck it to elliptical woman.

I've been in gyms for decades, and I don't often see confrontation like that. Most people mind their own business. But I loved it. Elliptical woman huffed and puffed, but knew she had been caught dead to rights. 15 minutes later, she finished her workout and departed straightaway without saying a word to anyone.

That mini cat fight was my entertainment for the day. But more importantly, lifter woman was exactly right in what she said to elliptical woman. I know I would have had no problem doing without the air circulation if the woman had asked kindly and deferentially to a few of us others, just out of respect. But the fact that she took it was just ugly, plain and simple. And it so happened that the both the guy and lifter woman weren't afraid to stand up to her.

The root of the problem in that situation is that no one ever really teaches most of us, like elliptical woman, how to act in a fitness center or gym. Some people assume it's just like being on the highway or in our own homes where we think we can take whatever we want. But it ain't so. And many folk, even though they have been in a gym before, never fully get the ethic.

So, one of the main things I constantly pound into the heads of the athletes and personal fitness trainers is gym etiquette, specifically the first law of the gym – deference. Deference is the one thing that makes the gym a cool and pleasant place to be and get some work done.

I have seen many people over the years be so incredibly selfish in a gym. And that rudeness has the power to make it such an ugly and unwelcoming place.

Further, it's not always the big, sweaty guys who are that way. In fact, it has been my experience that those types of folk are often the most courteous and deferential in any weightroom or fitness center. Why? Simple, they 'get' it. They don't have to be snotty, and they genuinely know that it can be hard for other people who might be intimidated by their big muscles or size. Plus, heavy lifters, whether they're women or men, just know the code of the gym, because they've spent so much time there and know what it takes to make it a good place to be.

Jesus Etiquette in the Gym of Life

I have become a very firm believer, over the years, that the ethic of the gym is almost exactly the ethic by which Jesus lived his life. On this issue it's not so much what he said as how he walked through life. It was his everyday mode of existence that was just as powerful as his words.

Jesus gave of himself each day. He was deferential to and protective of others, particularly those who were regular folks just trying to get by. He went out of his way to help others, even when he didn't have to. But, he also wasn't afraid to stand up against injustice, institutions, or people who were acting strictly out of self-interest or self-preservation.

You don't even have to be a Christian to see the amazing beauty in his kindness, his commitment to others, and his simple deference to the pain or situations of others.

It is so common for us in America, today, to become self-absorbed. It is so easy to get wrapped up in our own interests. And God wants us to feel fulfilled, no doubt. But the point we so fail, fail, fail to get is the overwhelming joy and peace that come from orienting our lives to bringing joy to others (and doing so in ways that are joyful to us just by doing them, regardless of the results or how the efforts are received).

We cling and cling to our own mad quest for happiness that we completely miss Jesus' call to other-centeredness. We completely fail to get what he was really about. We so prostitute his teachings on abundance, thinking its about 'things' rather than the real fruits, inside us, that those 'things' are intended to bring – peace, hope, joy, etc. We just don't get it! We just so fail to walk through life with the grace, graciousness, deference and other-centeredness that Jesus was truly about.

To be sure, what Jesus said and taught are certainly important. But there is something so fundamental about his way of carrying on in life that made words unnccessary. He was simply the embodiment of lovingkindness. He was the ultimate in graciousness and kindness, not just in words but in total life-orientation. Yet, simultaneously, his lovingkindness was one that wasn't afraid to kick butt when work needed to be done for others and when injustice needed to be fought.

And that is the balance we are called to walk – between working for justice on behalf of those in need and walking through life with deference and graciousness. It is the balance of fight and feel. Genuinely feeeeling the hurt of others, and willingness to fight in their defense. It is the balance of being able to be fully aggressive when others are being hurt and being fully tender and kind in all other pursuits. Jesus led by example, and that example was one of deference, bringing peace, and constant consciousness of the needs of others.

This is the very definition of the noble life. This is the very definition of grace. This is the very definition of the life well-lived and worthy of respect. These are the types of people who are beloved by many. These are the types of people who cause others to glow at the mere thought of them, for their graciousness is so infectious and pure.

Who is it you know or think of that defines that purity of graciousness and deference?

In what ways can you be more deferential in your life?

Who are the people (outside of your own family and immediate circle of friends) whose hurt you feel and for whom you are willing to fight?

Do you go out of your way to bring lovingkindness to others, or do you hustle through life oblivious to the needs, big and small, of others?

Chapter 18

Learning to Say 'No' to What You Love

The two body areas where most people want to lose weight are the thighs/hips (women) and the stomach/abs (men/women). The stomach is a major issue for a lot of people. That is a big reason why my lifters and trainees constantly hear me saying, "Abs are made in the kitchen, not the weightroom."

One of the biggest fallacies in fitness is that if I just do more situps, I'll lose weight in my stomach. Or, if I just do more leg exercises, I'll lose weight in my thighs and butt.

Yet, nothing could be further from the truth. There is no direct correlation or any correlation, at all, to working a body part and losing weight in that body part. The reason for this is two-fold: 1) Your body burns fat across the body, not in one specific spot you may be working; and 2) In order to lose weight in any body area you must learn to control your food intake.

You can do a hundred situps each day and have a killer set of abs. But, alas, you'll never be able to see those great abs if they are covered by a wall of fat because you can't control your food intake. The muscles are there and well-toned, but they're not visible because there is a curtain of fat there just below the skin, clouding the visibility of your great abs.

Like it or not, abs are made in the kitchen! The only way you will ever see your abs, or even just reduce the size of your stomach – or hips, or love handles, or butt – is by controlling how and what you eat. There simply is no other way.

The easiest way to understand it is to think of your body as a big balloon. On this balloon there are basically two openings rather than just one; one for intake and the other for output. If the intake valve is bigger than the output valve, that balloon is going to grow huge because it keeps taking in more and more and releasing little. But, if the intake valve is small and the output valve is quite large, the balloon is going to shrink, potentially excessively so. Thus, the goal is to either have valves of similar sizes, or have an output valve that is a bit larger than your intake valve; or, best of all, is to be able to control the openings of the intake and output valves.

You can do all the cardio in the world, but if you're not controlling your intake your hips and thighs will never get smaller. This is just one of the cold, hard realities of life. Making your best body has a price, and that price is not only self-discipline in the weightroom but self-discipline in life's most difficult room – the kitchen.

Food is nothing more than condensed energy. When you consume food you give your body energy. If you do not burn off that energy, it generally 'converts' into fat and simply sits on you, usually in your stomach or your hips. Thus, the only way to get the body you want is to use up that energy you are taking in and reduce the intake of energy. You must work out AND control your intake.

The problem is that saying 'No!' to your intake is one of the hardest things to do.

An Interesting Question

As you think about your own life and all the things you really enjoy doing and all the things you really hate doing, ask yourself this question: Is it harder for me to say 'no' to something I love doing, or say 'yes' to something I hate doing?

Think about it for a minute.

Sex. Working out. Going grocery shopping. Eating. Taking baths. Driving to work. Clothes shopping. Watching TV. Dating. Quitting a job.

Turning off the TV. Playing with your kids. Mowing the lawn. Getting the oil changed. Writing 'Thank You' notes. Going on vacation. Having a second or third can of soda each day. Running your business. Mowing the lawn. Paying utility bills. Volunteering time each week. Listening to your iPod. Spending time with friends.

As you think about these and other things, is it harder for you to say 'no' to something you love doing, or say 'yes' to something you hate doing?

I have asked this question to countless athletes, students, fit people and out-of-shape people, as well as tons of friends and acquaintances. If you're like most people your answer is that it is harder to say 'no' to something you love doing. Most people can motivate themselves to overcome unpleasant tasks, but find it difficult to deny themselves of things they really enjoy doing.

(This, of course, fits very well with American capitalism: If people just work harder at their jobs, even if they really dislike their jobs, they can relax and enjoy lots of fun or nice things that they do love. It is much harder to just say 'no' to having those extra things, and thereby be able to have a career and full life that you love. This is why people are so stunned and impressed when they read of some family that has cut its debt in half in two years or has wiped away all of its debt in 5 years, simply by cutting out luxuries and all self-indulgences.)

People, in general, just find it very hard to deny themselves the things they most love doing as well as engage in things they dislike doing. When it comes to the whole idea of getting in shape and staying in shape this means doing something they hate – working out – and denying themselves of something they love – eating yummy foods! It can be very hard to do, because it requires some amount of both – saying 'yes' to something un-fun and saying 'no' to one of life's most favorite things.

I believe the biggest mistake most athletic coaches and personal trainers make is teaching people about diet and pushing for changes right away in the beginning of trying to get them into shape. They make the mistake of expecting people *from the beginning* to both say 'no' to favorable things and 'yes' to unfavorable things, even though the fact that the person is out of shape or overweight clearly indicates that they have little capacity to do either.

Recognizing that it is very hard for most people to control their intake of food – that is, say 'no' to eating something they love – I rarely even mention intake/diet in my first month or two with a new client or athlete. Instead, I focus almost entirely on their ability to say 'yes' to something they don't like doing, working out.

I start them with easy, introductory workouts (*never* pushing them so hard that they are achingly sore the next day. Part of working out includes being sore and stiff the next day, but it helps nothing to run beginners into the ground. In fact, it only builds negative associations in their mind. Working out becomes equated with pain and dislike, making it even harder to get them into the gym consistently.). Each workout I gently increase the difficulty and the amount of weight being used, until they reach the level where I can push them harder. Also, I lengthen the time or distance of cardio, bit by bit, while keeping primary focus on resistance training.

Eventually, over a few months, I have built up in them the most important thing – discipline and mental toughness, at least in some small amount. The habit has begun. They have begun to learn how to work hard and push themselves, sometimes by doing extra reps on a set, or going a little farther in their cardio, or simply showing up in the weightroom on a day when they really didn't feel like working out.

In effect, they have learned how to push themselves through greater challenges and through things they don't like. By building up their discipline first in saying 'yes' to something they dislike I am then able to lead them into the more difficult task of learning to say 'no' to some things they love doing.

But another gain has been accomplished in these opening months, something equally significant – momentum. Before I ever start talking about intake control – how much, what types of food they consume, and when they eat – they have begun to see results from their working out. By my pushing them a little harder in every workout and constantly adding a little bit more weight, they have taxed their muscles, perhaps more than they ever have in their lives. As a result, the novice is beginning to both see some changes in his or her body, and he or she is beginning to just feel different. The trainee is beginning to experience the rush of a good workout, the confidence that working out brings, and the sense of accomplishment in knowing she is overcoming a great hurdle she has always been a bit scared of.

When I help my trainees to see all that they are accomplishing – both changes in their bodies and changes in their heads – a small amount of momentum begins to develop in the trainee. They begin to see the 'profits' from saying 'yes' to something they formerly disliked. Thus, they begin to be ready for more. This is when I begin to slowly implement my theories on intake. This is when they are ready to slowly conquer the beast of saying 'no' to that which they most love.

(**Note**: I prefer the word 'intake' to the word 'diet' simply because many people who cannot control their eating *absolutely hate* the word 'diet' and all that goes along with it. It has such strong negative associations. Also, 'intake' is a word that is obvious, makes sense, and everyone can understand.)

Oreos, Popcorn, and Cheddar Cheese with Peanut Butter on it

When the trainee/athlete has developed some measure of discipline and confidence I begin the discussion of intake control. I make slight mention of this very early. But I must stress that I generally wait, simply because even with advanced athletes this can be an incredibly difficult discipline to commence and master.

Usually, I offer my explanation for removing fat (discussed below) and then encourage the person to see if they can do one thing for me: Try to go one or maybe two nights per week where they don't eat anything after 6:30pm. No more nights than that. Just try to go one or two nights per week of stopping eating after 6:30pm.

I generally get curious looks when I first bring this up to a new trainee or athlete.

There is nothing harder in all of fitness than this one thing – to stop eating at night. Everyone loves to eat at night. It is soooo easy to do. It is comfortable. It is relaxing. Yet, there are very few things that have as great potential to radically change your body than this one act of ceasing night-eating.

Why only one or two nights? Rather than slam the trainee with trying to be far more disciplined than he/she is capable of, I ease them into it. Otherwise they will quickly grow discouraged. (Remember, lifting, fitness, and athletic success are all mental. Anything achieved physically is always driven by the mind! Thus, the mind needs to be slowly retrained. Fail to understand the impact of the mind, and you will fail to find success or teach success to your athletes.)

Whether it is popcorn during a movie or a bowl of cereal before bed, all of us love to have a late-evening snack or meal. I can remember as a child watching my father, who was always in decent shape because of his innate vigor, have a bowl of ice cream almost every night before bed. I used to like a peanut butter and jelly sandwich at bedtime. As an adult I have grown quite fond of sliced cheddar cheese with a bit of peanut butter spread onto it. (Yes, I know, very strange, but I love it, and now my kids do too.) And, of course, chocolate is a favorite any time of day. In the evening I like frozen semi-sweet chocolate chips to nibble on while I'm watching my favorite TV show or writing out the workout programs for my lifters.

Oh heck, I could go on and on about my favorite foods. And don't even get me started on Oreos or raw chocolate chip cookie dough!

But this lone act of stopping eating after 6:30pm dinner is unequivocally the most difficult thing to do in all of fitness. I can train anyone to do almost anything, but this is the hardest. The reason is because it pairs our two favorite things in life – feeling comfortable and eating.

The reason I want people to stop eating after their dinner is because any food eaten in the evening generally just sits on the body at night and doesn't get worked off (most people do not work out after their last meal of the day). That means each time you eat late in the evening you basically negate the hard work you might have done in the gym that day.

Further, by eating late at night most people cause themselves to not be hungry at breakfast. People then skip the one meal each day that both starts their metabolism going strong (imperative for burning calories) and gives them energy for the day.

Further still, people are setting themselves up for failure mentally. If you are already disinclined to eat in the morning, it means you are mentally strongest in the morning, at least in the area of resisting food. So, that would be the best time to actually eat, because you won't be eating all the wrong foods, because you really don't have the desire to eat in the first place.

But, people get mentally weak as the day goes on, at least as far as resisting food is concerned. As the day goes on people are more inclined to eat snacks, eat extra large meals, and eat late into the night. So it makes sense to devote your strongest efforts to when you most need it – late in the day.

In fact, when first starting out with new trainees I tell them I really don't care what they eat during the day. They don't have to change one thing during the day (except eating more protein), just stop a few evenings of night-eating.

And that one thing begins to have a radical impact on their weight. They can see it! It doesn't take it all off, but it has a profound effect on them.

Then, if it hasn't happened naturally already (which it often does after people start disciplining their evenings), I help people begin to discipline their daytime eating, both in amount and in what they're eating.

Granted, occasionally it is fun to eat something late or go out for a late dinner with friends. And that's great. Half the fun of working out is having the liberty to have more flexibility with your intake. That's why I tell folks to give themselves one night every week or two to eat in the evening. But, it's when we consistently eat stupid that we blow all of our hard work.

Now, most people I work with have difficulty stopping eating at 6:30pm for two reasons. One I already mentioned – they just love eating at night. But the second reason is because many individuals and families have moved their dinner time to 7pm, 8pm, or even 9pm, because of jobs, after-school extracurricular activities, or even because they aren't done with their workouts until that time (a cruel irony).

But, the one thing I assure them of is that there is nothing they can do that will have a greater impact faster than stopping eating after 6:30pm.[18] I have seen people drop 10 pounds right around their gut or in their thighs in 3-4 weeks, just by doing this one thing (big results demand stopping eating 6-7 nights per/week). Stopping eating in the evening is the hardest thing to do, but it yields the greatest payoff. I have seen it time and time and time and time and time again.

A coach friend of mine says, "Yeah Sven, I don't buy your theory. What's the difference if I eat in the morning or at night? My body is going to burn it, no matter what time I eat it."

To all unbelievers in my formula I simply say, "Try it for 6 weeks. Then tell me I'm wrong." Every single one of them who tries it discovers, to their amazement, that it totally works. You will always lose weight if you can accomplish this one deed. I don't claim to understand all the physiology behind it. I only know that it works exceedingly well, and can be exceedingly hard for some people to do.

Part of the reason it works is because if someone stops eating after 6:30pm, it does not mean they are going to eat more at lunch or have a snack in the afternoon, instead. It just means they are cutting out one unnecessary time of food intake. People's intake is pretty much constant during the day, assuming they're eating healthy meals. Further, your energy demands radically decrease in the evening. So the food taken in is neither needed nor used. So, nighttime food is just extra. Cut out that extra and you cut out unnecessary pounds.

That is why stopping evening/night eating is so critical to fitness. It is simply unnecessary food that is taken solely for pleasure, and which has a devastating effect on the body by countering all the hard work being done in workouts. I heard another trainer say, "Eat like a king in the

---

[18] Another biggy for losing weight is radically *increasing* consumption of vegetables (and fruit), even beyond FDA-approved levels. Basically, there is a direct correlation between the amount of vegetables eaten and weight lost. This is true not because, as our mother's told us, vegetables are good for us, per se, but because vegetables take up room in our stomachs, leaving less room for fatty and high-carb foods. And veggies (and fruit) are basically just water, which the body will flush out. If you eat 2-4 servings of vegetables per meal, you *will* lose weight.

morning, a queen at lunch, and a poor man at dinner." Your body will burn energy/food it consumes in the morning and midday, but will retain late-in-the-day food, fat, and calories.

Generally, I will start a trainee on one or two days per week of not eating past 6:30pm, and then scoot them up to 3-4 days per week. I tell them, "Don't break your regular routine entirely. If you normally eat at 7:30pm, keep doing so. Just only do that 4 nights per week. Then make yourself eat an hour-and-a-half earlier 3 nights." Or, with my college kids (all of whom love late night pizza, especially on the weekends; or who have chips and snacks in their rooms; or who love late night beer, despite its amazing capacity to quickly counter the positive effects of daily workouts!) I encourage them to still have their pizza at night on the weekend, but just give themselves 3 nights per week where they don't eat after 6:30pm, at all. That makes it easier to cut back tonight, knowing tomorrow night they can have a little snack.

Inch by inch.

After they have been doing that for a month or so I will encourage them to go to 4 nights per week of not eating after 6:30pm. Then after another few months I'll encourage them to go to 5 nights or even 6. Generally, I encourage all of my trainees and lifters, except for the most intense, to give themselves one night a week (maaayyybe two nights) where they don't worry about intake at night, and just relax and have something. It takes the pressure off. It makes intake control more do-able and less burdensome.

Most people want to look good without cutting themselves off from life. I find that people go a lot further in personal fitness if they can still enjoy parts of life, including eating. No, *especially* eating! Further, as all high-caliber bodybuilders and weightlifters know, there are actually significant physiological benefits to having an *occasional* day of eating a lot or even eating 'bad' food or eating late at night. Again, I said 'occasional' day, not 'frequent' day.

Further, it is always necessary to give the mind a break from disciplines. Like the body, the mind needs rest. You cannot constantly tax your mind without it growing fatigued and incapable of carrying out disciplines. Again, look at the example of pro athletes who quit the game in their late-30s. It is the mental taxation, not necessarily the physical demands, that fatigues them so. The mind needs rest.

But, once the athlete/trainee has begun to be able to control intake, a significant milestone has been accomplished. Once the person has begun to master the ability to say 'no' to that which is beloved, the person's whole life begins to change. She begins to say 'no' to other things in life that drain her or bleed life from her. She begins to take ownership of her life. And greater joy naturally follows!

Tough Words from Jesus

This stuff about intake control relates directly to one of the hardest verses in all of Jesus' teachings. It is found in Luke 14:26:

> **"If anyone comes to me and does not hate his own father and mother and wife and children and brothers and sisters, yes, and even his own life, he cannot be my disciple."**

Jesus could, indeed, be a cold person, at times. But, surely Jesus' words are not to be taken with icy literalness.

However, there is a strong measure of truth to what he says. And that truth lies in the realization that there is a pecking order to life – a hierarchy of priorities – and if you genuinely want abundant joy, peace, purpose, power, and nobility in life, then Jesus' teachings are at the top. Commitment to the life and teachings of Jesus must take priority over all other loyalties, if you desire to have the abundant and strong life of which Jesus spoke.

Saying 'yes' to Jesus' hard path, saying 'yes' to the joy and peace a life of faithfulness brings, demands saying 'no' at times to the things and people we love the most. It is far easier to only say 'yes' to Jesus' teachings than it is to also say 'no' to any person who would try to dissuade us or distract us from that path of following the call of God inside you and following Jesus' call to serve. And what Jesus says in this verse is that the strongest, most faithful, and most rewarding life is the one in which you have the courage to say 'no' to those you love if they would stand between you and the deepest calling of your soul, which is the voice of God inside you.

There are many who want a bit of God, a bit of church on Sunday, a bit of doing good things in the world. And that is fine...for them. That is where they are at in their spiritual journeys. But there are others, such as serious, intense athletes, who naturally long for a more powerful experience of life, who want so much more and are pressing toward the goal of a more intense relationship with God and a greater faithfulness to God's calling inside of them. There are those people in life who are not content with a mediocre existence or a compromised life. There are those, such as intense athletes, who simply desire a life lived at full-throttle, an existence lived at the edge of life. There are those who crave a life of passion and intensity, one driven by unflinching commitment to the highest path.

Once someone was talking to a great scholar about a younger man. He said, "So and so tells me that he was one of your students." The teacher answered devastatingly, "He may have attended my lectures, but he was not one of my students."[19] In other words, the student never fully bought into and lived the teachings of the scholar/master.

The great challenge in our spiritual lives is to have the courage to push out of our heads and hearts (even if not completely out of our lives) those people who pull us away from what we feel called to be, become, do, believe, follow, or lead. Just as the person desiring to lose weight must have the courage to say 'no' to food, we are to have the courage to say 'no' to the thinking of those people who might harm or undermine the path we feel called to take, whomever it might be. It is to have the courage to ask and boldly act on the question, "Does this person or action breathe life into me or suck life out of me?" For, that which breathes life into you is from God, and that which sucks life out of you is a distraction and not the path to which you are called.

---

[19] Barclay, William. *The Daily Study Bible Series: The Gospel of Luke* (Revised Edition). Westminster John Knox Press, Louisville, KY. 1975 (First Edition, 1953), p196.

Now, choosing your own path and sticking with it, no matter what others say, is no substitute for considered reflection. Surely, we are to weigh the paths and challenges life puts in our way. This is one way God strengthens our resolve, by yearly giving us new challenges and opportunities, so that we might re-choose our calling, or perhaps move to the next calling God has in store for us. That is why it is important to be open to change and new possibilities offered by others.

God is not in the business of the security that comes from contentment. God is in the business of passion, focus, and lives of noble purpose. Further, if God is in any security business, it is the security that comes from knowing no matter how treacherous or challenging the path is God is in it, teaching us, pushing us, sustaining us, and strengthening us.

But once the decision is made to choose a path, or once the path of another is rejected, or once you know the direction you are to go, you must have the courage to be diligent in not allowing others to undermine your work and your life, even if those people mean well and even if they are close loved ones. It is the courage to say 'no' to the enticement from those we love. Again, it doesn't have to mean cutting them out of your life entirely, but it does mean cutting back the influence they have in your spiritual life and your living out what you are called to be and do.

While in seminary I had a class in which one of my classmates was a nun on a year-long sabbatical from her ministry. This woman who had been a nun since her 20s and was now in her 60s told the story of how in her 40s she met a man whom she cared for very much and to whom she was deeply attracted. They talked often and drew very close, to the point where she strongly considered giving up her vows to the Catholic Church and to Jesus and taking vows with this man. As might be imagined, after 20 years of being a nun, this was no small decision. She prayed for months that God would give her clarity. In the end, she chose to say 'no' to a relationship with the man and a new 'yes' to her vows to the Church and God.

She told us, "Taking the vows 20 years before wasn't a once-and-for-all thing. I had to retake them again. And, in smaller ways, I retake them each day. And because I walk away from all the other things of life, my relationship with Jesus grows deeper each day."

Her continually saying 'no' to all that would pull her from her path only strengthens her commitment to that path. The greater the thing she says 'no' to, the more obvious it becomes how significant the thing is she is saying 'yes' to.

And this is an inevitable part of religious life and spiritual life. We all have times in life where we must choose what God is calling us to over what someone we love wants us to do. And sometimes the stakes can be quite high. But the bottom line is that your spirit will wither and your spiritual fitness will take a tumble if you choose something non-path over the path you love.

In stark contrast to the life of this nun, I have a friend who grew up in Ireland and was a Catholic priest/missionary in Africa in the 1950s and early 1960s. At that point he felt called – strongly called inside! – to leave ministry. He moved back to Ireland for a brief time and fell in love with a nun, who also felt called to leave her ministry! They moved to the U.S. where he bought a bar in a seaport town and she became a full-time nurse. There he won the trust of the sailors and other clientele, who would often entrust their paychecks to him when they came home on leave, so that he could monitor their money and they wouldn't blow it on women and the drink. His bar became his ministry, of sorts.

This former priest and former nun built a wonderful life together, and fully believed that their relationship with God and their following the teachings of Jesus radically *increased* by leaving church ministry. God had presented them with a new calling. And they chose to say 'no' to vocational ministry in the Catholic Church, which they loved, and say 'goodbye' to the people in church ministry they loved. Their new lives became ministries of love to each other, their children, and to those people they touched every day. And those ministries were fed by the joy and love they got from being married and living their new callings.

Trusting God means trusting the calling in your heart, even when it means saying 'no' to that which you love and those people whom you love, such as the Catholic Church in the case of that priest; and even when it means saying 'yes' to that which is not always fun, not always joyful, and not always easy, such as that priest leaving ordained ministry.

Relationship with God is inherently a life of abundance and joy, to be sure. But it is a life of challenge, hard decisions, letting go, embracing the new, re-embracing the old, and every other manner of decision that is unwelcome, unpleasant, and just damn hard! That is part of the rollercoaster of life with God. And it is part of the enormous joy, intensity, and exhilaration of life with God.

Are you ready for it all?

What is it that is hard for you to say 'no' to? What is hard for you to say 'yes' to?

Who or what is obstructing your path to fulfilling God's call in your life?

Do you have the courage to trust your calling and God's plan, and remove the obstructions in your life? Can you at least create more space for you to do what you are called to do with your life?

Chapter 19

SPEAK THE TRUTH IN LOVE

When I was young I spent a few years as a cadet and football player at the US Air Force Academy. One of the mottos at the Academy is 'every athlete is a cadet, and every cadet an athlete.' It is a successful D1 athletic program with many high-caliber athletes, but it was also an engineering school with the high percentage of those intense cadets going on to serve as pilots and lead in other technical fields in the Air Force. Therefore, we were constantly being taught the fundamentals and advanced practices of successful leadership.

One of the military lessons I've remembered most vividly from the Academy was how to effectively deal with an underperforming subordinate or athlete. We were taught what was called the 'sandwich approach.' Just as a sandwich is made up of two slices of bread and some meat in between, an effective means for dealing with subordinates is by making sure the 'meat' of what must be said is preceded and followed by honest and clear affirmation.

So, upon bringing an underperformer into his office, the boss might, for example, say, "Brendon, thanks for coming in. I want to go over a few things with you. As I have told you many times before, Brendon, you are an asset to this team and this office (and the boss should have, indeed, told Brendon many times what he does well). One, you have strong work habits. Two, you are excellent at developing new ideas and implementing effective solutions. And three, you bring excellent energy to the team. You're positive and give energy to others. I sincerely appreciate those qualities. You know that, because you've heard me say it to you and others before. However, there is a persistent problem with your inability to finish projects. You have started many, and you have great solutions. But they are never brought to completion, and usually get passed off to someone else, or even I end up having to clean up your work. You're a solid starter, but I need you to be a finisher. I just don't have enough resources right now for you to just get the projects off the ground and hand them off. I need you to finish each project all the way. And for the next few weeks we're going to sit down together on Thursdays to go over what might be missing and need to be tweaked in your projects. Then once you get the hang of what I expect, we can drop the Thursdays. Bottom line is, though, you need to start finishing every project. Now again Brendon, you *are* an asset to this team. Your energy is strong. Your problem-solving and solution-finding are excellent. Let's just bring up the standards on this other part."

Bread-meat-bread. What the boss genuinely (not fake or made up, but genuinely) appreciates about Brendon begins and ends the conversation so that Brendon is neither put on the defensive at the beginning nor sent away bitter. By focusing on what Brendon does well and by showing a pattern of behavior (not just a nagging for every little thing Brendon misses or goofs up), Brendon can take the critique as a positive motivator, rather than a negative one.

In sports it is no different. Every high level athlete needs real – no b.s. – feedback. The more clear and pointed it is, the more effective it is in solving the problem. But, every athlete also lives for appreciation and respect. Thus, if critique is done in an atmosphere of constant disapproval and/or constant put-downs, even the strongest athlete will eventually wither, become bitter, become de-motivated, or turn into a rebellious person. But if the critique in this area is conveyed with the utmost respect for genuinely strong performance in other areas, then the critique is far more likely to be heard and put to use positively.

Constant praise for underachievement makes the athlete weak. (Never praise poor performance.) But, constant critique makes the athlete bitter and constrained, or constantly worrying about screwing up. Out of respect for the athlete, honest critique is best served with honest praise when the athlete has earned it.

Paul's Tough Job for Us

The Apostle Paul talks about this very same thing in Romans 4:15 when he says that we are to

"...Speak the truth in love."

Every one of us has known people who only speak the truth, all the time. We sometimes refer to people like this as being 'brutally honest.' But often they are just that, brutal. And their touch is scathing, or they are just annoying to be around, over a long period of time.

Similarly, we have all known people who are only loving, all the time. They are never firm, only soft. They never speak against the soft path. They never speak against injustice, either. And if they have to choose between telling the truth or telling something that won't hurt anyone at all, they will choose the latter, sometimes fudging the truth or outright lying to keep from hurting anyone. These types of folks can be equally annoying to be around because they lack the strength to take a stand and just be strong. They aren't just loving; they're too weak or too soft.

It's easy to be harshly honest all the time. It's easy to be loving all the time. It is infinitely harder to speak the truth in love. It is infinitely harder to convey both love and the need for correction in the same sentence or in the same thought. One of the great challenges of life is to convey both love and areas for improvement.

This is what the very best coaches do. Their athletes not only feel loved or respected, but they also know and accept the truths and corrections the coach puts in their laps.

The best athletes are capable of not only critiquing themselves but honestly assessing their strengths. They are not overly critical of themselves and are not excessively self-praising. There is both objectivity and love.

It is this same truth and love we are challenged by Jesus to bring into the world. Just as Jesus railed against the religious authorities and fought for justice for the poor, oppressed, and the outcasts, and also brought great love to the people he interacted with everyday, so are we to be instruments of love and truth simultaneously. We are called to speak and live the truth in love. Only by this path can we change the world.

Do you tend to speak more truth and less love, or more love and less truth?

Are you capable of simultaneously telling someone what you genuinely appreciate about them and what they need to improve?

What truth are you called to speak? Have you already established an atmosphere of love, such that this truth will be more readily received?

Chapter 20

'DA CEO' AND THE 'COME TO JESUS' TALK: MORE CREATION AND DESTRUCTION

It is difficult to look into the heart and mind of an athlete and know what God has in store for her or him. Yet, on the other hand, there are always hints, always clues. Whether it be in mannerisms, words, things left undone, choices, or courses of action, every person drops hints of who they truly are, whether they realize it or not.

Within the very being of each and every person is latent greatness waiting to erupt. I believe that.

I have seen strength, beauty, charisma, brilliance, and excellence in many forms come seemingly out of nowhere, streaming out of what seemed to otherwise be a dead vessel. There are those who have broken through the culturally conditioned paths of: normalcy, taking the safe route, not pushing the limits, mediocrity, and blah-ness. There are those whose spark was lit, and who refused to let that spark be hidden.

Yet, it is the lighting of that spark – the ignition – that is the tricky part. Many people, when young, desire to be athletes. But rare is the one who catches fire. Rare is the one whose passion is equaled by a sense of fight – a fire that keeps driving him through the off-seasons of hard work and no glory. Rare is the one who tastes the hunger for greatness even when the lights have gone out and the season has long passed, and all that exists is the quiet, distant glimmer of a new season six or eight months away.

And so, what many teams below the professional level are littered with are athletes who talk of greatness and who may even possess the talent to do great things, but who utterly lack the internal flame – the hunger – that generates just plain hard work in the direction of his or her desired greatness.

'Da CEO'

I have worked with many athletes of this ilk. All talk, lots of flurry, and even some measure of talent, but no action, no fire, and not enough passion for the game to sustain and drive them to work hard in the off-season.

One guy, a wide receiver on a football team who bombastically referred to himself as "Da C-E-O," was this kind of guy when he first came into my weight room. While other guys pushed themselves in their lifting and pushed their buddies in between their own sets, this kid could always be seen sitting down between his sets and seldom encouraging his lifting partners when they were up.

Da CEO could be a real nice guy, one-on-one, but he never looked you in the eye and he never looked straight ahead. His apathy oozed from every pore. When you would talk with him his eyes were always darting about, a mark of nervousness and absence of confidence. He was full of bluster around his buddies, but when confronted with the pressure to produce at something other than talking, running fast, or catching footballs he was a wet rag, utterly useless and lacking inner strength.

Between the sitting down between sets, the darting eyes, and the shifting body that didn't stand still when under pressure, this kid was not much to speak of. There was potential, but nothing realized. When I got him he was a mediocre receiver in a tall body. He had the potential for me to pack some meat onto him. He had the potential to turn into something special. But he seemed all-too-content to be brash with no bite.

I started working with him in the off-season of his freshman year in college. It was obvious that he was trying to get through college football as he had gotten through high school – a good amount of natural talent but far too much talk and only average performance. He clearly saw no correlation between off-season work and in-season performance. Or, he just didn't care. And it showed.

The following season (his sophomore year) was similar to his first season. His performance on the field mirrored the level of effort he put into strength and conditioning off-season – mediocre. He was average, or below, and the team, itself, went 1-9, winning only the last game of the season against a team with no wins.

But it was in January of Da CEO's sophomore year that something happened. Later, the CEO and I would remember the setting differently, but neither of us forgot what was spoken…

The 'Come to Jesus' Talk

Every coach has one. And every coach has had to give it countless times throughout his or her career. Different coaches know it by different names. But the one I have heard used the most, and the way I refer to it, is the 'Come to Jesus' talk….and it has nothing to do with Jesus.

I've heard it called the 'Come to God' talk. I've heard it said that an athlete needs to 'find religion.' I've also heard it said that some particular athlete 'just needs to get his ass kicked.' Again, it has nothing to do with religion or God, and has nothing to do with physically harming a kid in any way.

Instead, it's about sparking an athlete who has potential to shift from a mindset of mediocrity to an ethos of fire and hard work. Sometimes it is taking an athlete who considers himself larger than life, larger than the coaches, and larger than the team and breaking him down with a dose of reality, a hard-hitting 'drop the attitude or we're dropping you' talk. Or it is taking a kid who has talent but no work ethic whatsoever and trying to put more fire into him, using this same 'get to work or get the hell off the team' talk.

With Da CEO it was mostly the latter mixed with a dose of just plain old condescension. Now, I am a firm and adamant believer in positive reinforcement and finding the good in every kid, and focusing on that good. That is my primary mode of operating with athletes. I love positive reinforcement, myself, and always respond favorably to it. So, that is what I use with my athletes and trainees. But I have also been in this business of sports long enough to know that sometimes there is no substitute for a swift kick in the metaphorical ass and a healthy dose of humiliation.

Now again, I have no idea where the phrase 'Come to Jesus' came from for the kind of talk that has the potential to turn a boy into a man. But I think it has to do with 'finding religion,' so to speak. It ain't about religion. It's about getting serious about life. It's the religion of hard work, fire, passion, and engaging life to the hilt. It's about taking life by the balls, rather than life leading you around, or rather than being all talk but no work. It's really about the kid finding himself; finding a spark deep within him that gets lit – finding the religion of his true potential. It's about breaking down who he thinks he is, so that he can become the greatness he was meant to be.

It was our 'Blue Chip' weekend. Our top high school recruits from around the state and region were on campus for two overnights. Friday night was the big dinner, videogame tournament on big screens, poker tournament, and basketball tournament – all for the recruits and for the existing team members whom these recruits would be shadowing all weekend, and on whose floors the recruits would be sleeping. If we were a D1 school, the recruits might be in a nice hotel. But at our D3 school the recruits got a sofa or a floor and some blankets, which, in the mind of most 18 year-olds, is somehow a cool experience.

Anyway, I had been asked to give the motivational speech to the players and recruits after the big dinner that evening. And I came early and stuck around after, in order to meet recruits.

At one point in the evening I was standing by a table mixed with some of my players and some recruits. Everyone at the table was either a wide receiver or a D-back. A few I respected, most I didn't. And on this evening, feeling a bit salty, I came right out and told 'em.

"Gentlemen, I'm going to be honest with you," I stated while looking each one in the eye. "I have no respect for wide receivers. You guys do no work but get all the glory. And I just don't respect that. Linemen, on the other hand, do all the work, both in season and off-season, but get no glory. Receivers are all flash, but no work, no grit, no balls to the wall hard work. And I really don't respect that." And I walked away.

They were mortified and hung their heads as I spoke and walked away. No doubt, more than one expletive was uttered in my direction. And, while it could be argued that saying such a thing on a recruiting weekend in front of high school kids looking up to these college athletes was highly unorthodox, something happened. Something clicked. Something was lit. Da CEO had found Jesus.

10 months later, while walking off the field after the last game of the season, Da CEO, now a junior, and I had a talk. The team had just won and finished the season 5-5, a radical improvement from the previous year. It had beaten one nationally-ranked team, and nearly beaten two other nationally-ranked teams, coming only a point or two short. Da CEO, himself, had twice been voted Offensive Player of the Week for all of Division 3 football after barnburner performances. He had crushed a school record or two. And, he even had a game in which he became third on the all-time list in Division 3 football for receptions in a game. Most significantly, as a junior, he had been named an All-American!

On top of that, his quarterback had set passing records for our school and the conference, as well as total yardage records. And his fellow receivers had banner games, too, each establishing himself as a niche receiver – one guy was brilliantly sure-handed and tough while another was fast, little, and had quick moves, while still another was tall and lightning fast. But Da CEO was clearly the leader of that band of brothers. And after that last game I wanted to make sure he knew how impressed I was by his season, by his self-control, by his discipline, and by his leadership among the receivers.

Da CEO looked me straight in the eye and said, "That last touchdown, coach, I danced after 'cuz I hadn't danced all season. I just worked all season. But that high-steppin after that touchdown felt damn good!"

"You earned it," I told him.

"It's because of you, coach."

"No, it's because of you, son."

"No, coach. It was what you said. It changed everything for me when you said that receivers don't work. I thought, 'Well, why can't I?'" Da CEO explained. "Why can't I work and earn respect? It was because of you, coach."

"No, and don't you ever forget this. It was because of you, your desire to want it, and your just plain hard work. And you can tap into this fire in any area of your life. Son, you not only became a great receiver through your hard work, you became a leader – a leader of other young men. This team could not have done what it did this year if the receivers hadn't become the hardest working section of the team (pound for pound the strongest position in the weightroom!). And there's no way in hell they would've become that fierce in their workouts in the off-season unless you had turned the corner, stepped up to the plate, and decided to become a leader, not just in words, but in action. YOU did this. YOU fired this team. YOU were the spark this team needed, and all of the coaches know it. You earned it, son."

In the previous off-season, Da CEO moved into the '1000-pound Club,' as did one other receiver, for the combined weight on the three primary lifts – squat, clean, and bench. Also, those two receivers were the most improved, strength-wise, posting the highest percent gain in overall lifts. The spark inside them had been lit, which gave life to an entirely new level of mental focus, which led to enormous physical gains, which led to Da CEO being named a team captain as a junior, all of which, in turn, sparked an entire team to improve their winning percentage 500% from the previous year!!

Had several other key players stepped up their game and their work ethic in the off-season? Absolutely. The offensive line, despite having no depth beyond the first five starters, coalesced well, worked hard, and provided great protection all year in a nearly injury-free season. The quarterback (mentioned in another chapter) played beyond himself, becoming the top QB in the conference. The linebacking core was bolstered by a few transfers from other schools after an incredible off-season of recruiting by the coaches. And the D-line, D-backs, and running backs stepped up at key times (though these would be the areas of greatest growth in the subsequent years).

And it is unequivocal that the Head Coach and his assistants had gone through the long, hard slog of frustration in recruiting, injuries, and setbacks of all types. The success of that team that year and the years that were to come belonged squarely in the lap of the Head Coach. He was the man! And he was a pleasure to work for, leading by his example of hardcore work.

But it was indisputable to anyone who knew the team that the power source on the team level and the individual player level had become the receivers and their insane focus and work ethic.

As an aside, after his senior season, Da CEO was named an All-American, for the second year in a row, and has been considered for a possible pro career, which is not easy to accomplish coming from a D3 school!

According to Da CEO, the 'Come to Jesus' talk changed his life!

Humiliating Peter with a 'Come to Jesus' from Jesus

Wielded accurately, humiliation can be a powerful tool in cracking us open. It is a tool that is best when rarely used. But it is often precisely what is needed to break off that which is old, decaying, useless or impeding one's movement forward and upward to higher ground.

And this course of action was not foreign to Jesus, either. In fact, one time, in particular, Jesus comes off as a real SOB in his humiliation of Peter. Unafraid to cut loose and breathe a little fire, Jesus laid into Peter.

Jesus had just previously commended Peter for his understanding of who Jesus was – "the Christ, the Son of the living God," Peter said (Mt 16:16) – and said that Peter was the rock on whom Jesus' church would be founded. Jesus then went on to tell the apostles what was going to befall Jesus when he went into Jerusalem – i.e. that he was going to be tried by the elders and chief priests, and then be killed. Peter, unable to handle the thought of his Jesus suffering and being killed told Jesus that it could not be so. It just could not be!

Riled to anger by Peter's cowardice, Jesus tore into him,

"Get behind me, Satan!
You are a hindrance to me;
for you are not on the side of God but on the side of men"
(Mt 16:23)

The very man that was just said to be the rock on which the church was to be built was now being called Satan. And while there are some non-Christians who would say that the Christian Church has acted more like Satan over the years, the point here is that Jesus allows his anger to burn white-hot, even against one of his most treasured friends and apostles.

Humiliated in front of the other apostles, Peter was cowed, yet still not fully convinced. He was clearly put-down in front of Jesus, and would be put down again by Jesus when, in the Garden of Gethsemane, he starts a fight for Jesus to try to defend him. Peter's humiliation still not complete, he would yet go on to deny Jesus three times in Jerusalem on the night of Jesus' trials before Caiaphas, Herod, and Pilate (a situation in which Peter humiliated himself, likely reminding him of Jesus' condemnation of Peter and Jesus' prediction that Peter would deny him those three times, thereby breaking him down even further with extreme guilt). But something was cracking open.

And upon cracking Peter in calling him Satan, Jesus uses the opportunity (in the very next verse) to insert into Peter and the other apostles his core teaching,

"If any man would come after me, let him deny himself and take up his cross and follow me. For whoever would save his life will lose it, and whoever loses his life for my sake will find it"
(Matthew 16:24)

The best coaches have always known how and when to play this card of humiliation. And the worst coaches either overplay this card or never play this card. But a severe rebuke and condemnation of a flagging player is often precisely what the doctor ordered.

Jesus did it with Peter. And it, along with other teachings of Jesus, began to fill Peter up and point him in the new direction for his life. And the rest, as they say, is history. Peter (along with the evangelism of Paul and the other apostles) went on to become the foundation of Jesus' church. The one who had been severely and publicly humiliated by Jesus became the very cornerstone of Christianity, just as Da CEO had become the cornerstone of a fast-improving team!

It's interesting to note that shortly after Jesus' tongue-lashing of Peter, Jesus himself would learn from the real master just what humiliation truly was, and just how powerful it could be in cracking open something incredible.

God hands Jesus a 'Come to Jesus'

It makes you wonder – this whole story of Jesus' betrayal, trial, death and resurrection – just what the hardest part was for Jesus. After the placid quiet of the Garden of Gethsemane wherein Jesus breaks down and pleads with God to not make him suffer as he knows he's about to, Jesus is thrust immediately into what had to be a heart-breaking event. One of his most trusted friends (Judas) betrays him, turning him over to the vultures that were the high priests and scribes.

But Jesus manages to keep his cool through his trials before Caiaphas and later Herod and Pilate. He even manages to grit his teeth through the scourging of his body, as well as the public humiliation of him by the soldiers doing the torture. Further, we have no account of Jesus crying out in pain when the nails are driven into him as he is put on the cross.

But it is then, in the end, in front of God and all those who were still assembled that even Jesus was humiliated, left to die alone by the God who needed him broken and dead before He could use Jesus to his fullest potential. It is then that Jesus twice cries out to God.

"My God, my God, why have you abandoned me?"

Jesus was humiliated and alone, and then died….beginning a chain of events that would go on to change the world! Whether you believe the man's body literally came back to life or not, it is indisputable that his Spirit would utterly and completely change the course of human history in ways even the most avowed atheist or secularist cannot deny. His radical teachings on love and his unflinching self-sacrifice catalyzed the world to a whole new level of existence.

It was the act of being broken that was absolutely critical to the fulfillment of his God-designed destiny. Until Jesus, until Peter, until Da CEO, and until you and I are broken down, humiliated, torn asunder, and squashed of our belief in our own independence and invincibility, we are of little use to the purposes of God.

So, you must ask three questions:

1. Where is God humiliating you? Or, through what life humiliations might God be trying to break you open and teach you?
2. What is the rough edge that the Master Sculptor is trying to break off you before you become the piece of art that God can use for his designs? What is it about you that only the strongest of chisels with the hardest of blows can crack from you?
3. Ultimately, what is God trying to teach you, show you about yourself, or help you understand about life and your place in it? What is God saying in your 'Come to Jesus' talk?

For the truth is that there can be no butterfly without the cocoon. There can be no great sculpture without the hard chisel of the sculptor. There can be no excellence without the severity of the coach. There can be no new life without the breaking open and stripping away of the old life and the stripping away of our mad desire to always cling to that which is safe and easy.

It is only in our humiliation that we are cracked open, broken down, and prone to God's truths finally entering us. Only then can we become the excellence God wishes us to be and perform the excellence God needs us to do in order to change the world and bring it more fully into relationship with his Spirit of love.

Chapter 21

THE 'GET BACK' GUY AND GOD'S VOICE

Roughly a 3-foot distance is required.

That space is what the rules say must separate the actual sideline in college football from where the team is allowed to stand during the game. Teams are not allowed to stand right on the sideline. In fact, most football fields actually have a second white line drawn *3 feet outside the sideline* as a reminder to the players to stay back, away from the sideline.

Coaches are allowed in that 3-feet area, as well as players exiting or returning to the field of play. But, otherwise, it is intended to be a space that is clear for coach movement and overflow play from the field, thus reducing potential injuries and infringement on referee calls. Regularly obstruct that 3-foot space and your team can be penalized.

Unfortunately, it is the natural inclination of players to want to get closer to the game and, therefore, crowd into that 3-foot zone. This is why many teams at the college level will employ one of their coaches to serve as a 'Get Back Guy.' The Get Back Guy is simply the coach who is heard throughout the game shouting at players to "Get back!" away from the field and out of the 3-foot zone, thus avoiding potential penalties and giving the other coaches room to move and think.

On many teams the job of Get Back Guy falls to a member of the strength and conditioning coaching staff. For, they know the players well, but don't generally have on-field responsibilities during a game.

It was no different for me. As the Head Strength and Conditioning Coach I was, of course, asked to be on the sideline to motivate the players and to serve as the Get Back Guy. Routinely, however, I turned down this request. I enjoyed being on the sideline and motivating the players, and regularly did so. But I refused to serve as the Get Back Guy.

Why?

While I tried to do as many things as I could to help and serve all the teams I trained and coached – spending countless hours off-the-clock working to improve the capacities of my athletes and the influence of the coaches I worked with – there were certain things I would not do, on principle. Specifically, I refused to do anything that used my voice for anything other than training or some form of motivation. And being the Get Back Guy was the perfect example of misappropriation of my voice.

Was it that I had some sort of complex about speaking in public or something like that? No. Was it that I had vocal chords that demanded great care, like those of a singer? No. Was it that I was just surly and lived by my own set of rules? Well, yes, but that personality trait had nothing to do with why I wouldn't be the Get Back Guy.

I simply believed very strongly that the more I used my voice for non-training-related and/or non-motivation-related activities, the more I diluted the impact of my words when I was training or motivating my players. The more I spoke about non-essential things, the less I was heard when I spoke about essential things.

Don't get me wrong. When I am in a training setting or when I am giving a motivational speech I have no problems speaking at length or hectoring athletes in need of pushing, improvement, or adjustment. But, again, those are essential things. Being a Get Back Guy – nagging players like a mother nags her sons to clean up their rooms – was non-essential to maximizing the impact and power of my athletes.

And, I had the good fortune to work with coaches who understood and saw value in my point, encouraging me to be on the sidelines with no responsibilities beyond motivation.

Diluting the Voice

After going back into church ministry as a Sports and Recreation Pastor, I was conscious of this theory in much that I did. For example, I was explaining this theory to the Worship Director at my church. I was telling him that it is precisely this notion of diluting the impact of my voice that caused me to refrain from reading the announcements in worship, using my voice on the church voicemail, or speaking in situations beyond the non-essentials of a spiritual leader, whenever possible.

To this, the Worship Director added, "Oh, of course. I don't need God's input on every miniscule decision. But I darn sure want to know God's will on the biggies, like who I am to marry, what my calling is, work-wise, whether to have (more) children, what should I say at my brother's funeral, and so forth. The big stuff! It's in the big decisions that I most need Him. The big decisions I neither can do nor want to do alone. I gotta handle the little stuff on my own."

For years, this is how I, too, thought God operated. After years and years of what I felt were unanswered prayers and petitions seeking God's counsel, I came to believe that God acts on a similar principle of not wanting to dilute his voice: "The less they hear my voice, the more they're inclined to listen when they do hear it." I used to think that God doesn't want to be the Get Back Guy with a diluted voice. So, I fell out of the discipline of prayer, simply because I felt it was ultimately fruitless – all questions and no answers.

But, cliché as this may sound, as my life began to change and I began to slow down, I began to realize that the problem wasn't God's lack of speaking. The problem was my frantic life and inability to listen.

But what does this mean, really, to 'hear God's voice?'

According to the Bible, at the baptism of Jesus by John the Baptist (Mt. 3:13-17) four miracles happened, all within a few minutes, all confirming for those present that Jesus was the Son of God and the Chosen One:

1) The 'heavens' opened up
2) Jesus was lifted into the air
3) A dove descended from the opened heavens and alighted on Jesus
4) God spoke from the heavens and said, "This is my beloved son, with whom I am well pleased."

Now, whether you believe these miracles actually literally happened isn't the point. You can talk that out with God on your own. The point here is simply that, like the people present at the baptism of Jesus, some people have the benefit of literally hearing God speak to them in a voice from heaven; some people have the benefit of having miracles happen that confirm God's presence or confirm Jesus or confirm God's will for their lives.

But some people simply have some major (or minor) event or happening in life that speaks God's will for their life in a way that is ***as if*** God spoke to them.

There is no actual voice. But, the happening is so clear and so strong that it is the closest they have ever come to actually hearing a voice from heaven or receiving a nature-defying miracle.

And when I speak of the 'voice of God' in this book that is one of the types of occurrences that I am talking about. One of the ways God does communicate is through unusual or highly improbable sequences or timing of events. Perhaps it is a strange sequence of events. Perhaps it is an incredible coincidence. Perhaps it is through uncanny timing.

The Other Voice

But, there is another way God speaks to us, one I have spoken of at other points in this book.

I believe that deep within us the voice of God unifies with our own voice, becoming indistinguishable. It's just that we are so wrapped up in the speed, commotion, and anxiety of life that we cannot hear. But, when we quiet our lives and just relax we are finally able to hear what the prophet Elijah experienced as a "still small voice" (1Kings 19:12). And this is less an actual 'voice' and more of a knowing. That is, I experience a person's voice as being outside me, coming in. But this type of knowing is *as if* from outside, but is already in me. It was not previously known to me, but now is known inside me. Further, it is less a 'voice' and more a feeling, a knowing, a sensing, or an intuiting. This is what most of us experience when we have asked in prayer for an answer to a particular question or need. We just sense the answer inside.

And the more disciplined we are to quiet ourselves on a moment's notice, the more able we are to hear that 'voice,' just know what 'feels' right, or intuit very deep within us what it is God is saying to us.

The problem I had been having in years of 'unanswered prayer' is that I was too damn busy to hear the voice speaking quietly from within. God was speaking, even in the small stuff, but I didn't have ears to hear. I didn't have quiet 'ears.' I didn't create the stillness in my life to feel the vibrations of what felt right.

Sound a little New Agey? Well, in a way, it is. In a very real and powerful way, the New Age movement and some other religions have done a far better job of putting new words to and re-articulating the experience of communication with the Divine. The Christian language has grown so overwrought as to be bled of meaning. Further, much of New Age, at least on this one topic, has changed the locus of experience of God's voice from two of the five senses to a third – from the ear and the eye to the feel.

It is no longer a head experience. It is not even so much a heart experience. Though, both head and heart are integrated into this experience. Instead, it is much more an experience in the viscera, the intestines, the guts, and the solar plexus.

And, given the removal of all the anxieties of life that knot our insides and churn our stomachs, we can actually feeeel God leading us in the direction that is just right for each of us. But as long as our lives are stirred and confounded by a billion other things that we think are more important, from the great to the banal, we can never hear the answers to every little prayer and question we utter toward God.

Is that quiet inner voice always the voice of God? I have no way of knowing, for sure. Truth is, none of us can know with absolute certainty what is and is not God in any situation. What we say are answered prayers, we sometimes later say couldn't have been answered prayers. What we today say are blessings often turn out to be curses. What we today say to be curses often, in fact usually, turn out to be blessings.

In my own life, when I heed that 'voice' – that feel, that knowing – what follows always feels right and fits with who I am, and seldom needs correction. I look back on decisions where I trusted that feel and 100 times out of 100 that was exactly the path that I needed to take.

None of us knows exactly what God is speaking in our lives. At least, there is no way to prove it, one way or another. Instead, we affix God's name and blessing to that which feels good or right in our lives. Objectively speaking, there is no way of empirically confirming that something is or is not – or was or was not – God's will. Instead, we most often say something is from God when it feels right with who we are. Even if it is not a 'good' or 'prosperous' event but often when it is a hard or suffering-related experience, we say that it was likely or definitely from God.

In other words, there is no way of knowing definitively if something is from God. But we call it 'from God' if it feels right with who we are in the long term. And the best we can do in the short term is trust the feel, the voice, the knowing, and the gut, as well as the flashes of insight, the epiphanies, and the fleeting revelations. The best we can do is *hear* the *voice* of God speaking in what feels right and seems right deep within us.

And, really, this notion of God communicating to us through a 'feel' is not all that great a stretch for those Christian denominations that believe Jesus is literally physically present in the Eucharist, or is "in, with, and under" the Communion bread and wine. For, if Jesus truly is present, bodily, then Jesus would be digested and turned into cells, blood, synapses, mucus, pancreas tissue, cilia, ganglia, and the like. And, when you inquired of the Divine or asked God for insight, knowledge of His will, or any other thing you would quite literally be able to feel God's answer being communicated to you through your very own cells, limbs, organs, skin, heart, brain, and gut, because God/Jesus was quite literally part of your actual physical body.

God's Undiluted Voice

Unlike my own work as a coach and pastor, I believe that God does not concern Himself with diluting his voice, but speaks to me everyday, as much as I please, in even the smallest and insignificant of circumstances. I am human and my voice loses impact and power, the more it is heard. But God's voice inside never declines, never wanes, and never loses its import in our lives.

But, hearing that quiet voice of God puts a greater onus on me. I can hear God's voice, if that's what I want. But I have to have the discipline to shut down, temporarily shut out the world and really be able to feeeel what it is saying.

God's presence in the world is not some intellectual concept to which we must assent. It is a felt, *affect*-ive interconnection and relationship.

To spend your days expecting a larger than life miracle or voice from heaven to answer each one of your prayers and requests is to consign yourself to a lifetime of waiting. But, to trust that God will answer you strongly *inside* in your big decisions and little decisions is to live in the confidence and assurance that you can move forward in life. To know that God speaks through all your senses, particularly your own feeeel of yourself, is to live in the quiet assurance that you can have all your prayers answered; perhaps not always the answers you think you want, but at least answers with clarity.

Similarly, you have the power to tap into God's 'inside voice' (and keep Him from 'yelling' by breaking down your life) if you will only quiet your life and begin to feel what feels right, and sense what you know you must do in each situation. You must remove those things from your life that alter your physical state and your ability to feel yourself and know what you are truly feeling at any given moment. For if God truly is inside you (as is stated in the Eucharist, and as more Christian denominations need to acknowledge), then you most certainly can feel Him communicating to you what His will is for your life.

And, really, isn't that all we really want – to know God's will for our lives, to live in that confidence and clarity of knowing we are on precisely the exact path that is our destiny and calling?

The 'voice' of God is there in life. But if you want it for more than the big things, you gotta be able to quiet yourself to hear it, feel it, know it, and experience it.

The Problem

This listening for God's voice inside and doing as it commands is what I referred to in previous chapters as 'reading the chip' that God implanted in you when He made you. To hear and heed what God is saying to you on this chip from within is what it means to 'Love God.' It is to listen for that deepest, quietest voice inside that is the union of the voice of God and your own truest voice, to the point where they are indistinguishable. It is to honor and live who you truly are and what God made you to be. And if you are truly in tune, it doesn't feel like something outside you, but like it is your own truest expression of your own self, just as God originally made you to be.

But the problem for the Church and many Christians in considering this possibility is, "You can't trust your own voice inside, because the human creature will always lean toward doing bad things. It's not God's voice inside you. It's your own sinful voice."

But the truth is, God made you; and God does dwell inside you, as the Bible states, time and again. And this is where "Loving God" is balanced with the other part of Jesus' command, "Loving Neighbor."

What makes an inner calling truly in line with Jesus' teaching is if what you are called to do not only feels right inside but is also done in service of others. The great balance of Jesus' prime command is that it not only sits right with who you are inside, but it is oriented toward the service of humanity. It is loving the call inside from God, and it is loving the neighbor outside you whom you are called to serve. This is the consummation of the "love God and love neighbor" command, which Jesus made his first and greatest!

So, what is God trying to get through to you?

What were you put on this earth to do?

Chapter 22

PASSIVE INCOME IS A LOT LIKE FAITH

There is a term in economics known as 'passive income.' Simply put, if 'active income' is earned by going to work and earning a paycheck, then when I take that paycheck and invest part of it in rental property, stocks/investments (portfolio income), or something in which I am not actively involved, the money I make off my investments is known as 'passive income.' It's called passive income because I am not actually working to earn it. I already earned the original money at my job. The money itself is now doing the work by multiplying from interest and investment, while I am at home playing catch with my son or mowing the lawn.

Growing your muscles through resistance training is little different. Basically, as mentioned in an earlier chapter, lean muscle burns calories at a higher rate than other cells do. Thus, by building muscle mass you raise your resting heart rate, increase blood flow, and improve overall efficiency of your body system.

What this means is that a person with high muscle mass is burning more calories than the non-athletic or non-active person. But where it really gets interesting is in the fact that people with high muscle mass are actually burning calories at a higher rate *even when they are inactive.* A person with more muscle mass can be sitting at home watching *The Simpsons* on the sofa, and still be burning more energy, carbs, and calories, and doing so at a higher rate, than the person who is not training, not training as hard, or strictly doing cardio to try to lose weight. This is why trying to lose weight by only doing cardio is a fool's errand.

Passive income.

You don't have to be in the gym working out, you don't always have to be active, in order to reap the fruits of hard work on the weights.

What is 'Faith,' really?

Faith is no different. Faith is basically passive income. It's stuff getting done even when we're not doing a darn thing to get it done.

We so often hear people say, "God helps those who help themselves." But we quickly forget the other side of it, which says, "No, that's not quite true. Jesus' whole message is for people who cannot help themselves – the weak, the broken, the despised, the outcast. For, we are all weak, broken, and cast out, at times. And, more importantly, Jesus' whole message is that *we foolishly spend all our time thinking life is about what we do rather than about what God does in our lives*." Jesus was constantly banging on the disciples for their lack of faith – their lack of trust in God's actions in life.

In other words, while putting 'faith in action' is extremely important, there is also that thing called 'trust in God' that we so often forget about, especially in our mad lives that are driven by activity, consumption, overdoing, and rush, rush, rush.

Faith, really, is putting trust in God – trusting that God will provide; trusting that God is at work, making things happen, especially when we're not. And we're generally so bad at it because we believe that nothing happens in life unless we do it ourselves.

We don't believe that God can be trusted. We think we have to do it all ourselves. It is all about our own activity. But faith is the trust that God is at work in our lives, *even when we are not at work in our lives.* Sorta like passive income.

We forget the words that resound throughout the Old Testament after Abraham first boldly stated them in Genesis 22:14:

"The Lord will provide."

We forget that religion and faith are ultimately not about belief in a story or even in a list of principles or beliefs. Religion, faith and spirituality are ultimately about *trusting* God's activity in our lives, based on the fact or in part motivated by the fact that others have had really kickass lives when they trusted in God's activity.

Ultimately, nothing matters except, "The Lord provides." This is the very core of the Bible, faith, and relationship with God. Jesus' entire life, death, and teachings were intended to convey this lone point: Trust God, because God will provide.

The more we trust God, the more we step into that abundant life Jesus promised. The more we trust God, the more capable we are of moving mountains here on earth. The more we trust God, the more our after-death concerns are taken care of.

Instead, we try to move life's mountains ourselves. We try to do it all with our own sweat, blood, and toil. We completely lack the ability to simply turn it over to God and trust that God will show us what to do and when to do it, and in the meantime we are to do nothing. Yes, that's right: nothing. Sometimes the life of faith means doing nothing; and that is often the hardest of all things to do.

We are so geared into being active and doing, doing, doing, that we push God out of the equation. We are so good at forcing life. We worry and fret, and worry and worry. We scurry about like squirrels preparing for winter. We frantically try to amass those things that make us feel secure. We are so unwilling to trust that the Lord will provide. We are so unwilling to just let go and trust that God can handle it and will take care of it. And so, we get busy doing action for action's sake; often cluttering and confounding what God is trying to accomplish.

Faith is fundamentally trust. It is trust that I don't have to force life. It is trust that if it feels forced, it ain't the right path. It is trust that when God wants me to do something it will be abundantly clear and obvious, and the path will flow effortlessly. It will feeeel right.

If you lack the ability to trust that God will act when God is ready and that you don't have to force it, you lack faith. If you lack the belief that God is continually creating new life in your life, you lack faith. If you lack faith/trust, you will never accomplish one-tenth of what you could if you did trust. Jesus said:

"Truly I say to you, if you have faith as a grain of mustard seed, you will say to this mountain, 'Move away,' and it will move; and nothing will be impossible to you"
(Matthew 17:20).

It is, in fact, this very verse from which we get the expression 'move mountains.' And Jesus *says it is not by our activity that we move mountains but by our passivity* – our faith that God will move it. It is not we who move the mountains, but God who moves the mountains, if we would only trust that God will do so.

Passive income.

Often the most work is accomplished not by what we do, but by what we don't do. It is meditation, prayer, and walking away from or forgetting a problem – *trusting that God is at work* – that often have the biggest and most powerful impact on any situation. That is faith. That is trust in God's providence.

So, what is the biggest challenge for you, personally, in attempting to fully trust God with your life?

Are you ready to trust God even more with your life, rather than depending upon your own flurry, commotion, and worry, worry, worry?

Are you ready to place your effort and intention out there, and then trust God is at work bringing it to fruition?

Can you trust that when it is time for you to act, God will make it clear?

Can you allow for the radical possibility that sometimes doing nothing is the best course of action?

Chapter 23

SPIGOTS AND UNLEASHING YOUR CRAZY

I do quite a bit of motivational speaking. One question I regularly ask groups of high school and college athletes is if they know what a 'spigot' is. More often than not, not even one person raises his or her hand with the right answer. It seems that word is not as common as it used to be.

A spigot, I explain, is that nozzle on the side of your house that you screw your hose onto to water your lawn. 'Spigot' is, more or less, just an old-fashioned word for a faucet of some sort, whether on your house, in your sink, or what have you.

But, I explain, it is important to remember that a faucet or spigot is not just a nozzle where something such as water comes out. It also has some sort of handle, dial, or knob to control the flow of water coming out. Without the dial/handle there would be no way to control the flow, and water would simply be streaming onto your lawn 24 hours/day. A spigot enables us to control the flow.

We have 'spigots' in our head, too, so to speak. Each and every athlete I work with, and each and every one of us, has several flows of thoughts into our heads: a flow of thought about working out, a flow about a girlfriend or boyfriend, a flow of thought about family, a flow of thought about work, a flow about their sport, a flow about going out with friends this weekend, a flow about their favorite sports team, a flow about God stuff, and on and on. And every one of these flows of thought has a spigot on it. Every train of thought can be controlled – turned on, turned down, turned up, and turned off.

And the real challenge, as discussed in the chapter on mental focus, is to control these spigots so that when you are engaged in one activity the other spigots are turned off. That is what focus is – the ability to have one spigot on at a time, and possibly turned on full blast, while all the other spigots are turned off. That way thoughts of one thing are not invading your mind and taking your energy when you are focused on something entirely different. Self-control, self-discipline, intensity, and focus are all just different names for having this ability to turn off all non-relevant spigots, and crank wide-open the spigot or spigots necessary for success at a given task.

Fundamentally, this is where excellence in sports comes from and what heavy lifting in the weightroom teaches – the ability to tune out distractions ('turn off the other spigots') and totally focus on the task at hand ('crank open the spigot for this event'). Sports excellence is fundamentally *not* a physical thing, especially weightlifting, not to mention working out for personal fitness. *Excellence in sports, as with life, is directly and perfectly correlated to the capacity to focus your mind.* As I have stated at other points in this book, there is no success in sports or any venture in life without the ability to control your spigots, without the capacity to focus your mind.

The amount of physical energy that has to be called forth to lift double or even triple one's own weight in one or two seconds is massive. It requires a physical explosion that is first conjured in the mind. The lift begins and is carried through in the mind. Thus, without the ability to fully unleash the spigot flow and tune out all distractions (or turn off the other spigots in the mind), an athlete will only achieve mediocre results.

If I can mix metaphors here, it's like the equalizer on your stereo (or the mixing board in a recording studio) that has all those different dials, knobs and levers that control everything from bass to tone to mega-hertz to loudness to everything else. By controlling the feed of the sound from a CD or the radio, the quality of the sound flowing to and out of the speakers can be perfected. Similarly, controlling your excellence means being able to perfectly adjust and tweak the flow of every piece of input that enters your mind and body and flows out of your mind and body.

The problem with so many young athletes is that they lack the ability to focus. They lack the ability to turn their spigots on and off. They were simply never taught how.

So, they'll be sitting in class thinking about baseball, and on the baseball field thinking about their girlfriend, and with their girlfriend thinking about going out with their buddies, and rarely thinking about studies. So, they're never really fully present in anything, and thereby they are seldom fully successful in anything, because their mind and their body are always in two different places; seldom fully working together.

The only way to break through this focus barrier is to keep upping the ante. We only lack focus for bigger challenges because we have been able to get by at lesser tasks with less focus and less intensity. But, if the athlete genuinely wants to be successful, he or she must be taught to bring more mental focus.

The only way to increase focus is to increase the challenges in the direction a person wants to go. It is to take the athlete to higher levels where greater focus is demanded; where lesser focus will only bring failure.

This is why resistance training (weight training) is such a powerful vehicle for training for all sports. It is simply the athlete interacting with gravity, eliminating all other extraneous variables. Thus, it is possible to apply increased challenge (and exact greater focus from the athlete) at consistent increments, day after day, month after month.

By going to ever-increasing levels of mental focus, the athlete is then prepared when confronted with adversity, fatigue, pain, and distraction in a game situation or high-pressure environment (such as a test in class) where the possibility of losing control of one's spigots is exacerbated by a multitude of stimuli.

You got Crazy?

This brings the discussion to one of the most important spigots in the human mind, particularly in the mind of young males, but especially in the mind of young male athletes.

There's a spigot in the head marked 'Crazy.' Handled poorly, it can wreak havoc. Handled well and channeled with excellence, this is perhaps the single most majestic and powerful of all the spigots in an athlete's being.

Most of the young athletes I have coached – D1, D3, Olympic hopefuls, professionals, or competitive powerlifters and bodybuilders – have this 'Crazy' spigot and it is turned on. After dealing with athletes for decades, I can see the degree to which it is turned on in the first three minutes of talking with any young kid. I see it especially in the athletes of aggressive sports – wrestlers, boxers, football players, rugby players, ultimate fighters, hockey players, and sometimes basketball players. Other athletes have it, but often it is most quickly obvious among contact sport athletes.

And, whether it is because of testosterone, socialization, or something else, all young males have it. Again, it's only a question of degrees. And their ability to tap it is directly related to how much those people around them have tried to squash it.

The problem is that our culture, our youth sports, our families, our adult males, and far too many coaches have taken to not only cranking that 'Crazy' spigot way off in young boys, but then taking a sledge hammer and breaking off the control knob, so that no crazy ever comes out of boys and young men. Rather than ever teaching boys to control the flow of massive power that courses through them, we think it is best to dam up that power, pretending it doesn't exist or shouldn't exist. But the flow behind the 'Crazy' spigot valve is so strong that it *will* flow, somehow, somewhere. If the young male is not taught how to control that flow, the spigot of 'Crazy' will eventually break off and craziness and destruction will dominate that man's life, again whether it is as a young man or much later in life. Because we have a culture that so fears the male crazy and is so utterly inept at both respecting it and metering it, we have boys that are never taught how to be men and control their crazy (and so the young athlete is essentially 'out of control'). For, being a man means being able to fully control *all* that God has given you. For if you don't, these other energies in the male being will find expression somewhere, somehow.

Sadly, as a culture, we seem to think that tapping and harnessing the 'Crazy' just happens naturally in young men/boys. It doesn't. Or, we think that if we ignore it, it will go away. It won't.

And the wild ones – the boys whose crazy spigot is constantly on (not just on the court or rink, but always) and is going at a hundred miles/hour –

simply have not met men who are quite in control of their own flow of crazy and who know how to teach boys how to control that flow. These are boys who get mixed up in drugs, vandalism, stealing, or serious rebelliousness. These are the athletes who go around punching walls (the perfectly stupid, yet ridiculously common athletic example of uncontrolled crazy), or the guys who are constantly getting in bar fights. Their innate young male crazy (as well as the anger and rage it can birth if not harnessed) is unchanneled, diffuse, and doing them more harm than good.

But when that crazy is harnessed it can be the most powerful tool for accomplishing amazing things.

"Cross-country is a mental sport…
…and we're all crazy!"
-- seen on the back of a high school running team sweatshirt

Harnessing the Crazy

To harness the flow of crazy in a young athlete it is not enough to just say 'be good; don't be bad.' It's not enough to simply break off the spigot handle. The boy must be taught to control and *use* the power coursing through his veins.

Imagine a light bulb being turned on in a dark living room. Rays of light are shooting out of that bulb in a million directions, illuminating the entire room. That's what most younger males are. Their energy is totally unfocused and is going in a million of uncontrolled directions.

But, then someone came along and invented the laser. A laser takes all that energy of thousands of light bulbs and, rather than letting it shoot light in a million directions, focuses all that energy and light in one tight, tight, tight stream of light. And that is why lasers are so powerful. A laser is tightly concentrated energy focused into a stream of enormous power aimed in one lone direction.

Teaching a late-teenage boy who is on fire with testosterone and unyielding crazy to condense, tighten and direct his energy and focus is essentially teaching him how to become a laser. It is teaching him how to turn off all the other spigots, and unleash the massive power within him in one direction, so to accomplish enormous good! It is also about teaching him how to turn the crazy down and even off at times when it will only create problems or do damage.

The thing is, accomplishing this spigot control ain't always pretty. Teaching young men how to become men demands older men who know and have mastered their own power. Teaching young men about controlling their own power demands older men whose power is greater and who are unafraid of the power of young men. This is all too rare in our society. Many men think they can do it, but they can't, which is part of why our culture is in such a state. This isn't about being macho or acting tough or hardcore. This isn't an act. It is a spiritual thing, really. It is about men who have truly mastered themselves…all of themselves.

A "Crazy" Beijing Olympian

In her August 20, 2008, article from Beijing, China, *The New York Times'* Juliet Macur reported on the stunning and largely unexpected silver medal-winning performance of American gymnast Jonathan Horton, touching on the notion of crazy and the coach who simultaneously harnessed it and set it free.

> "High above the arena floor where Jonathan Horton was about to unveil a dangerous and daring horizontal bar routine, his parents, Margo and Al Horton, held their breath.
>
> "Their son had told them to expect something extraordinary, so they braced themselves. For the Hortons it was nothing new.
>
> "'Ever since he was a little boy, he's always been doing crazy things,' Margo Horton said of her 22-year-old son. 'He thrives on crazy things. In fact, he does better gymnastics when he's doing crazy things.'
>
> "Indeed, Jonathan Horton, who has the energy of a hyperactive toddler and the guts of a stuntman, won an Olympic silver medal on the high bar with those crazy things.

> "Just three days before the Olympic final on Tuesday, he patched together a new horizontal bar routine, hoping to raise his score and put him into medal contention. He added one risky release move, then upgraded another, lifting his difficulty mark by a half point.
>
> "The crowd at the National Indoor Stadium noticed. It roared each time his hands and his body twisted and flipped in the air, snubbing gravity…
>
> "In the days before, Horton's competitors seemed stunned that he was performing the new routine in the first place. Preparing a performance like that for the Olympics usually takes months, not 72 hours…
>
> "'It pretty much went silent in the gym when I was practicing and everyone was coming up to us and asking, "Is he really going to do this?"' said Horton, who was fourth in the all-around at last year's world championships. 'But I didn't want to hold back. I didn't want to have any regrets. I want to go big or go home.'
>
> "'He's always been kind of a riverboat gambler,' [Mark] Williams [Horton's coach] said. 'We took a risk, and it paid off.'
>
> "Horton's mother said: 'When he does these things we're always saying, "Oh my goodness?" When he lands them, though, there is nothing more beautiful.'"

Simply dealing with a 'riverboat gambler' who has the energy of a 'hyperactive toddler' and who thrives on doing risky and crazy things is no small task. But teaching that young man how to actually use those wild traits to his advantage is both a rare gift and an acquired skill. More to the point, harnessing that wildness invariably demands techniques that an outsider might call crazy, unnecessary, inappropriate, or uncalled-for. But dealing with crazy is no place for the normal.

Unorthodox Training Techniques

The Athletic Director[20] of one college at which I worked pulled me into his office one day to tell me that he had received complaints from

[20] He has since left this position.

one or two other staff/faculty about my coaching style. These other staff regularly heard swearing in my gym, and they didn't like it. These staff people thought it could make the gym intimidating for girls. They also thought it projected unfavorably on the college. And I was asked to clean it up.

Knowing full well that this was a discussion I was going to lose, not by logic but by the unquestioned cultural mindset toward swearing, I laid out my thinking anyway.

First, I explained, this is not just a 'guy thing.' Over the years I have actually had countless female athletes, even at a Christian college, who are very intense lifters, train very hard, and who swear with regularity and flair.[21] But, as with my male athletes, it is not always loud or frequent. It just happens, sometimes, at least for the athletes lifting heavy weight.

And I want to create young people who attack life with a sense of noble purpose, and I believe you cannot do that without teaching them how to turn on, turn up, and turn off their power, at will. Further, I believe the weightroom to be a controlled environment perfectly suited for executing such an endeavor.

I went on to explain to this Athletic Director, who was now into his 60s and nearing retirement, that, contrary to the feelings of many of the male coaches at the college, I was strongly in favor of our college's practice of providing women-only weight training classes during the day (mostly for novices), where the gym is shut down to anyone outside the class. In my time at the college I had always been an advocate of this practice. Most coaches are upset by this practice because it eliminates chunks of time that their athletes can be in the weightroom. I, however, was in favor of it, because I knew some girls just have personal fears, insecurities, and body issues about being around boys in any sort of setting,

---

[21] A trait I particularly welcome in my young female athletes as it shows a willingness to think and act outside convention and social expectation, which is a trait that will suit them well as they move into adulthood and are confronted with difficult and often unpopular decisions that demand courage and…well, a willingness to think and act outside convention and social expectations for women. The swearing isn't the point; the courage to act independently and against convention is.

not to mention an athletic one. And these classes are a great way to introduce them to resistance training (weights) in a controlled and safe setting. I attempted to help my friend (the Athletic Director) see that I do understand the needs of girls.

Second, I then explained that just as some female lifters have special needs so also do many of my male athletes. The nature of heavy lifting is such that massive amounts of energy are being conjured and released. It just takes so much more energy to lift radically increased amounts of weight. That's why heavy lifting (or even lifting high reps) is so hard. It demands more energy!

Therefore, when reps are hit or missed there is a massive release of breath and energy, whether accompanied by an expletive or not. However, when the rep or set is missed it is only natural – in fact, primal – to express frustration through some sort of curse word. (For the record, I've heard the most devout Christian athletes swear in such circumstances.) It releases the anger and the energy in a way that "Oh darn" or "Phooey" just can't do. Further, it gets it out of one's system, so that the athlete can let go and move forward. If you've never lifted seriously heavy weight, way beyond anything you've ever lifted before, you will never understand what I'm talking about. It's just a different world that demands different rules.

I told my Athletic Director that I was trying to create athletes and students who are the very best ambassadors for our college. And I believe, just as we provide novice female lifters with a safe space to begin working out, when working with young men in their late-teens and early-twenties it is necessary to provide them with a safe space, as well, where they can simply be boys, let out their frustrations, and bang some heavy weight around.

By giving them a safe place (the weightroom) to be boys, and by telling them that is what we are doing, we actually decrease the likelihood that they will act like mongrels when they are out with their friends on Friday night.

Spigot control! By giving them a controlled setting to release their crazy and learn to control their crazy, we actually reduce the wild and uncontrolled release of it later.

Young men have enough testosterone in them to kill a horse, it seems. We can delude ourselves into thinking that they should just never express their aggressive, head-banging side. We can try to break off that 'Crazy spigot' handle, or we can provide them a safe space (gym) where the chance of them doing any harm, at all, is close to nil. We can then place on them the expectation that because they have been given a place where boys can be boys they must then conduct themselves as men outside the weightroom walls.

The trick of turning boys into men is not to turn off the crazy, but to give boys a place to release as much of the crazy as possible, so that it doesn't get backed up and build up more and more and more pressure, until it finally explodes out! If boys have a regular place to cut loose, release massive amounts of energy through lifting, aggressive sports, and occasional swearing and pushing each other around, then the crazy energy will have a release, and it won't come out in bars, with girlfriends, or alone with a bottle.[22]

I saw this in nearly all of my male athletes. When they knew I would protect and respect their release of power, crazy, and rage (and keep the gym safe for others while they did so), they began to mellow out a bit around campus and off-campus. They began to act less like uncontrollable boys and more like tall, confident young men who knew themselves and could control themselves. They began to master themselves. When their true needs were recognized and respected, they respected the needs and wants of others. It's so simple!

And it also works for my female athletes and all my non-athletes because I am constantly educating them, as well, about the different needs of different people in the weight room, just as I educate my big lifters about their responsibility for the needs of others.

Lastly, I told my A.D. that to use me as a nagging mother – who tells the athletes not to swear and to just be good – to these boys is a mistake.

[22] There is an old adage in psychology, "Boys bond bloody." Essentially, one of the biggest things that bonds males together is scrapping, teasing, wrestling, and getting in each other's grill and then getting past it. It is the shared energy, the power, and the respect that flows through it all. It's just a guy thing. Young men simply cannot be treated and effectively raised the same way young women are. Sheer biology precludes that as an effective method.

They have enough mothering in their lives from their parents and from the college, itself. They need someone who treats them like a son, a kid brother, a subordinate, a mentor, and a friend. They need someone who gives them space, but also places on them firm expectations of performance, and instills in them a greater sense of nobility, which is not precluded by swearing.

All told, allowing swearing, shouting, and boisterousness to happen in the weightroom can be a good thing, because it shows our boys that we protect them and their needs just as fervently as we protect those of young women.

As expected, however, I was told, in so many words, that the needs of the top athletes and the males will all be brought down to the level of the beginning lifters. In other words, rather than the weak and the strong living in harmony by understanding each other, the strong shall be neutered, to some degree, so that the occasional beginning lifter that is in there during peak athlete hours will not be offended. The spigot shall be only allowed to be part-way open, just a teeny little bit.

Rather than understanding and harnessing the crazy in young athletes, that college preferred to ignore that crazy even exists, an all-too-common head-in-the-sand response that, in the end, only makes the problem worse.

This incident brought home to me the fact that we have failed to instill in boys and young men a sense of their own power and how to channel it, control the force of its flow, and simply turn it on and off. Further, we have failed to instill in boys and young men a sense of nobility – *a sense of what to do with all that power they have*. We have confused noble purpose with simply being good. We have substituted the high life of bravery and valor with following the rules, having good behavior, acting 'appropriately' (Yech!), and having males do what they're told.

And I am a firm believer that unless we teach young men how to use that power that is in them, they will become nothing more than hollow versions of themselves; weakened by their inability to even know their own power; and certainly lacking any sense of noble purpose that they can invest their power into.

Living with honor is not about 'doing the right thing.' In fact, living with honor and valor can at times mean doing the very wrong thing. Jesus was constantly accused of doing the 'wrong' thing. It can mean breaking the law (consider Gandhi or Martin Luther King Jr. for strong examples). It can regularly mean defying what those around you think you should do or what the institution thinks you should do. It can mean standing up against all that is supposedly good and right, just as it at times means following that which is good and right.

To accomplish the great good God has written on your soul to do demands having the ability to harness your power, turn the crazy on, fight the fight, and use all the tools God has given you, including those traits that ain't always pretty.

Greg

In all my years of lifting and coaching, I have acquired a few favorites. Sometimes it is the strongest guy. Sometimes it is the most intense female. Sometimes it is the weakest guy who just wants it bad enough to work his tail off. Sometimes it's the joker who lightens me up, but works when I tell him to. More often than not, it's the badass. There's just something enchanting about those people who live on or near the edge of life. They are vivacious and exuberant, and ultimately inspiring.

Greg was a serious badass. He was a 190-pounder who lifted with ferocity and who, on the field, hit like a ton of bricks. All of this mad intensity was no surprise considering his past. The kid was no more than 21 years old, but he had seen more life than most 40 year-olds.

Greg was a former drug addict, former heavy boozer, and a formerly out of control young man. However, by the time he got to our college he was already well into his recovery.

Augsburg College in Minneapolis has a nationally-recognized program for young adults in recovery from alcohol or drugs, known as the 'Step-up Program,' where they can simultaneously be mentored, complete their college degree, and get the close interaction and support that the recovering addict often needs. The goal is to help them become fully functional contributors to society who also happen to possess a college degree. Essentially, Augsburg and its Step-up Program give troubled kids a second chance. And, given Augsburg's inner-city location and national recognition for this program, I was constantly interacting with young men who possessed a whole lot of crazy, such as Greg.

In fact, after a very short time at Augsburg, Greg was getting almost straight-As, and was establishing himself as a new leader on our football team. But in the weightroom he was something else, altogether. Pound for pound one of the three strongest lifters I had at that school. He was just all badass and focus. Well, almost. He did require occasional reining-in when he would joke around in between sets, something I absolutely do not tolerate during team workouts. But on the whole, he was simply a treat to have on the team.

Part of what I loved about Greg was that he was real and had truly seen a hard patch of life. Here was a kid who had come from good parents, but had simply taken a few wrong turns in life and gone way down the rabbit hole of following his unharnessed crazy. But by the time he got to me he was a success story in the making. He had met some men in his life that began to teach him how to channel his crazy badass self; and who taught him that if he didn't channel it, he would quite simply die or become seriously, seriously messed up!

But, what also made Greg so doggoned special was his matured attitude, the fact that he did whatever I told him to do in the weightroom, and that he was such a nice guy. Greg was in so many ways totally opposite from me. A self-described redneck, he wore Mossy Oak camo undershirts, and regularly went hunting or just shooting guns with his buddy from Texas. Once, at a talent show during football camp, Greg wanted to display his expertise at hatchet-throwing by plucking an apple off the head of a fellow player (who was also sort of a Grizzly Adams-type) using a hatchet. (Needless to say, I stepped in with a firm "No f---ing way am I allowing that!")

Greg's greatest attribute, however, was that he knew his spigots, including his crazy spigot, and had been taught more spigot control than 90% of kids his age. He had truly learned to master himself. When he was in class or the library, he was all academics; and his grades proved it.

When he was in my weightroom or on the field, he was all aggressiveness and business. When he was with friends, fellow Step-up members, or people he liked, he was focused with graciousness and a good spirit. As a D-back on the football team, he once unloaded with such massive force on a receiver coming across the middle that the receiver not only had the pass blown out of his hands, but his helmet popped-off five yards, and the receiver himself was jettisoned backwards several feet!

Was Greg our top leader? No. Was he our strongest guy? No. Was he easy for every person to get along with? No. Was he our best baller? No. But he was always *one of* the very best at everything he did.

Why? Spigot control; all spigots. And most importantly, he knew how to channel his crazy.

Biblical Crazies and Changing the Course of Humanity

The only people who change the course of history are those who have crazy, have power from within, and can channel all their energy. No exceptions.

The great story of life has been written by men and women who have spigot control, and who have tapped into the ferocious God-given power within themselves.

The Bible, itself, is rife with stories of Biblical madmen (and madwomen). The history of Christianity after Jesus is one where the greatest changes were accomplished by men and women of intense personalities, unusual and even anti-social habits, and colorful lives. It is not the nice and the good followers of Jesus' teachings who have changed Christianity the most and changed the world the most, but the men and women of controlled and channeled power and fire.

Who were the great crazies of the Bible? Perhaps the better question is who wasn't a crazy? The list of great Bible figures who channeled a massive amount of power and fire, and lived way outside the box is almost endless:

- Abraham: Attempted to kill his son, because 'God told him to do it' (Genesis 22);
- Jacob: In cahoots with his mother, he stole his brother's inheritance, and believed he was blessed by God for doing so (Genesis 27);
- Jacob: Had sex with two sisters and was married to them both *simultaneously* (Genesis 29);
- Jacob: Had sex with and married the maid of one of the sisters while still married to both sisters (Genesis 30);
- Jacob: Had sex with and married the maid of the other sister (Genesis 30).
- Joseph: Interpreted dreams and was accused of sleeping with his boss's wife (Genesis 37-41);
- Moses: Was literally a killer before God called him to lead the Hebrews out of Egypt (having killed an Egyptian who was beating a Hebrew); then after leading them out, kept murdering wayward Israelites by the thousands (not to mention enemies by the tens of thousands), because 'God told him to' (Exodus 2:11-12; Exodus 32:25-29), once slaughtering 3,000 Israelites right after getting the commandment 'Thou Shalt Not Kill';
- Aaron: Led an orgiastic pagan worship of a cow made of gold (Exodus 32);
- Deborah (and other Israelite leaders and generals throughout the Bible): Led an 'army of God' in the slaughter of thousands of enemy soldiers (Judges 4);
- Jael (a woman who was partisan to Israel/Deborah's army): Gave comfort to General Sisera, who was fleeing Deborah's forces, and while he slept Jael drove a tent peg into his temple and through his head so hard that it stuck into the ground when it came out the other side (Judges 4:17-22);
- Ruth: Provided for her family by getting the king drunk and sleeping with him, thereby currying his favor (Ruth 3);
- Samson: Killed a lion with his bare hands, reportedly killed a thousand men with the jawbone of an ass, and later killed a party full of bad guys by tearing down the house (Judges 14-16);
- David: As a boy, he not only slew the ferocious giant, named Goliath, but the part most Sunday School kids

aren't taught is that after dropping Goliath with a stone from his slingshot, David went over in a fit of bloodlust and cut off Goliath's head (1 Samuel 17);

- David: As an adult and king, he slept with another man's wife, then had the man, who was one of his soldiers, sent to the front lines of the war to be killed so that David could have his wife to himself (for the record, God made David fry for this one) (2 Samuel 11);
- King Solomon: Had 700 wives and princesses, and 300 concubines (1 Kings 11:3);
- Jeremiah: A firebrand prophet who unleashed God's fury on his own people and was hunted by many who did not like him and his message (Jeremiah);
- Elijah: Killed 450 prophets of the enemy's god (1 Kings 18:22,40)
- Jonah: Walked into the middle of an *enemy city* and basically told them that they were screwed if they didn't fall on their knees and ask God's forgiveness! And they actually did it (Jonah 1-4);
- Daniel: Told the corrupt leaders to 'stick it' by refusing to bow down and worship the king – an act that guaranteed that Daniel would be thrown into a den of lions to be mauled and devoured (Daniel 6; he ended up surviving);
- John the Baptist: Lived on locusts and honey, raged on religious authorities of his day (about 100 times moreso than Jesus did), and was beheaded upon the request of a teenage girl, who was being seduced by the king (Matthew 3:1-6, 7-12; 14:5-12);
- Judas: Defied one of the most powerful men to ever walk the face of the earth (Matthew 26:47-56);
- The 12 Apostles: According to some accounts, most of them were killed for proselytizing in foreign lands, often in horrific, gruesome ways;
- Stephen: Stoned to death for having the guts to stand up for his beliefs (Acts 6:8-7:60);
- Paul: Killed Christians, literally for a living, before becoming a Christian (Acts 8:1; 9:1-2), and, according to some accounts, was himself killed for being a Christian;
- John of Patmos: As if dropping acid, had colorful and wild delusions about the end of the world (recounted in

> the Book of Revelation, a book considered largely heretical [*antilegomena*], due to its dubious origin and usefulness, that only barely made it into the canon of scripture; a book that is disputed by some of the greatest theologians in the history of Christianity, such as Martin Luther).

Jesus: The Ultimate Crazy Badass!

That, of course, leads to Jesus. He was the consummate badass, the ultimate in crazy.

And it is precisely because of his madness, his mad actions, his mad beliefs, and his mad, mad love that he has been venerated by centuries of people, not the least of which is the madman in you. Jesus is the ultimate in spigot control, focus, and channeling all of his energy and life in one world-changing direction. He is a man who had truly mastered himself. Jesus is the consummation of ferocity and intensity directed toward changing the world and bringing the world into relationship with God.

Jesus Story One:

Talk about unleashing your crazy:

> Now as Jesus was going up to Jerusalem, he took the twelve disciples aside and said to them, "We are going up to Jerusalem, and the Son of Man will be **betrayed** to the chief priests and the teachers of the law. They will **condemn** him to **death** and will turn him over to the Gentiles to be **mocked** and **flogged** and **crucified**…"

Here in Matthew 20: 17-19 we read that toward the end of Jesus' ministry he went up to Jerusalem *knowing* he was stepping into a maelstrom that would sweep him up and suck him down into a flurry of madness, chaos, and excruciating torture and pain.

He *knew* that by going to Jerusalem he was choosing his death. But he chose it anyway! Jesus *knew* he was about to get his ass kicked and killed by the steamroller of the religious institution.

He had advance knowledge that by choosing this particular course of action he would be killed – little different from the man who jumps from a 40-story window or off a bridge into fast-moving traffic who knows in advance that he will be killed. Jesus *knew* he was going to his torture and death.

Martin Luther and John Hus knew that by standing against the Roman Catholic Church they would be hunted and likely killed. Hus was burned at the stake. Mohandes Gandhi knew that by standing against the British Empire in India he would very likely be killed; and he was. Martin Luther King, Jr., knew that by standing against racism in America he would quite possibly be killed; and he was.

Jesus Story Two:

In the story of Jesus and the cleansing of the temple I here highlight one tiny piece that is frequently overlooked. It is a small point that sharply accents how ferocious and calculating Jesus could be. Taken from John 2:13-17, note the italicized word:

> The Passover of the Jews was at hand, and Jesus went up to Jerusalem. In the temple he found those who were selling oxen and sheep and pigeons, and the money-changers at their business. And ***fashioning*** a whip of cords, he drove them all, with the sheep and oxen, out of the temple; and he poured out the coins of the money-changers and overturned their tables. And he told those who sold the pigeons, "Take these things away; you shall not make my Father's house a house of trade." His disciples remembered that it was written, "Zeal for thy house will consume me."

Note the word *fashioning.* Some translations use the word *made*.

In either case, the point is that Jesus did not *grab, seize,* or *pick up off the ground* a whip. Instead, he deliberately and methodically took time to weave together a whip of cords. As he seethed and fumed, his anger just below the surface, his hands worked the cords slowly and with malice into a whip. Slowly, methodically, intently this crazy man planned his vengeance on those crowds defiling the house of God.

This wasn't Jesus-the-badass-who-loses-his-cool-when-he-gets-pissed-off. This is hold-that-thought-while-I-go-stew-in-my-rage-and-create-the-instrument-of-your-destruction-before-coming-back-to-seriously-fry-your-soon-to-be-sorry-asses Jesus. This isn't hot-tempered Jesus. This is cold and calculating Jesus, opening an angry can of whoop-ass, and bent on a serious cause and whatever is necessary to make it happen.

Jesus Story Three:

And here is the ultimate in crazy. In every gym the biggest and baddest athletes are often the quietest or most docile. They don't have to prove themselves. They know their power, and so does everyone else. The biggest and strongest defer not out of weakness – quite the opposite! Instead, their deference is born of an acute knowledge of just how powerful they truly are. Jesus is such a fierce badass who knew how powerful he was and that he didn't have to respond to every affront or swing back every time someone took a swing at him. Not only that, he could keep turning the other cheek, because he knew that if he needed to he could pound the living hell out of a man. Read in Luke 6: 27-36:

> "But here is what I tell you who hear me. Love your enemies. Do good to those who hate you. Bless those who call down curses on you. And pray for those who treat you badly.
>
> "Suppose someone hits you on one cheek. Turn your other cheek to him also. Suppose someone takes your coat. Don't stop him from taking your shirt.
>
> "Give to everyone who asks you. And if anyone takes what belongs to you, don't ask to get it back. Do to others as you want them to do to you.
>
> "Suppose you love those who love you. Should anyone praise you for that? Even 'sinners' love those who love them. And sup-

pose you do good to those who are good to you. Should anyone praise you for that? Even 'sinners' do that. And suppose you lend money to those who can pay you back. Should anyone praise you for that? Even a 'sinner' lends to 'sinners,' expecting them to pay everything back.

"But love your enemies. Do good to them. Lend to them without expecting to get anything back. Then you will receive a lot in return. And you will be sons of the Most High God. He is kind to people who are evil and are not thankful. So have mercy, just as your Father has mercy."

True power, true strength, and true control of one's crazy is often most visible in the capacity to ***not*** *engage.* To truly control your crazy means that no one else can control you or incite you to action. Only you control when and where your crazy is engaged, which means you then have the power to use it for the most noble of endeavors.

To truly master yourself is to own your own spigots and control them, so that no one else can set you off or 'push your buttons.' It is to be able to take the blows of life when it is pointless to fight back, all the while saving your fire for the causes that really matter.

The Ultimate Goal of Crazy and Spigot Control

The goal of unleashing and channeling crazy is to change the world, nothing else. This is the goal of learning to control all the other spigots, as well.

It's not enough to be able to control yourself unless you then put your power to good use. That is the whole point of Jesus' life. It ain't about you. It ain't just about your happiness. It ain't about keeping yourself at the center of the universe.

The goal of life is to master yourself, and then use that mastery for a purpose bigger than yourself. It is to give your life, your abilities, your power, your control, and your crazy in the most focused and white-hot service of those who need your power most – the outcast, the crapped-on, the oppressed, the poor, the hungry, and the hurting, as well as other crazies who haven't been taught how to channel their fire.

Jesus didn't lead a group of nice people. Jesus never hung out with nice people. Jesus never really even was preaching to the nice people. Jesus simply wasn't about being 'nice' to people or hanging out with nice folk, or even teaching people how to be nice.

Jesus was infinitely gracious and kind. But this lovingkindness is very different from just being 'nice.' His entire life was spent with the 'bad' folk, the crazy folk, the badasses, and the folks who were 'good' not because they never did bad things but because they spent their lives fighting for others and fighting against injustice!

To be crazy like Jesus is not about being macho or about being some tough guy on the outside. It is about truly going the spiritual path to find and master all of who you are, not just act in ways that our society says men are supposed to be. It is to sharpen your blade as much as you can and tighten your laser as fiercely as you possibly can. It is to then unleash all that power for those who need your power most! The easy path is to use all your energy and fire for you and yours. The lesser path is one of self-interest. But Jesus' radical path, for those rare souls who have the courage to go it, is one of insane commitment to those who are most hurting and who most need what you bring to life.

This is the noble life. This is the definition of a life well-lived. This is what it means to remove yourself from the center of the universe, and place God and neighbor there. This is, in the end, the very definition of a life lived in Love of God and love of neighbor. This is what it is to fulfill Jesus' first and greatest commandments, to which God proudly smiles and says, "This is my son (or daughter) in whom I am well pleased."

Got crazy?

Ready to kick some ass?

Ready to finally do something with your life?

Aspire to something great! Aspire to a noble life!

It is time to unleash your inner lion!

It is time!

ANNOTATED BIBLIOGRAPHY

Armstrong, Lance and Sally Jenkins. *Every Second Counts.* Broadway Books, 2003.

One of the world's greatest athletes shares the gritty and insightful wisdom he has learned from life's sufferings and self-punishment on the road to becoming the best and becoming himself. A challenge to traditional Christianity's notion that suffering is bad.

Bach, Richard. *Illusions: The Adventures of a Reluctant Messiah.* Dell Publishing, 1977.

The perfect introduction for the adult beginner (and an excellent reminder for the longtime spiritual traveler) on the spiritual journey, which challenges inside-the-box thinking. Told in delightful story form.

———. *Jonathan Livingston Seagull.* Macmillan, 1990.

Brilliant; a child's introduction to the nobility and beauty of the compassionate hero's spiritual path.

Barclay, William. *The Daily Study Bible Series.* Westminster John Knox Press (Revised Edition), 1975.

The best Biblical commentary series available for the moderate-to-left-leaning Christian seeking strong spiritual guidance.

Perfect as a daily devotional, packed with quotes, poetry, historical references, and excellent Biblical scholarship.

Bonhoeffer, Dietrich. *The Cost of Discipleship.* Macmillan, 1959.
One of the few pastor-theologians who stood up to the Nazi regime, he offers his theory on how religious conversion that is not followed by "works" cheapens the grace offered by God.

Campbell, Joseph. *The Power of Myth* (Betty Sue Flowers, editor). Anchor Books, 1988.
The one religion must-read of the 20th Century! It completely revolutionizes religious thought by putting it in a world-history/myth context. Extremely popular because it is a broadly-accessible, absolutely intoxicating read.

———. *A Joseph Campbell Companion* (Diane K. Osbon, editor). Perennial (Reprint), 1995.
A poetic synopsis of his work to be always kept on hand for the advanced Campbellite.

Collins, James C. *Good to Great: Why Some Companies Make the Leap ... And Others Don't.* HarperBusiness, 2001.
Based on hard research of the long term, very-top producing companies in America, this book hammers out a solid formula for the successful advanced growth of any organization. Obvious religious as well as personal spiritual crossover applicability. New York Times Bestseller. If you desire relevant religion, you must read this book.

Dwoskin, Hale. *The Sedona Method: Your Key to Lasting Happiness, Success, Peace, and Emotional Well-Being.* Sedona Press, 2003.
A brilliant non-religious supplement to faith, enabling the reader to release the negativity in life which obstructs the flow of joy and abundance.

Erlandson, Sven. *Rescuing God from Christianity: A Closet Christian, Non-Christian, and Christmas Christian's Guide to Radically Re-Thinking God Stuff* (2nd Ed.). Llumina Press, 2006.

Strong new Biblically-based theology for a new world.

----------. *Spiritual But Not Religious: A Call To Religious Revolution In America.* IUniverse, 2000.

Articulates the roots of the American spiritual crisis, and what must be done to solve the crisis.

———. *The 7 Evangelical Myths: Untwisting the Theology behind the Politics*. Llumina Press, 2007.

A scathing indictment and deconstruction of evangelical/conservative Christianity and its theology in light of its overreaching in American politics.

Ford, Debbie. *The Secret of the Shadow: The Power of Owning Your Story.* HarperOne, 2002.

A powerful tool for finding your power from the hardships you've lived. Excellent author!

Gawain, Shakti. *Creative Visualization: Use the Power of Your Imagination to Create What You Want in Your Life.* Nataraj Publishing, 1978.

A New Age classic.

———. *Living in the Light: A Guide to Personal and Planetary Transformation.* Nataraj Publishing, 1986.

Challenging insofar as it offers spiritual seekers and Christian leaders who are searching for new words for Christian themes a stripped-down and redressed version of many Christian truths (whether intentional or unintentional on the author's part). Also, delves into the inherent societal-global-responsibility of the spiritual journey.

Grabhorn, Lynn. *Excuse Me, Your Life is Waiting!* Hampton Roads Publishing, 2000.

Simply a brilliant book for finding and following the positive flow of energy in your life.

Hamilton, J. Wallace. *Ride the Wild Horses: The Christian use of our untamed impulses.* Abingdon (Reprint), 1980.

12 of the best sermons you will ever read. Argues not for a change in human instincts, but for a harnessing of them for use in God's work.

Hillman, James. *Soul's Code: In Search of Character and Calling.* Warner Books, 1996.

The most accessible of his writings (though still very dense) for those on the spiritual journey. He explores archetypal patterns of spiritual seekers.

Keen, Sam. *Fire in the Belly: On Being a Man*. Bantam, 1992.

Pushes for males to develop spiritually beyond traditional stereotypes to a new definition of man as passionate in the heart and fired in the belly.

Luther, Martin. *Martin Luther's Basic Theological Writings* (Timothy F. Lull, editor). Fortress Press, 1989.

A compilation of works of perhaps the single most pivotal Christian figure since Jesus. Offers a deep understanding of the underpinnings of much of Protestantism, as well as the spirit of fighting for societal change, and the heart of a man torn and strengthened by his own spiritual struggles.

Maxwell, Robert. *The 21 Irrefutable Laws of Leadership: Follow Them and People Will Follow You*. Thomas Nelson Publishers, 1998.

A brilliantly insightful and powerful look into the natural laws of who humans follows and why.

CPSIA information can be obtained at www.ICGtesting.com
Printed in the USA
BVOW071341080212

282455BV00002B/216/P